WESTMINSTER COMMENTARIES

EDITED BY WALTER LOCK D.D.

LADY MARGARET PROFESSOR OF DIVINITY
IN THE UNIVERSITY OF OXFORD,

AND D. C. SIMPSON D.D.

ORIEL PROFESSOR OF THE INTERPRETATION
OF HOLY SCRIPTURE, CANON OF ROCHESTER

THE SECOND EPISTLE

TO

THE CORINTHIANS

THE SECOND EPISTLE

TO

THE CORINTHIANS

WITH INTRODUCTION AND NOTES

BY

H. L. GOUDGE, M.A., D.D.

REGIUS PROFESSOR OF DIVINITY
IN THE UNIVERSITY OF OXFORD

METHUEN & CO. LTD.
36 ESSEX STREET W.C.
LONDON

First Published in 1927

PRINTED IN GREAT BRITAIN

PREFATORY NOTE BY THE GENERAL EDITOR

THE primary object of these Commentaries is to be exegetical, to interpret the meaning of each book of the Bible in the light of modern knowledge to English readers. The Editors will not deal, except subordinately, with questions of textual criticism or philology; but taking the English text in the Revised Version as their basis, they will aim at combining a hearty acceptance of critical principles with loyalty to the Catholic Faith.

The series will be less elementary than the Cambridge Bible for Schools, less critical than the International Critical Commentary, less didactic than the Expositor's Bible; and it is hoped that it may be of use both to theological students and to the clergy, as well as to the growing number of educated laymen and laywomen who wish to read the Bible intelligently and reverently.

Each commentary will therefore have

(i) An Introduction stating the bearing of modern criticism and research upon the historical character of the book, and drawing out the contribution which the book, as a whole, makes to the body of religious truth.

(ii) A careful paraphrase of the text with notes on the more difficult passages and, if need be, excursuses on any points of special importance either for doctrine, or ecclesiastical organization, or spiritual life.

But the books of the Bible are so varied in character that considerable latitude is needed, as to the proportion which the various parts should hold to each other. The General Editor will therefore only endeavour to secure a general uniformity in scope and character : but the exact method adopted in each case and the final responsibility for the statements made will rest with the individual contributors.

By permission of the Delegates of the Oxford University Press and of the Syndics of the Cambridge University Press the Text used in this Series of Commentaries is the Revised Version of the Holy Scriptures.

WALTER LOCK

PREFACE

THE purpose of this Commentary, like that of the whole series of which it is a member, is to interpret to English readers the meaning of Scripture in the light of modern knowledge. But the writer has certain convictions which it may be well to explain.

The first is that no hard and fast line can be drawn between the interpretation of Scripture and its practical application, between what the words meant when they were written and what they mean for the Church to-day. With the original meaning we must no doubt begin. But we cannot fully understand the words immediately before us without considering the mind and teaching of the writer as a whole ; nor can we fully understand this mind and teaching without considering its relation to our own problems. The strong distinction sometimes drawn between principles and their application is not a sound one; for principles are but abstractions apart from the facts to which they apply. No doubt the modern commentator, unlike the ancient, generally feels it to be his duty to eschew "homiletics"; and, if by "homiletics" he means moral and doctrinal teaching which, though perhaps suggested by the words of Scripture, really proceeds from the general furniture of his own mind, he is certainly right. But if by "homiletics" he means what the 17th century commentator Bernardine à Piconio calls the "Doctrinal Corollary," or the "Corollary of Piety," which necessarily follows from the words which he is explaining, to eschew "homiletics" means to fail to explain.

Now there is perhaps no part of the N.T. in which these considerations are more important than in the Second Epistle to the Corinthians. It is commonly said that no satisfactory Commentary upon this book exists. That is a hard saying, in view of the admirable work done upon this Epistle in modern days. The older commentators failed to understand its historical background, because they failed to understand the scope and purpose of the Acts of the Apostles. They supposed that S. Luke, in the period with which he dealt, gave us a full account of S. Paul's travels; and that S. Paul therefore could not have paid any visit to Corinth, of which S. Luke's history does not inform us. But modern commentators are free from this mistake, and they have done most valuable work in making the historical background clearer. Why then do they fail to satisfy us? Why do so many good and scholarly books leave so confused an impression upon our minds? It is because the Epistle with which they are dealing is a jungle of details, which the clearest understanding of the historical situation will not enable us to penetrate, unless we grasp, not only S. Paul's character, but his view of his own position and authority, and (as far as we may) the deep and abiding truth which it contains. Now this view has to be discovered largely by the study of this very Epistle; no other is in this matter equally illuminating. But it is difficult to grasp it, both because in some of its aspects it is to modern English readers strange and unwelcome, and because it is not until the last chapter of the Epistle has been studied that we clearly see what it is. Indeed there is more to be said. It is only when we have grasped S. Paul's outlook that we can fully understand the historical situation itself. We only see it through his eyes, and so cannot reconstruct it before we know what his angle of vision is. Thus those, who refer to this Commentary for the interpretation of particular texts, must not be surprised if they find assumptions made, which have no adequate justification in the immediate context. The justification will be found in the teaching of the book as a whole, and especially in the view which S. Paul takes of his position, and which it has been thought well to explain in the Introduction, before considering the historical situation.

Secondly, the present writer believes that the advance of learning has made it impossible to write Commentaries which will satisfy the needs of all readers alike. Now the best modern Commentaries are mainly historical, critical, and philological in character; they are written mainly for scholars;

and this inevitably means that the needs of readers, whose interests are mainly doctrinal, moral, and devotional, are little considered. A commentator to-day must envisage clearly the readers whom he has in view. The present writer has primarily considered the needs of those engaged in practical Christian work, who have neither money to buy very expensive books, nor time to read very long ones; and who thus ask of a Commentator that he should tell them what they want to know, and nothing else. Above all it is intended for those who, like S. Paul, are members of the ministry of the Church, and wish to learn from him how they themselves ought to think about their calling, and deal with those to whom they are sent. Readers of this kind do not require proof of the authenticity of an Epistle which nobody doubts; or discussions of alternative readings which hardly affect the sense; or references to books which are beyond their reach; or *catenae* of the various interpretations which scholars have suggested. What they do require—especially in this Epistle— is help to discover the treasure hid in it for themselves, and for those to whom God sends them. Many desirable things will not be found in this Commentary for the simple reason that the writer does not know them; but some will be absent because in his judgment they would make the book longer, without making it more useful to the readers whom he has in view.

Thirdly, it may be well to explain what in the writer's view is S. Paul's position in Christian thought. He does not believe that there is any such thing as Paulinism, if by that is meant a view of Christianity peculiar to S. Paul[1]. He

---

[1] The following words of a modern French writer admirably express the truth :

"Sans aucun doute, ses conceptions portent un cachet distinctif, et on a le droit de parler d'une théologie de Saint Paul ; il est non moins certain que Dieu, qui l'a fait docteur des Gentils, l'a préparé à ce rôle et l'y a conduit par des révélations qui ont enrichi le dépôt de la foi chrétienne.... Il pouvait donner à la foi commune une forme qui lui était propre, il pouvait même l'enrichir et la développer, il ne la créait pas, et il était assuré que son enseignement provoquait dans l'Église entière un écho profond." LEBRETON, *Les Origines du Dogme de la Trinité*, p. 352.

believes that the highest religion of the O.T., the religion
taught by the Lord, that taught by the Twelve, and that
taught by S. Paul, are all one and the same religion, though
at different stages of development. This was certainly the
belief of S. Paul himself. With Marcion's repudiation of the
O.T. he would have had no sympathy. Always he maintains
that the O.T., rightly understood, gives the fullest support to
what he teaches, and that Pharisaism is a heresy. Always he
bows to the word of the Lord, as the one authority superior
to his own; always he claims that his teaching differs neither
from that of the Twelve, nor from that everywhere "delivered"
to the "churches of God" (1 Cor. xi. 16). Had it differed, he
would have "run in vain" (Gal. ii. 2); and that, not because
the authority of the Twelve is superior to his own, but because
the authority of the Lord is living in all the Apostles whom
He has chosen, and there cannot be more than one "Jesus,"
or "a different Spirit," or "a different Gospel" (2 Cor. xi. 4).
Moreover, though with all respect for those who think otherwise, the present writer has a similar belief about the relation
of the mind of S. Paul to the mind of the Church of later
days. The Church of the early centuries spoke of him as
par éminence "the Apostle": it had no suspicion that his
writings were out of harmony with its faith or authorized
practice; and just as little that it had understood him less
than it had understood his fellow-Apostles. That is still the
Church's attitude; and, though no doubt it may be violently
assailed, the charge of paradox lies, not against its defenders,
but against its assailants. When S. Paul wrote to the churches
which he had founded, he expected to be understood; and
there is no reason to suppose that he was not. The view
sometimes expressed, that, except for a glimmer of light
vouchsafed to S. Augustine, no one understood him until
Martin Luther, seems to the present writer the very reverse
of the truth. It is precisely these two great writers, who have
most seriously misunderstood S. Paul, and led others to misunderstand him. To-day the characteristically "Protestant"
view of his teaching seems to be coming to the end of its
reign. That his view of the Church is the "Catholic" view is

now generally admitted; that his view of the Sacraments is the "Catholic" view is very widely admitted; and the present writer believes that in the doctrine of the Christian ministry too, though here there is greater obscurity, it will come to be seen that S. Paul's view is at any rate nearer to the "Catholic" than to the "Protestant." May he add that to the best of his belief, these convictions are not convictions which he has brought to the study of the N.T., but convictions which he has derived from it, and that he is quite willing to be shewn that he is mistaken?

One thing more. The present writer does not accept everything which S. Paul incidentally says as being necessarily true. S. Paul was a Jew of the first century, brought up at the feet of Gamaliel. His outlook upon the world was not that which modern science has taught us, and our methods of historical criticism were not at his disposal. Of the real history of his nation and its institutions he knew less than we could wish, while of such lesser inhabitants of the world unseen as angels and demons he thought that he knew more than we to-day generally credit him with having known. Perhaps, as Bishop Lightfoot has suggested, he did not trust his Jewish authorities on the orders of angels quite as implicitly as we may at first suppose; certainly he never makes their statements part of his gospel. These and similar beliefs, though affecting the imaginative clothing of his deeper convictions, do not appreciably affect their substance. His deepest convictions rested, the present writer believes, upon facts of history and experience interpreted to him by the Spirit of God. Here not only did he know, but he knew that he knew. The modern scholar, as a rule, if he speaks at all about the deep things of God, speaks with a very uncertain voice; he neither claims any authority, nor exercises any; and only too often he regards S. Paul as no better endowed than himself, and as changing his mind between one Epistle and another. But S. Paul never speaks tentatively, except when he is dealing with questions of casuistry. About Christian doctrine there is in his case no example of a change of mind; though of course there is development in his thought, and his own position and the immediate needs of his converts lead him to dwell now upon one and now upon another element in the one truth. On the deep things he speaks with calm authority and consciousness of inspiration, and does not regard it as possible that he is mistaken: on these things therefore the present writer accepts what he says. He has also a profound admiration for S. Paul's character; and, as the Commentary will shew, is prepared to defend him at every point at which he is assailed.

I have to thank Dr Lock, the General Editor, for reading the Commentary, and for the suggestions which he has made. He is, of course, not responsible for what I have written.

I have also to thank my sister-in-law, Miss M. L. Colleneter, for the Index.

H. L. G.

" What an admirable epistle is the second to the Corinthians ! How full of affections ! He joys and he is sorry ; he grieves and he glories ; never was there such care of a flock expressed save in the Great Shepherd of the fold, who first shed tears over Jerusalem, and afterwards blood."

GEORGE HERBERT, *The Country Parson*, ch. vii.

INTRODUCTION

The Apostleship of S. Paul

The Second Epistle to the Corinthians is S. Paul's *apologia pro vita sua*; and that not just as a man, but as an apostle of Jesus Christ. He has to deal, as we shall presently see, with a Jewish-Christian mission, which attacks not only an important part of the Gospel which he preaches, but his apostolic position. In Galatia, where this mission had at first considerable success, both forms of attack seem to have been equally violent. The first two chapters of the Epistle to the church there are a defence of his apostleship; the last four of his Gospel. But, when he writes the Second Epistle to the Corinthians, a change seems to have taken place in the method of his adversaries; for the whole situation had been altered by that Conference at Jerusalem, of which we read in Ac. xv. The Epistle to the Galatians was almost certainly written before it. Had it not been so, it would be impossible to explain why S. Paul, in writing to them, did not mention its decision. He uses in this Epistle a great variety of arguments in defending his teaching. If the question of the freedom of the Gentiles from the obligation to observe the law of Moses had been already settled in his favour, why did he not say so? But the Second Epistle to the Corinthians was written some time after the Conference, and violent attack at Corinth appears now to be directed against his apostolic position alone. The Jewish Christians who oppose him have not indeed bowed to the decision of the Conference; they still maintain in some form the importance, if not the obligation, of observing the Mosaic law (cf. 2 Cor. iii; xi. 4, 13–15). But S. Paul is now known to have on the main issue not only the elder Apostles behind him, but even S. James of Jerusalem, in spite of his attachment to the law; and the most promising line of attack is now to deny his apostolic position. An evangelist he may be; and an evangelist of the true, not of a corrupted, gospel. But an Apostle, with the powers and rights of an Apostle, he certainly is not; the decree of the Conference had said nothing about that. "The apostles and the elder brethren" may have expressed regard for S. Paul as one who had hazarded his life for the name of the

Lord Jesus Christ (Ac. xv. 25, 26); but they did not speak of him as an Apostle, nor could they have done so. In claiming to be on a level with the Twelve, and to exercise authority over the Gentile churches, he is making a claim which he has no right to make. It is this line of attack which is being adopted at Corinth, and the Epistle will shew us what his answer was.

But before we turn to it there is a preliminary question to be faced; and, if we give to it what may seem too large a share of our attention, the reason is that upon a right answer being found for it a right understanding of the Epistle depends. The question is this: What is meant by an Apostle, and what is the authority which an Apostle possesses? Plainly, he is much more than a missionary sent forth to preach the Gospel. Let us hear S. Paul himself as he speaks of the gifts of the Ascended Lord. " He gave some to be apostles ; and some, prophets; and some, evangelists; and some pastors and teachers" (Eph. iv. 11). Here, as in 1 Cor. xii. 29, 30, we find a definite order. An Apostle is higher than a prophet, and a prophet than an evangelist. Now an evangelist is one who has been sent to preach the Gospel; and in the early days of the Church there were many evangelists. When the Church of Jerusalem was persecuted after the death of S. Stephen, "they that were scattered abroad went about preaching the word" (Ac. viii. 4). We do not hear of any ordination in the case of these evangelists, any more than we do in the case of the prophets. But they were none the less the gifts of the Ascended Christ, since it was the call of His Spirit which they had heard and were answering. Is it for a moment conceivable that any one, who had been forced to the admission that S. Paul's gospel was the same gospel as that of the elder Apostles, denied to him recognition as a Christian evangelist? We shall assume then that S. Paul claimed a position far greater than this. An evangelist, a "minister of the gospel," he certainly was; indeed he was also a prophet (cf. 1 Cor. xiv. 5, 6); but, if he had claimed no more than this, he would never have had to write the Epistle before us.

How then shall we understand the position which S. Paul claimed? The word "apostle" means "envoy," one who is sent out as an authorized representative of the person, or body, from whom he goes. It was e.g. used of those who were sent out from Jerusalem to collect the tribute for the temple service. Similarly, Epaphroditus is called the "apostle" of the Philippians (Phil. ii. 25), and the delegates of the Macedonian churches who go with S. Paul are called the "apostles" of these churches (2 Cor. viii. 23). When in Ac. xiv. 4, 14, S. Paul and S. Barnabas are called Apostles, the reference seems to be to the way in which they had been sent out by the Holy Ghost speaking through the lips of the prophets of Antioch (Ac. xiii. 1-4). In that early Christian book, the *Teaching of the Twelve Apostles*, travelling missionaries bear the title; and this usage still prevails in Eastern Christendom. But, as we have seen, S. Paul claims much more than to be a missionary. He claims (Gal. i. 1, 17; ii. 6-10) a position on a level with that of the Twelve as an Apostle of Christ Himself; and the question that arises is what this position is[1].

Now, if we wish to understand the thought of the N.T., we must almost always go back to the O.T. Not only were the Apostles by their Jewish education familiar with it, but they regarded it as a great source of guidance to themselves. The Church, they believed, was continuing the life of Israel; the things which had happened to God's people of old had "happened unto them by way of example,"

---

[1] S. Paul's use of the title "Apostle" presents points of difficulty. Apart from the use of the term in 2 Cor. viii. 23 and Phil. ii. 25, where "Apostles of Christ" are not in question, it is uncertain whether he ever uses the term of any one except the Twelve and himself, except in 1 Thess. ii. 6. Thus (a) it is not clear that S. James of Jerusalem is called an Apostle either in 1 Cor. xv. 7 or in Gal. i. 19; or that in the former verse the meaning of "Apostles" is extended beyond the Twelve. In both verses we must take account of S. Paul's "rudeness of speech" and want of clearness in expressing his meaning, and it is difficult to suppose that the title is really given to one so tied to a particular city as S. James. In any case the suggestion that he took the place of S. James, the son of Zebedee, after the martyrdom of the latter is certainly to be rejected. The place of Judas was filled, because he had ceased to be an Apostle; but James, the son of Zebedee, is an Apostle for evermore (cf. Rev. xxi. 14). (b) A similar uncertainty rests upon S. Paul's view of the position of S. Barnabas. In Gal. ii. 1-10, though S. Barnabas goes up with him to Jerusalem (v. 1), and is recognized by the elder Apostles and S. James as a missionary to the Gentiles, his position is entirely subordinate to S. Paul's. So again in 1 Cor. ix. 5-7, no privilege is claimed for S. Barnabas that has not been claimed for the "brethren of the Lord," and that is not claimed for all Christian labourers. Bishop Lightfoot goes much too far when he says that S. Paul "claims for his fellow-labourer all the privileges of an Apostle, as one who like himself holds the office of an Apostle and is doing the work of an Apostle" (Commentary on the Epistle to the Galatians, Additional Note on the name and office of an Apostle). But it is difficult to escape the conclusion that S. Silas is called an Apostle in 1 Thess. ii. 6; and, in view of this, it is not unlikely that in some other places S. Paul uses the term in the wider sense. In any case he regards S. Peter as in a special sense intrusted with the gospel of the circumcision, and himself as in a special sense intrusted with the gospel of the uncircumcision, each having a primacy among any other "Apostles" who assist them in their several spheres (Gal. ii. 7).

and were written for the admonition of the later Church (1 Cor. x. 11). No doubt, the long-expected Christ had done great things for His people; He had indeed made all things new. But the new Church was built upon the "rock" of the faithful remnant of the old (Mt. xvi. 18); its "perfect law of liberty" (Jam. i. 25) was the old law "filled full" (Mt. v. 17), and transformed by the Lord; its baptism was apparently the old baptism given to proselytes, but now enriched with a new spiritual power; its Eucharist was the Passover feast of a new and greater divine deliverance. All, and far more than all, that Israel of old had been, the Catholic Church was now. "Ye," says S. Peter, "are an elect race, a royal priesthood, a holy nation, a people for God's own possession, that ye may shew forth the excellencies of him who called you out of darkness into his marvellous light" (1 Pet. ii. 9). Thus the first Christians would expect those, who under the new covenant were called to represent God and His Messiah to men, to be appointed and empowered much as God's representatives had been appointed and empowered under the old. The new representatives, like the new law and the new sacraments, would be greater than the old; they would have the Spirit of Pentecost, as the old had not; but their relations both to God who sent them, and to men to whom they were sent, would resemble those with which the O.T. had made God's people familiar.

What then are the fundamental principles that we shall be led to apply to the understanding of all forms of the representation of God to men? They are the principles inherent in the O.T. theocracy. The constitution of Israel, according to its true idea, had been that neither of an earthly monarchy, nor of an oligarchy, nor of a democracy; Israel in the divine intention was the Kingdom of God. That is why such men as Gideon (Judg. viii. 22, 23), Samuel (1 Sam. xii. 12), and Hosea (Hos. xiii. 10, 11) are so suspicious of visible heads of God's people; they endanger the recognition of the true king. The God of Israel had undertaken towards His people the kingly office in its every aspect (Is. xxxiii. 22). He was their Champion, the Vindicator of their rights; their Law-giver, directing their lives; the Provider for their every need (Mt. vi. 33). Now, of course, it was part of the king's prerogative to make appointments to office in his kingdom. If a man is to represent the Divine king in any capacity, the king Himself must have bestowed his office upon him. Does the God of Israel require a "judge"—a vindicator of His people against their enemies? Then He must Himself call

and empower the judge, as the story of the vindicators of Israel from
Moses to the Christ Himself sufficiently shews[1]. The puppet-kings
elected by the people in Northern Israel have neither divine authority
nor success. Or does the God of Israel require a prophet to declare
His will? Then He must Himself call the prophet, give to him his
message, and confirm by action the word He has sent him to proclaim.
To speak in God's name without God's call and message is to be a
prophet of "wind and falsehood" (Mic. ii. 11). Or, once more, does
He require a priest for the reconciliation of His people to Him?
Then the priest too must have the divine commission. For sacrifice
is not a human device, but a divine institution (Lev. xvii. 11); and
"no man taketh the honour unto himself, but when he is called of
God, even as was Aaron" (Heb. v. 4). When Jeroboam "made
priests from among all the people, which were not of the sons of
Levi" (1 Kgs. xii. 31), when Saul offered sacrifice (1 Sam. xiii. 9), and
Uzziah incense (2 Chr. xxvi. 16), their action was disallowed[2]. The
representatives of God in the O.T. are of many different kinds, and
have many different functions to perform; we must beware of as-
signing to the priests an importance which never belonged to them.
But all God's representatives are alike in this, that they neither appoint themselves, nor derive any part of their authority from the
people to whom they are sent. It is God, the King of Israel, who in
one way or another appoints them, and their authority comes solely
from Him. So of course it is expected that it will be with the great
Messiah, upon whom the hopes of God's people are so largely resting.
God will raise Him up, appoint him to his office, by His Spirit empower
him, and give him the victory, and the rule which will follow it.
Thus, when we come to the N.T., we shall expect to find the same
theocratic principle everywhere prevailing. If a man is in any way
to represent God, it must be God and not man, who has called and
empowered him. The call, as in the O.T., may come in a great

---

[1] Jephthah (Judg. xi. 4–11) seems to be an exception.

[2] It may be urged that no attention is here paid to the conclusions of O.T.
criticism. The reason is that we must always ignore them in interpreting the
N.T., since the writers of the N.T. were ignorant of them. S. Paul e.g. did not
distinguish the Priestly Document (P) in the Pentateuch from the earlier J and
E. He would have supposed that in the great sacrifice described in 1 Kgs. viii. 5
the part taken by the priests was what according to P it ought to have been;
and, when he laid hands on men to make them presbyters, he would have had
in mind such passages as Deut. xxxiv. 9.

variety of ways—by vision, by audition, by the voice of God speaking n the heart with self-authenticating power, or even by the call of a prophet. But it is from God in some way that the call must come. The duty of the people is not to call or appoint representatives of God; but to recognize those whom He has Himself appointed, and bow to their authority.

But now we must turn to a less familiar principle, though one of the highest importance. The representatives of God to His people, whatever their position, are not substitutes for Him, but the instruments of His personal activity. Thus they never possess any authority or power which they can use as they please; they can only say what God sends them to say, and do what He sends them to do. What we are to recognize is always God Himself working through those whom He has appointed; the constitution of Israel always remains theocratic, and never becomes bureaucratic. Just in so far as any officer of the divine kingdom abuses his position, God ceases to act through him. If e.g. a "judge" engages in an unauthorized war, he will be left to himself to carry it on. If a prophet speaks a word in God's name presumptuously, it will have no fulfilment (Deut. xviii. 20–22). If a priest offers an improper sacrifice, it will have no effect (Mal. i. 8–10). The great characteristic of "spiritual," or divine, power is not that it is sacrilege to abuse it, but that it cannot be abused. No one has any authority unless he represents God; and no one does represent God, unless he truly represents Him. From this a conclusion follows of the highest importance. Just because the only authority to which we are subject is the divine authority, there is always appeal from the minister to the King; and, if it is justified, the King will hear it. His calls to men to represent Him are profoundly real; as long as His representatives truly represent Him, He will support them to the uttermost (Jer. i. 18, 19). The "gainsaying of Korah" (Jude 11), his appeal to the holiness of all the Lord's people, and their supposed equality, has a tragic issue. But, if God's representatives misrepresent Him, all that they say and do is null and void, even though their original call was from Him. In a word, "they can do nothing against the truth, but for the truth" (2 Cor. xiii. 8). In the Kingdom of God, though not elsewhere, human government, prophecy, and priesthood are simply veils, the more transparent the better, for God's own activity, in ruling, teaching, and reconciling His people (cf. 2 Cor. iv. 7).

It is then these principles that we must apply to all representation of God, and not those which we derive from modern democracies or bureaucratic empires. The possession of divine authority is never a thing which can be proved by argument. Divine authority is "numinous," to use Otto's excellent word; it proves itself to those capable of recognizing it. It first shews itself in a divine right to command in the closest association with a divine power to convince; and the evidence of its reality is first found in the response which the conscience and the mind make to it, though, if it is set at nought, it can be practically vindicated (cf. 2 Cor. xiii. 3, 4). It is something which is felt; like heat and cold, like colour and sound, it cannot be described in terms of other things. Indeed the more we attempt to prove by purely intellectual argument that we have divine authority, the less likely it is that we possess it.

But, before proceeding further, we should observe how clearly these principles appear in the activity of the Lord Himself. He Himself as King-Messiah is the Ruler, the Judge or Vindicator of His people, as well as their Prophet and Priest, and all by divine appointment. But not even the authority of the Lord is delegated authority, which He can use as He will. He has it because He is in the Father, and the Father in Him (Jn. xiv. 10); because His activity is that of the Father abiding in Him, and doing His works (Jn. xiv. 10); because the words which He speaks are not His, but the Father's (Jn. xii. 49); and His priesthood is just God reconciling in Him the world to Himself (2 Cor. v. 19). "All authority" has indeed "been given unto" Him "in heaven and on earth" (Mt. xxviii. 18); but if there is in fact no appeal against His claims for our obedience to His kingly rule, or against His teaching, or against His means of reconciliation, it is because He makes present the Father who sends Him. If in the New Testament we find that everything which is done for us is done through the Lord Jesus Christ, that does not mean that the Father has been supplanted, or has in any way receded from our view; it means that for the first time nothing is being allowed to supplant the Father, and that in the Lord for the first time the Father is perfectly seen (Jn. xiv. 9).

Now so it is with the Apostles, and with all who truly represent Christ to men. A divine call is necessary. They never derive their call or their authority from the Christian laity; the democratic principle is unknown; it is the Lord who calls and empowers them. But they do not form a bureaucracy; they are transparent veils for the Lord's personal activity. "Peace be unto you : as the Father hath sent me, even so send I you" (Jn. xx. 21). Just as the Lord has not been sent to take the Father's place, but Himself to bring the Father, so the Apostles are not sent to take the Lord's place, but themselves to bring the Lord. Indeed, through this double representation the Father Himself is still present and active. "He that receiveth you," says the Lord to the Apostles, "receiveth me, and he that receiveth me receiveth him that sent me." God, Christ, the Apostles—that is the order. But it is not an order, in which the second takes the place of the first, or the third of the second. It is God—God in Christ—who in the persons of the Apostles is dealing with the Church and the world still. There are three questions to consider, in seeking to understand the apostolic office. First, how are the Apostles called? Secondly, what are the functions, and so the powers, of the Apostles? Thirdly, what are the conditions under which their functions can be performed, and their powers manifested? The Second Epistle to the Corinthians adds little, if anything, to what is found elsewhere in the answer which it gives to the first of these questions. But it has a real contribution to make in the case of the second; while the answer which it gives to the third is its greatest contribution to Christian theology, morals and devotion.

How then, we first inquire, were the Apostles called? The Twelve were called by the Lord. The Church had nothing to do with their calling, nor did they volunteer their services; on this the Gospels particularly insist (Mk. iii. 13, 14 ; Jn. xv. 16). Nor does any different principle appear in the case of S. Matthias (Ac. i. 24); if the use of the lot seems strange, we must remember that the Holy Ghost was not yet given. So it was with S. Paul too. The Church did not call him, nor was he a volunteer, though he may have wished to have been one. He had a "stewardship intrusted to" him, a definite office in the household of God ; and it was only by refusing the steward's pay, that he could have a share in the exultation of the volunteer (1 Cor. ix. 15–18). It is the Lord who calls all His Apostles, because all authority has been committed unto Him as Lord and Christ—because He is not only the Bringer, but the Head and Centre, of the divine kingdom, and the Father's rule is exercised through Him. Moreover, with the Apostles, as with many of those who under the old covenant received the highest calls, it is by a visible theophany, except in S. Matthias' case, that the call is given.

So it had been with Moses (Ex. iii. 1–6), with Gideon, the greatest of the "Judges" (Judg. vi. 11–14), and with Isaiah (Is. vi. 1–8); and so it was with the eleven, and with S. Paul on the Damascus road. Though there was an early call to companionship given to the Twelve, and an early temporary mission to the cities of Galilee (Luk. vi. 13–16; Mt. x. 1–15), that was not the call to full and abiding apostleship; it was the manifestation of the Risen Lord which conferred that. So it is that S. Paul says "Am I not an Apostle? Have I not seen Jesus our Lord?" It is not only that an Apostle must be able to bear personal witness to the resurrection and present glory of the Lord; no one but the Risen Lord can call him to his office. To make a man an Apostle it is not enough that "the word of the Lord" should come to him with self-evidencing power. The prophet may be called in that way, but not the Apostle. It is this clear personal call, and the resulting responsibility, not to the Church, but to the divine Caller (1 Cor. iv. 1–4), which, as we shall see in the Second Epistle to the Corinthians, gives to S. Paul his independence of his converts, and his dignity and power in dealing with them. Like the Lord, S. Paul is humble, if humility is understood to mean readiness for the lowliest service: but, like the Lord again, he is not at all humble, if by humility is meant a low estimate of his own position and authority.

So, once more, though we cannot deal with the subject here, we find that it is with every office in the divine kingdom. The theocratic principle everywhere prevails, while the democratic is wholly absent. Calls may come directly from the Lord by His Spirit; the N.T. prophets and evangelists have, as far as we know, no other ordination than this. They may come also from the Lord through His representative, as so commonly in the O.T. The laying on of hands, as the O.T. shews, symbolizes the transmission of the Spirit's power from one who possesses it to one who is called to share in his work (cf. Numb. xi. 16 ff.; 24–29; xxvii. 18–20; Deut. xxxiv. 9). But the calls never come from the Christian laity, though (as in the O.T.) they may suggest the names of the men to be ordained[1].

---

[1] In connexion with efforts after Home Reunion, it has been suggested that Nonconformist ministries should be accepted, if ordination has taken place by laying on of hands with prayer. But the laying on of hands symbolizes the transmission of spiritual authority and power; and, unless the ordainer possesses them, the laying on of hands is devoid of meaning. When, on the other hand, a Nonconformist minister bases his claim to be a minister of Christ on the

Secondly, what are the position and functions of an Apostle? Here it is most important to dismiss from our minds the idea that an Apostle is just "a clergyman." We may call him a minister of Christ; but, if we do, we should give to the word minister its political rather than its ecclesiastical sense. Our Lord is a King and the Catholic Church is His Kingdom; the Apostles are primarily men through whom His rule is exercised. No doubt our Lord is not only our Ruler, but our Priest and Teacher also; and among the functions of the Apostles who represent Him are those of uniting men to God by the sacraments, and teaching them by His word. But we never find the Apostles thinking of themselves as priests[1]; and, though of course bearing witness to the Lord and preaching His Gospel is a very important part of their work, it is not this which is distinctive in apostleship. What is distinctive is the government of the people of God. There is no Papacy to be found in the N.T. Though the primacy of S. Peter among his fellow-Apostles is very marked, where

---

inward call that Christ Himself has given to him, and the recognition of his call by his fellow-Christians and fellow-ministers, he takes up a far stronger position. His claim is parallel to that made by the prophets of the O.T., and probably by those of the N.T. also.

[1] Much stress is sometimes laid upon the fact that the Apostles and presbyter-bishops of the N.T. are never called priests. That they should have been so called is almost inconceivable. For (a) "a Christian priest" would mean a Levitical priest converted to the faith, but continuing to exercise his old ministry in the Temple (Ac. vi. 7). (b) "Priest" was far too humble a title even for a presbyter-bishop. The Levitical priests neither taught nor ruled by reason of their office, and even the Temple worship had lost much of its importance owing to the rise of the synagogues. (c) Though there is little doubt that presbyter-bishops in the absence of the Apostles were the celebrants at the Eucharist, and the ministers of the other sacraments, it would not then have occurred to anybody that there was much parallel between these functions and those of priests. S. Paul gives the title of priest neither to the Christian presbyters, nor to the Christian laity, nor to the Lord Himself. Outside the Epistle to the Hebrews, and a few references to the O.T. thought of the corporate priesthood of the Church, references to any priesthood among Christians are confined to a few metaphors (e.g. Rom. xv. 16; Phil. ii. 17; 2 Tim. iv. 6). Indeed the whole conception of "the clergy" as a body of men separated for the peculiar service of God only appeared at a later date. The early presbyter-bishops probably carried on their ordinary trades, and resembled Jewish "rulers of the synagogue" rather than Levitical priests. The heathen would hardly know which Christians held office in the Church. If we mean by a priest a man whose office is to unite men through Christ to God, the title is quite appropriate to the clergy; and the celebration of the Eucharist may be regarded as taking the place of the sacrificial worship of ancient Israel. But we must not expect to find our modern language in the N.T.

the Jews only are concerned, the Apostolic "College" has authority over him rather than he over them (Ac. viii. 14). The Papacy, when it arose, was, like the earthly kingship set up in Israel, a human institution with a strong tendency to obscure the sovereignty of the unseen King. But, though there is no one Apostle to succeed to the Lord's place, as Joshua succeeded to that of Moses, the authority of the Lord as King lives on in the apostolate as a whole; the Apostles are far more than ministers of the Gospel.

Now this authority to rule we find bestowed by the Lord during His earthly life. The Lord says to the Apostles : "I appoint unto you a kingdom, even as my Father appointed unto me, that ye may eat and drink at my table in my kingdom ; and ye shall sit on thrones judging the twelve tribes of Israel" (Luk. xxii. 29, 30). These words are not altogether devoid of difficulty; and the question may be raised whether the Lord is speaking of His present kingdom in the Church, or of the kingdom of the future, or of the one as the foretaste and earnest of the other. But the words which follow suggest that the Lord's present kingdom in the Church is chiefly in view, though the parallel passage in the Gospel of S. Matthew emphasizes in S. Matthew's characteristic way the kingdom of the future (Mt. xix. 28). As we have already seen, the Apostles are from Christ, as Christ from the Father; He will live and rule in them, as the Father lives and rules in the Lord Himself. By the Resurrection and Ascension God will make Him both Lord and Christ (Ac. ii. 36); in the outpouring of the Spirit at Pentecost, the King-dom of God will come with power (Mk. ix. 1); and thereafter the Lord, the unseen King, will be reigning in the Church (cf. Rev. i. 12–20). It is His sovereignty, which the Apostles are to exercise, though, as we have seen, simply as the agents of the unseen King. They are the members of His court, eating and drinking at His table, as Mephibosheth did at the table of David (2 Sam. ix. 10); they sit on chairs of state, exercising judgment over the twelve tribes of the people of God. It is the same position, which is implied in Mt. xvi. 19, in Mt. xviii. 18, and in Jn. xx. 22, 23. To bind and to loose is a Rabbinical phrase used in connexion with the interpretation of the Mosaic law. To "bind" is to declare unlawful; to "loose" is to declare lawful. It will be for the Apostles to interpret with authority the law of Christ, to declare what it forbids and what it allows. To forgive and to retain sins is to admit or refuse to admit men, to restore or refuse to restore them, to that union with Christ and His people, through which sin is done away (1 Jn. i. 7). All these powers we find the Twelve exercising in the Acts of the Apostles. The Church there appears as a visible kingdom; its members are just as definite a body as the Jews or the Greeks (cf. 1 Cor. x. 32); and it is the Apostles who are its acknowledged rulers. S. Luke, who records the Lord's promise of sovereignty, records also its fulfilment. The distinctness of the Apostles from other Christians is very marked, as is also the general recognition of their position. "Of the rest durst no man join himself to them...the people magnified them" (Ac. v. 13). The "fellowship" of the Church is their fellowship (Ac. ii. 42; cf. 1 Jn. i. 3); the authorized teaching of the Church is their teaching (Ac. ii. 42). They alone, by the laying on of hands (Ac. viii. 14–16), bestow the Spirit, the Church's characteristic blessing. They alone ordain (Ac. vi. 6); they alone at first administer the Church's property (Ac. vi. 1–3). When controversy arises as to the obligation of the Jewish law, it is they, with the elders appointed by them, who in the power of the Holy Ghost promulgate the final decision (Ac. xv. 23–29). Indeed awful powers lie in reserve, when there is need for their employment, as the stories of Ananias and Sapphira (Ac. v. 1–11) and of Elymas (Ac. xiii. 10, 11) plainly shew.

Thus it is not possible to regard the position of the Apostles as due only to their long companionship with the Lord, and the spontaneous reverence of their fellow-Christians: their position rests upon their appointment to rule by the Messianic King. Their sovereignty is not a sovereignty of this world administered on this world's principles; warnings against such a misunderstanding had just been given when the sovereignty was bestowed (Luk. xxii. 24–27). Just because it depends upon the presence of the Lord living and acting through them, it cannot be exercised except in accordance with His principles. But it is real sovereignty none the less, the sovereignty of the Lord Himself, and of the Father in Him; and if it is denied or resisted, it can be, and is, vindicated by the divine power.

Now it is this authority which S. Paul claimed, and which his opponents denied to him. Like his Master, he is all gentleness when his position is not disputed; in writing to the Macedonian churches—notably in the Epistle to the Philippians—he writes as a friend to friends, and the note of authority scarcely appears. His spirit here is that which we see in the Epistle to Philemon, "Though I

have all boldness in Christ to enjoin thee that which is befitting, yet
for love's sake I rather beseech" (Philem. 8, 9). But just in so far as
his authority is denied or resisted, this authority is claimed and
vindicated. In the First Epistle to the Corinthians, though he writes
as one who expects his teaching to be accepted, and his directions to be
obeyed, we can see that he is conscious that his claims are not recognized by all (1 Cor. ix. 1, 2); and his tone is therefore different
from that which we find in the Macedonian Epistles. Thus he speaks
of the orders which he gives "in all the churches" (vii. 17; cf. xvi. 1);
he refuses to argue with his converts beyond a certain point (xi. 16;
xiv. 37, 38); with the Corinthian guilty of incest he deals with
appalling severity (v. 3–5); and threatens to "come with a rod'
(iv. 21) to the Corinthian church as a whole. Between this, and
our Second Epistle, as we shall presently see, came an Epistle now
lost; and so severe was this that there was a time when he repented
of having sent it (2 Cor. vii. 8). But it is our Second Epistle itself
which is most illuminating as to S. Paul's conception of Apostolic
authority. In the earlier chapters indeed, when his mind is full of
thankfulness for the success of his severe letter, the authoritative
tone is not prominent. "We preach not ourselves, but Christ Jesus
as Lord, and ourselves as your bondservants for Jesus' sake" (iv. 5;
cf. 1 Cor. iii. 21–23). Even here, however, he can say that it was to
"spare" the Corinthians that he "forbare" to go to Corinth (i. 23);
that he had written, that he might "know the proof of" them,
whether they were "obedient in all things" (ii. 9); and that his
delegate Titus had been received with fear and trembling (vii. 15;
cf. Phil. ii. 12). But it is in the final chapters that both his
authority itself, and its divine source, are most clearly exhibited.
The beautiful reference in x. 1 to the meekness and gentleness of
Christ, and to the lowliness of his own bearing among the Corinthian
Christians, makes the language of the verses which follow the more
remarkable, since it is deliberately chosen in full view of the Lord's
example of humility. S. Paul is Christ's (x. 7), and as such he
possesses an "authority," in which he might "glory somewhat
abundantly" (x. 8). He speaks of the "peremptoriness" (so Moffatt),
with which he may have to deal with those who deny the divine
authority which he bears (x. 2); he has weapons "divinely strong"
to overthrow the strongholds of the enemy (x. 4); he is equipped
for the punishment of "all disobedience" (x. 6). What he un-
questionably has in view is not stern language to be used to his

opponents, but stern action, like that which we see in his dealing with the incestuous Corinthian. "What we are in word by letters when we are absent, such are we also in deed when we are present" (x. 11). Just as plain is his language in ch. xiii. He will act as a judge holding his court (xiii. 1); if he comes again, he "will not spare" (xiii. 2); he may have to "deal sharply, according to the authority which the Lord gave" him "for building up, and not for casting down" (xiii. 10). S. Paul's attitude is not in the least that of a Protestant minister towards his congregation; it is far more like that of a reforming Pope. But it arises simply out of his relation to Christ as His representative, and he is quite sure that the power of God in Christ will vindicate his bold words. "Ye seek a proof of Christ that speaketh in me; who to you-ward is not weak, but is powerful in you: for he was crucified through weakness, yet he liveth through the power of God. For we also are weak in him, but we shall live with him through the power of God toward you" (xiii. 3, 4). The meaning of such words is plain. In an Apostle we have to do with the indwelling Christ. But that indwelling Christ is not Christ as He was in the days of His human weakness and humiliation, but Christ as He is now, in the glory and power to which the willing acceptance of weakness and humiliation has brought Him. The "signs and wonders and mighty works," which manifest the true Apostle (xii. 12), are no doubt normally wonders and mighty works of mercy, foretastes of the blessings of the divine kingdom, like those of the Lord in His earthly life; the primary purpose of apostolic power is building up, not casting down (x. 8). But there may be wonders and mighty works of judgment too, though even these with a hidden purpose of blessing behind (cf. 1 Cor. v. 5; xi. 30-32). Thus S. Paul claims over the churches of his own foundation all the authority that the Twelve could claim over the Jewish Christians (x. 13-16; cf. Gal. ii. 7-9). Just as they are Apostles of the Jews, so is he an Apostle of the Gentiles (Rom. xi. 13); and, when he appeals to the Corinthians themselves as the proof of the reality of His Apostleship (2 Cor. iii. 1-4; cf. 1 Cor. ix. 2), his appeal is not to the fact that they are Christians—an "evangelist" might have effected that—but to all that his whole apostolic activity, and the gifts of the Spirit received from his hands, have together made them. (Cf. Rom. i. 11; Gal. iii. 5.)

Thirdly, what are the conditions under which the functions of the Apostles are performed, and their powers manifested? Something has been said about this already, and much will be said in the course of the Commentary, but it may be well to deal with this question a little more fully at this point. To English readers unfamiliar with N.T. thought the account which has been given of the meaning of Apostleship may be unwelcome; it may but increase that dislike of S. Paul which is so widely manifested to-day. "What you have done," it will be said, "is to make S. Paul the incarnation of that priestly assumption which all Englishmen detest, and which it was the task of the Reformation to abase and destroy. All that you need to add is that the Bishops of the Catholic Church are the successors of the Apostles, and the whole Catholic system of priestly domination will have emerged complete. This claim, which we hear so loudly made to-day, that S. Paul was a Catholic, and that Catholicism is simply the doctrine of the New Testament, does not affect us in the least. If you are right, we reject the doctrine of the New Testament, and intend to work out a religion more suited to modern ideas of freedom and commonsense." Now in view of the real tyranny which the Church has undoubtedly exercised only too often, and which, where it is possible, it sometimes exercises to-day, this attitude is entirely intelligible. But before S. Paul is condemned, the deepest teaching of this Epistle should be understood, and especially that profound difference between theocracy and bureaucracy, to which reference has already been made.

Let us leave S. Paul for a moment, and turn to that old Breviary hymn which, in its English translation, stands alone among our hymns in rightly describing the position of the Apostles. It will shew how profound and Scriptural is the best thought of the Church about apostolic authority.

> Aeterna Christi munera,
> Apostolorum gloriam,
> Laudes ferentes debitas,
> Laetis canamus mentibus.
>
> Ecclesiarum Principes,
> Belli triumphales Duces,
> Caelestis aulae milites,
> Et vera mundi lumina.
>
> Devota sanctorum fides,
> Invicta spes credentium,

Perfecta Christi caritas
Mundi tyrannum conterit.

In his Paterna gloria,
In his triumphat Filius,
In his voluntas Spiritus,
Coelum repletur gaudio.

"The princes of the Churches"—"the soldiers of the heavenly court"—there is the echo of Luk. xxii. 29, 30. "The eternal gifts of Christ"—there is the echo of Eph. iv. 11, with just the thought added from earlier in the same Epistle (Eph. ii. 20) that on them as foundation the Church rests until the end. But what is it which makes them all this? "In them is the Father's glory." So too says S. Paul. "It is God, that said, Light shall shine out of darkness, who shined in our hearts, to give the light of the knowledge of the glory of God in the face of Jesus Christ" (2 Cor. iv. 6). "In them the Son is triumphing." So too says S. Paul again. "Thanks be unto God, which always leadeth us in triumph in Christ, and maketh manifest through us the savour of his knowledge in every place" (2 Cor. ii. 14). It is not the Apostles who triumph, but Christ in them—Christ who lives in them, and speaks in them, Christ who is "not weak" in His dealing with those to whom the Apostles are sent, but "powerful in" them (2 Cor. xiii. 3). "In these is the will of the Spirit." Once more we hear the echo of S. Paul, as he says that the weapons of his warfare are "not of the flesh, but divinely strong to the casting down of strong holds" (2 Cor. x. 4).

Moreover, when we turn to the human conditions of apostolic power, the great hymn is equally faithful to the Apostle's teaching. "The devout faith of the saints" recalls to us 2 Cor. iv. 13; "the unconquered confidence of believers" 2 Cor. iv. 16–18; and "the perfect love of Christ" 2 Cor. v. 14. It is these things, and not only the calling of God, as S. Paul will shew us, that are the conditions of apostolic power. For how do the Apostles represent Christ? Is it just an official representation? On the lower levels of their work it may be so. When the Lord sent out His Apostles first, it was but to repeat a simple message and cast out demons in His name (Mk. iii. 14, 15); Judas could do that as well as S. Peter or S. John. But it is far otherwise with the Apostles as "ambassadors on behalf of Christ" (2 Cor. v. 20) after His Ascension.

Their representation is no mere official representation. It is one which rests upon a progressive identification with Christ in experience and life through the sufferings borne for Him. Like the Lord Himself, S. Paul will shew us how he had not only to preach the Gospel of glory won through pain and death, but himself to become the embodiment of that Gospel ; and that it was only as he did embody it that the power of Christ could be manifested in him, and he himself become an Apostle indeed. The call to Apostleship was one thing ; the fulfilment of the call was another; and it was upon this fulfilment through the hard discipline laid upon him and accepted, and not upon the call only, that his apostolic power rested. That hatred of clerical domination which characterizes Englishmen is a thing entirely right. No office in the Church, however lofty, can give to a man the right to dictate to his Christian brothers. But clerical or official authority is one thing, and spiritual authority —the authority of Christ recognized in those servants of His whom He has not only called to mediate it, but made so like Himself that they are able to mediate it—is altogether another ; and it is the second, not the first, which S. Paul claims. " If any man thinketh himself to be a prophet, or spiritual, let him take knowledge of the things which I write unto you, that they are the commandment of the Lord" (1 Cor. xiv. 37). S. Paul undoubtedly issues commands, and expects them to be obeyed by those who can recognize in his voice the voice of Christ Himself. But he would not even wish to be obeyed on any other ground; that would be to take the place of the one Lord, instead of bringing Him near. In the Church, as in all other forms of human society, official authority, and some measure of obedience to it, there must necessarily be ; we ought to "obey them that have the rule over " us in the Church, as in the State, "and submit to them " (Heb. xiii. 17) in the interest of seemliness and order, if for no higher reasons. But in the Church official authority ought to be confined within narrow limits, if the Church is not to become just one of the kingdoms of the world ; and both in Eastern and Western Christendom, under the influence of conceptions of authority drawn not from Christ but from the pagan Empire of Rome, official authority has largely taken the place of spiritual authority, and claimed a position which belongs only to the latter. To spiritual authority, on the other hand, there is no limit to be set except that which results from want of power to mediate it; and the chaos which Protestant Christendom presents to our view is the natural result of the fact that here not only has spiritual authority been very largely lost, but its very meaning has been forgotten. It is the great Epistle now before us which of all Christian writings can best teach both "Catholics" and "Protestants" what spiritual authority means, and how necessary is the imitation of Christ's suffering, if we desire to possess it. We shall find S. Paul basing his claim to be an Apostle not alone upon his call, and the vision of the Risen Lord then vouchsafed to him; not alone upon the signs of an Apostle in wonders and mighty works; and not alone upon the witness to his apostleship found in the life of the Corinthian church. He will base it also upon those sufferings which have made him an Apostle indeed.

HISTORICAL INTRODUCTION TO THE EPISTLE[1]

The First Epistle to the Corinthians was written from Ephesus, probably in the spring of A.D. 55 or 56 (1 Cor. xvi. 8); the Second from Macedonia towards the close of the same year. The long stay at Ephesus was now over. S. Paul, after leaving it, went first to Troas (2 Cor. ii. 12), and then crossed to Macedonia (ii. 13). It was here that Titus met him (vii. 5, 6), and here that he still is, as he writes this Epistle (ix. 2). Thus all that we read seems to accord, both with the Apostle's plans, when he wrote the First Epistle, and with the story of S. Luke in the Acts of the Apostles. When the First Epistle was written, Timothy was apparently on his way to Corinth, though the letter would reach the church before he did (1 Cor. iv, 17; xvi. 10); and S. Paul was expecting to follow him later in the year, after visiting the Macedonian churches (1 Cor. xvi. 3–9). To this S. Luke's account substantially corresponds. He tells us that S. Paul, when his stay at Ephesus was drawing to a close, intended to pass through Macedonia and Achaia on his way to Jerusalem; and that he sent Timothy and Erastus in advance into Macedonia, while "he himself stayed in Asia for a while" (Ac. xix. 21, 22). There is some obscurity about the movements of Timothy, as S. Paul makes no reference to them in the Second Epistle. Probably Timothy never went farther than Macedonia, as S. Luke's words seem to suggest. Timothy was evidently timid (1 Cor. xvi. 10, 11), and may have remained in Macedonia till he

---

[1] For Corinth and its church, see the Introduction to the Commentary on the First Epistle to the Corinthians in this series of Commentaries.

was joined by S. Paul. S. Luke, writing at a later date, simply
mentions what actually took place, without concerning himself with
S. Paul's original intention. He relates at length the story of the
riot at Ephesus; and, very briefly, S. Paul's journey through
Macedonia into Greece, his three months' stay there, and his return
to Macedonia on his way to Jerusalem (Ac. xx. 1-3).

Thus we approach the Second Epistle to the Corinthians without
any anticipation of historical difficulties. Nor is our confidence at
once disappointed. S. Paul and Timothy are again together (i. 1),
and the opening paragraphs suggest the happiest relations with the
Corinthian church. S. Paul speaks of his recent sufferings, and of
the divine consolation which has more than repaid him for them,
with the fullest expectation of sympathy; and asks for his converts'
prayers (i. 3-11). We observe indeed that the "affliction which
befell" him "in Asia" must have been far greater than S. Luke's
account would lead us to suppose. But there is as yet nothing to
suggest that the Corinthians themselves have had any share in
bringing it about; on the contrary, they are described as themselves
sharers in the affliction, and in the comfort which follows it (i. 6).
Nor, again, do we at first find any difficulty, as S. Paul bears witness to the clearness of his conscience (i. 12-14), and speaks of his
change of plan (i. 15-23). We naturally suppose that this change
had been involved in the course outlined in the First Epistle (1 Cor.
xvi. 5-9). At an earlier time, before the First Epistle was written,
S. Paul had intended to visit Corinth before going to Macedonia,
and after a visit to Macedonia to return to Corinth; but, when the
First Epistle was written this plan had been abandoned, and the
Corinthians deprived of one of the intended visits. As, however,
we pass from the first chapter to the second (i. 23-ii. 4), difficulties
begin to arise; and, as we proceed, they multiply. Indeed this
Epistle perhaps provides more historical difficulties than any other
book of the N.T. Our best course will be to take note of them as
they appear, and endeavour to solve them. As we do so, the story
that lies behind will become clearer.

The first difficulty arises when we consider more carefully S. Paul's
change of plan. "I call God for a witness upon my soul, that to
spare you I came no more unto Corinth" (i. 23). Why, we ask,
this intense solemnity in so simple a statement? Bad news of the
Corinthian church had reached S. Paul, before he wrote the First
Epistle; the possibility that, when he came, it would have to be

"with a rod," had been distinctly before his mind (1 Cor. iv. 21). What more natural than that S. Paul should have thought it well to send the First Epistle to bring the church to a better mind, before paying his personal visit? Yet apparently his change of purpose is under such strong suspicion that he must take an oath to clear himself from it. Was then this change of purpose the simple matter which at first we thought it? Moreover, our doubt is confirmed when we come to the second chapter. "But I determined this for myself, that I would not come again to you with sorrow. For if I make you sorry, who then is he that maketh me glad, but he that is made sorry by me? And I wrote this very thing, lest, when I came, I should have sorrow from them of whom I ought to rejoice; having confidence in you all, that my joy is the joy of you all. For out of much affliction and anguish of heart I wrote unto you with many tears; not that ye should be made sorry, but that ye might know the love which I have more abundantly unto you." Two difficulties here leap to the eye. In the first place, while S. Luke has told us of but one visit of S. Paul to Corinth before the despatch of the Second Epistle, these verses seem to speak of two. In the second place, S. Paul seems to refer to a letter, as well as to a visit, of which we know nothing; for it is not easy to suppose that he would refer to the First Epistle in the language which he here employs. The consideration of these two difficulties will take us into the heart of the historical problems.

Let us consider the former difficulty. Did S. Paul pay a visit to Corinth from Ephesus, of which S. Luke tells us nothing? S. Luke's silence would present no difficulty. He is a historian, not a mere chronicler. He writes with a definite purpose, and selects his facts in accordance with it. We can see this even in his Gospel, and it becomes clearer still, when we study the Acts of the Apostles side by side with S. Paul's Epistles. S. Luke's primary interest is in the advance of the Gospel, as the apostolic witness is borne "in Jerusalem, and in all Judaea and Samaria, and unto the uttermost part of the earth" (Ac. i. 8). He does indeed draw a beautiful picture of the church of Jerusalem in its earliest days; there, he seems to say, is the model which all churches would do well to follow. But he pays little attention to the life of the Gentile churches, after they have once been founded, or to S. Paul's relations with them. Who would suppose, from anything which S. Luke tells us, that S. Paul had any trouble with the churches of Galatia, or

that the church of Corinth ever caused him any serious anxiety?
What S. Luke ever desires to shew is how "mightily grew the word
of the Lord and prevailed" (Ac. xix. 20). Whether when men had
believed, and been baptized, they were henceforward all that they
ought to have been, is a question into which he hardly enters.
Thus the only visit of S. Paul to Corinth which S. Luke relates at
length is the first (Ac. xviii. 1–18); the only other visit which he
mentions, though it lasted for three months, is dismissed in half a
verse (Ac. xx. 3). Indeed, he does not definitely mention a visit to
Corinth in this case, but a visit to "Greece"; we only assume that
S. Paul was at Corinth, because no other important church in
"Greece" is known to us, and a Jewish plot against him as he was
"about to set sail for Syria" could hardly have occurred anywhere
else. If then S. Luke dismisses a three months' sojourn in this way,
we should hardly expect him to relate a hurried visit paid from
Ephesus. Moreover, S. Luke tells us little of S. Paul's doings
during the long period of his Ephesian work (xix. 8–10); half the
chapter devoted to Ephesus is filled by the riot which sent him
again upon his travels. If then, in order to explain S. Paul's words,
we must assume a visit to Corinth, of which S. Luke tells us nothing,
the assumption may be made without hesitation.

But does S. Paul's language force us to accept this additional
visit? All scholars are not here agreed, but its acceptance appears
to be inevitable. In 2 Cor. ii. 1, which has already been quoted, the
translation of the A.V. has been made from an incorrect text, and
even the R.V. has failed to make clear the Apostle's meaning. The
word "again" should be separated from the word "come," and
closely connected with the words "with sorrow." S. Paul speaks not
of two visits, the second of which was likely to be with sorrow, but
of two visits, the second of which was likely to be as sorrowful as
the first had been. Now it is most unlikely that S. Paul would
speak of his first visit to Corinth, in which he had founded the
church, as markedly a visit of sorrow. Sorrow no doubt he had
there in abundance even at his first visit; always he bore about "in
the body the dying of Jesus" (2 Cor. iv. 10); but the main feature
of the first visit was the success which attended it. The verse therefore before us, rightly interpreted, leaves it almost beyond doubt
that S. Paul paid a visit to Corinth, of which the Acts tells us
nothing. But this verse does not stand alone. The thirteenth
chapter will afford us even clearer evidence. The opening words

"This is the third time I am coming to you" are quite plain in their meaning. Even if in themselves the words could mean "This is the third time that I am intending to come," the context would render such an interpretation inadmissible. That S. Paul was always coming, and never came, was one of the sarcasms which he was meeting; the last thing which he would have done at this point would have been to dwell upon intentions, and not upon facts. Plainly, his meaning is that he has been to Corinth twice, and is coming this time prepared for definite action. The ambiguous words of xii. 14, "This is the third time I am ready to come to you" must be explained by the plain words of xiii. 1, and not the plain by the ambiguous. In xii. 14, that is to say, we must connect the words "the third time" with the word "come," and not with the words "I am ready." All this being so, it becomes plain that xiii. 2 must be translated as in the text of the R.V., and not as in the margin. The correct rendering is "as when I was present the second time," and not "as if I were present the second time." We conclude without hesitation that in our reconstruction of the history we must find room for a second visit to Corinth before the despatch of the Second Epistle. Nor need we have much hesitation in placing this visit after the despatch of the First Epistle, though great names may be quoted for the opposite view. The evidence lies in the First Epistle itself. If S. Paul, when he wrote it, had already been twice to Corinth, he would almost certainly have distinguished the two visits, as he does his two visits to the Galatians (Gal. iv. 13). But, on the contrary, he always looks back to his first visit, and to that alone (1 Cor. ii. 1–5 ; iii. 1, 2 etc.), and evidently derives his later information from the reports of others (1 Cor. i. 11; v. 1; xi. 18).

We return now to ii. 3, 4 ; and, having accepted as a fact this additional visit to Corinth, we are at once forced to the conclusion, that the reference in these verses is not to our First Epistle, but to another which has been lost to us. For this Epistle, on the view we have accepted, was a substitute not for a second visit, but for a third, which S. Paul had once intended to pay. Moreover, the language of v. 4, in which the circumstances and purpose of the letter are described, itself makes it most improbable that the First Epistle is in view. It is not that we cannot think of that letter as having been written "out of much affliction" and "with many tears." Tears probably came to the eyes of the Apostle more easily than to those of his modern commentators; he was not trained, like the modern Englishman, to an unnatural repression of emotion. Many tears may have been shed over the First Epistle, tears not without a touch of bitterness, as he wrote ch. iv. 8–13, of burning shame, as he wrote v. 1–8, and of exultation as he wrote the great paean of love in ch. xiii. But his words in 2 Cor. ii. 4 describe the character of the whole Epistle, to which he is referring; and they are not appropriate to the First Epistle. Here too we have to take into account the light thrown by later passages of our Second Epistle; and, when we do this, we find abundant confirmation of the conclusion that we have reached. Indeed the very next paragraph (ii. 5–11), though it has often been explained by 1 Cor. v. 1–8, does not find there any satisfactory explanation. It is true that 2 Cor. ii. 9 suggests that S. Paul had demanded, as he did demand in the First Epistle, the punishment of a member of the Corinthian church. He accepts the punishment imposed by the majority as adequately meeting the demands of the situation, and urges that the offending member should now be forgiven and restored. But for two reasons we cannot accept the identification of this offender with the offender of 1 Cor. v. The latter had been delivered unto Satan for the destruction of the flesh, that his spirit might be saved in the day of the Lord Jesus; discipline in his case, as in that of Ananias and Sapphira, was to take the form of death. Had S. Paul's sentence proved a *brutum fulmen*, the confidence, with which we shall find him speaking of his apostolic powers in xiii. 1–10, would have been quite impossible. Moreover, the language of S. Paul in ii. 5 and 10, where he speaks of his personal sorrow and personal forgiveness, makes it almost certain that the offender had in some way insulted or injured S. Paul, or some one who represented him. To this passage we should add a later one (vii. 5–16) which is still more illuminating. So painful in character was this lost Epistle that S. Paul (*v.* 8) was at one time sorry that he had sent it; while evidently he was personally much concerned in the matter with which his letter dealt. Probably we should not identify S. Paul himself in *v.* 12 with the man who "suffered the wrong"; in the latter part of the same verse, he speaks of himself in plain language. But evidently he was himself personally affected by the injury done, and *vv.* 7 and 11 describe a strong revulsion of feeling in his favour. Thus again we have definite facts for our historical reconstruction. S. Paul, after his second and painful visit to Corinth, instead of paying a third visit, as at one time he had intended, wrote a letter, which it cost him much to write, and the Corinthians much to receive. It was a letter full-charged with love and sorrow; and it demanded that the Corinthian church should take definite action against one of its members. That this letter has not come down to us need occasion no surprise. Many of S. Paul's Epistles have been lost, including, as 1 Cor. v. 9 shews, one to the Corinthians sent earlier than our First Epistle. The painful letter was probably short; and contained little of permanent value to the church.

The discussions which have occupied our attention have brought us nearly to the end of the second chapter. We can now advance more rapidly. Important as the chapters following are in many ways, they are less important for historical reconstruction. But there are two questions, upon which, if we read between the lines, they throw much light. What, as S. Paul writes his Epistle, are his real relations with the Corinthian church? That is the first question. And the second is closely connected with it. What are the chief dangers to which the church is exposed? We shall have, at a later stage, to consider very carefully the integrity of the Epistle. There are commentators of great name who think that we have in it, not a single Epistle, but fragments of several which have been artificially combined. It is therefore of particular importance to examine the situation which the earlier chapters presuppose, without reference to the later, in which it is maintained that the situation is different.

We consider then, first, the question of S. Paul's relations with the Corinthian church. Are they the same as those which we find in our First Epistle, or is there a noticeable change? In the first Epistle S. Paul writes as one who is on the whole master of the situation. The Corinthian church even then exhibited very unsatisfactory features. There was much party-spirit; there was teaching unworthy of the one foundation, Jesus Christ; there was self-satisfied intellectualism; there was heathen vice, and far too much compromise with the world; there was much to blame in the conduct of public worship, and serious error with regard to the resurrection. But the church had written to ask for S. Paul's instructions, and he replied as one who expected to be heard and obeyed. Of course, we must not overestimate the strength of his position. There were many, who were attached to other teachers rather than to himself (1 Cor. i. 12); and he has to defend the character of his teaching (ii. 1–iii. 2). There are signs of suspicion

(iv. 3–5), and of forgetfulness of the debt owed to him (iv. 8, 15).
S. Paul in ch. ix insists upon the reality of his apostolic position,
as he would not do, were it altogether unchallenged. But none the
less the whole tone of the Epistle, the clearness and confidence with
which, without a trace of apology, he issues his commands, and
delivers his doctrinal teaching, presuppose that by the church as a
whole his authority is accepted. We can hardly say the same of the
Second Epistle. S. Paul, no doubt, has just won a great victory; the
news brought of the church by Titus has filled him with joy; and
he makes the most of all this (vii. 13–16). But his satisfaction with
the result of his painful letter is not the measure of his satisfaction
with the situation as a whole. He writes indeed most affectionately;
there is an advance here upon the First Epistle; but the reason
appears to be that he feels that these expressions of affection are
more necessary. He is really, even in the early chapters, upon his
defence. He feels that he is being treated as a stranger; "need we,
as do some, epistles of commendation to you or from you?" (iii. 1).
He has to meet, not merely unworthy suspicions, but definite hostility and misrepresentation. He protests his sincerity again and
again (i. 12, 23; iv. 2; v. 11); and such words as those of ii. 17—
"but as of sincerity, but as of God, in the sight of God, speak we in
Christ"—prove how necessary he feels such protestations to be.
Though he disclaims the desire to commend himself, he feels that
he must not leave those who are faithful to him without material
for effective reply to his rivals for their allegiance (v. 12). Moreover,
the vindication of his ministry and apostleship is, even in the early
chapters, more lengthy and pronounced than in the First Epistle.
To this we must presently return. Evidently all is not right with
the relation of S. Paul to his Corinthian converts.

The second question is that of the dangers to which the church
is exposed. S. Paul, in his dealing with the churches he has founded,
is frequently obliged to conduct a war upon two fronts : he has to
combat both Gentile license, and Jewish legalism. Now in the First
Epistle he is chiefly concerned with the former ; in the Second he is
at least as much concerned with the latter. Gentile license is not
at all forgotten, as the solemn warnings of vi. 14–vii. 1 sufficiently
shew. This passage is indeed by many regarded as an interpolation,
and it certainly comes in most awkwardly. But there is no authority
in the manuscripts for omitting it ; and its awkwardness may be due
to the fact that S. Paul feels that its warnings must not be omitted

even in an Epistle mainly concerned with other things. It is the too intimate association of the Corinthian Christians with the heathen around them which is in part responsible for their alienation from himself; and warning must be given, though it is given by the way. A similar recollection of the sins, by which many of his converts are still stained, probably lies behind the appeal of v. 20—"we beseech you on behalf of Christ, be ye reconciled to God." But the chief danger, when S. Paul writes our Second Epistle, is evidently of a different character. It is a corruption of the word of God, for which Jewish teachers are responsible. If we regard the last four chapters of the Epistle as part of the same letter as the first nine, there can of course be no doubt of this. But we have not to wait for these later chapters; little reading between the lines is necessary to see that the same danger is in view in the earlier portion of the Epistle. "We are not as the many, corrupting the word of God" (ii. 17). "We have renounced the hidden things of shame, not walking in craftiness, nor handling the word of God deceitfully" (iv. 2). "We henceforth know no man after the flesh: even though we have known Christ after the flesh, yet now we know him so no more" (v. 16). What is the implication of such words as these? Gentile license might reject the word of God, but it could not so naturally be said to corrupt it; and Gentile Christians were not likely to have claimed to know Christ after the flesh. S. Paul is now face to face, as in the First Epistle he was not, with the danger which he had already had to meet in the churches of Galatia, the opposition of Judaistic or Pharisaic Christianity. The Ghetto at Corinth was large, and its people bitterly opposed to S. Paul, who had so largely robbed them of their Gentile adherents (Ac. xviii. 5-17); a few months after the despatch of the Second Epistle, he nearly lost his life at their hands (Ac. xx. 3). If Pharisaic teachers had been able to work serious mischief in Galatia, we need not be surprised if we find them at Corinth attacking S. Paul's teaching there also. We must remember that in S. Paul's time there was no such separation between Jews and Christians as that to which we are accustomed to-day. To the eyes of the Gentile world Christians appeared to be merely a sect of the Jews; S. Paul himself is described as "a ringleader of the sect of the Nazarenes" (Ac. xxiv. 5). Though the Jews might find a crucified Messiah a great stumbling-block, it was not so much S. Paul's proclamation of Jesus as the Christ, which incensed them against him, as his insistence upon the equality of Gentiles and

Jews in the body of Christ, and his attitude to the Mosaic law. The early church of Jerusalem had been popular with most of the Jews (Ac. ii. 47 ; v. 13); and, but for S. Stephen, might have continued so. Thus we cannot doubt that everywhere among the Jewish communities scattered over the Empire there was an opening for "another Gospel" than that of S. Paul, a gospel which would indeed maintain that Jesus was the Christ soon to return from heaven to set up the Kingdom of God, but which would insist that the law which He had obeyed must be obeyed by all who claimed to be His followers, and that the Kingdom which He would soon set up would be one in which none but the circumcised would find any but a very humble place.

Now it is just such a corruption of the word of God as this, which S. Paul has to fight and overcome at Corinth ; and even the earlier chapters of our Epistle shew this. Why, for example, does S. Paul in iii. 12–18 introduce so seemingly ungenerous a contrast as that which he draws between Moses and himself? The Moses of whom he speaks is plainly not the Moses of history, the deliverer even more than the lawgiver of his people, but the Moses of the Pharisees ; and the contrast drawn between the effect of the law and the effect of the gospel is precisely that with which the Epistles to the Romans and to the Galatians have made us familiar. If we do not find controversy as to circumcision and the law so prominent or so detailed as in Galatia, that is because circumstances have altered. The struggle at Corinth is not so much between the law and the gospel as between S. Paul and certain false apostles. The Conference of Jerusalem (Ac. xv) had taken place before the Second Epistle to the Corinthians was written ; it was no longer possible to maintain that the observance of the law was necessary for salvation (cf. infra, p. 125). But S. Paul's opponents understood what scholars in their studies do not always understand, that for the vast majority of mankind the acceptance of truth primarily rests upon the trust which they repose in the character and competence of their teachers, and not upon understanding of the intellectual grounds upon which their teachers base what they say. "Abide thou in the things which thou hast learned and hast been assured of, knowing of whom thou hast learned them" (2 Tim. iii. 14). The great battles are won not so much by doctrines as by personalities, though no doubt it is the doctrine which forms the personality identified with it, and judgment upon the one involves judgment upon the other. Arius e.g. was defeated by S. Athanasius, as the Pharisaic teachers by S. Paul, not so much by argument, as by greater suffering and nobler action. Thus the most effective method of undermining S. Paul's teaching was to attack his character, and to deny the reality of his apostleship. S. Paul was a master both of the kind of dialectic which appealed to the Jews, and of the deeper appeals to the real needs of the human mind and heart; those who met him on his own ground would be likely to fare ill. It was far more effective to say that he had never been one of the personal followers of the Lord, and knew little about Him; that the little which he knew he had received at second hand; and that Jewish Christians, who had known Christ in the flesh, were far more trustworthy guides than S. Paul could be. Moreover, if S. Paul was a true Apostle, why did he not, like other Apostles, claim maintenance from those to whom he had proclaimed the Gospel, as Christ had authorized His Apostles to do? Thus we find that, in the Epistle to the Galatians, S. Paul defends his apostleship first, and only passes to dialectic afterwards; and that, in the Second Epistle to the Corinthians, his apostleship is evidently the main issue. S. Paul makes a personal matter of the controversy, because it was for the Corinthians essentially a personal matter, and could be decided upon none but personal grounds.

Now it is only when we recognize this that we understand S. Paul's words, even in the early chapters of the Epistle. In i. 13, 14 the acknowledgment of the truth of S. Paul's words is bound up with the acknowledgment of S. Paul himself. He cannot pass by a charge of "lightness," since he knows that, if they make light of him, they will also make light of his message (i. 17-20). So too all that follows is intensely personal. S. Paul never wearies of speaking of his love for his converts, of the closeness of his union with them, of the glory of his ministry as seen in its results, of the depth of the union with his divine Master which his life of suffering has brought about. Everywhere behind his words we can see the charges brought against him, and which in the interests of the Gospel he is obliged to meet. If, unwillingly enough, he commends himself, it is because he cannot successfully commend his gospel without doing so. If we ourselves weary a little of his explanations of his refusal to be supported by the Corinthians, and think that he "doth protest too much," we must remember what a lethal weapon for the attack upon his apostleship his action in this matter afforded. S. Paul is entirely selfless; "all things are for your sakes" (iv. 15).

But he knows that that detestable maxim of the world "Never explain" is a maxim of pride, not of Christian charity; and that one dangerous form of vanity is the vanity of those who cannot bear to be thought vain. In the early chapters, he holds himself in leash; he will let himself go later. But he is preparing for the final attack from the first. Behind the contrast between S. Paul and Moses we can see the *a fortiori* contrast between S. Paul and the present champions of the Mosaic law; and he dwells upon his sufferings because he knows that it is by these sufferings and the identification with Christ which they have brought, that God has made him the Apostle he is.

In chapters viii. and ix. S. Paul deals with that collection for the Church at Jerusalem which lay so near his heart, both because of the poverty of the Jewish Christians, and because of the opportunity which it provided for demonstrating and deepening the unity of the whole Church. This collection will be dealt with in the course of the Commentary; we are at present concerned with these chapters simply as providing materials for our historical reconstruction. We learn from viii. 6 that Titus has already been to Corinth at least twice, the second time as the bearer of the Epistle of sorrow which has been lost to us. In viii. 10 we learn that the collection had begun at Corinth in the previous year. In viii. 16–24 we see that Titus is now going to Corinth again to carry our Second Epistle. In *vv.* 17, 18, and 22 the past tenses are what are called epistolary aorists; they refer to the moment at which S. Paul is writing, a moment which will lie in the past when the Epistle is read; in English in each case we should use the present tense. So it is again in ix. 3 and 5. No serious historical difficulty occurs in these chapters. But, before leaving them, we should observe the tone in which S. Paul writes. It does not seem quite the same as that of the First Epistle, where he deals with the same subject. In the First Epistle the tone is authoritative. "As I gave order to the churches of Galatia, so also do ye. Upon the first day of the week let each of you lay by him in store, as he may prosper, that no collections be made when I come" (1 Cor. xvi. 1, 2). The tone of the Second Epistle is different. "I speak not by way of commandment" (viii. 8). "Herein I give my judgment" (viii. 10). The two chapters are most tactful, and very effective; they are a rich mine of argument and appeal for Christian generosity. But S. Paul does not seem altogether at ease. His position has been shaken, and the collection is imperilled.

Very significant is viii. 5. The Macedonians, he says, first "gave their own selves to the Lord, and to us by the will of God." Let the Corinthians take note of that. The two things go together. They cannot be at once devoted to the Lord, and disloyal to His Apostle. Very significant also is viii. 20, 21. S. Paul has to be very careful. He must guard against the slightest suspicion of making personal profit in the matter.

We have now reached the last four chapters; and it is here that the main *crux* of the Epistle occurs. We expect it to draw to a close with some such words as we shall find in xiii. 11–14. S. Paul speaks of the "collection for the saints" both in the First Epistle to the Corinthians and in the Epistle to the Romans, and in each case at the end. His Epistles generally become more directly practical towards their close; and the right use of money is one of the most practical of our duties. But here, after speaking of the collection, S. Paul makes a fresh beginning, and the change of tone is startling. "Now I Paul myself intreat you by the meekness and gentleness of Christ, I who in your presence am lowly among you, but being absent am of good courage toward you: yea, I beseech you, that I may not when present shew courage with the confidence wherewith I count to be bold against some, which count of us as if we walked according to the flesh" (x. 1, 2). The rest of these chapters are in accordance with this beginning. Stern and strong disciplinary action, S. Paul says, may have to characterize his approaching visit. His chief opponents are attacked with strong invective, and caustic irony. But the church itself comes under the lash. Its moral corruptions are denounced as severely as in the First Epistle. "I fear, lest by any means, when I come, I should find you not such as I would, and should myself be found of you such as ye would not; lest by any means there should be strife, jealousy, wraths, factions, backbitings, whisperings, swellings, tumults; lest, when I come again, my God should humble me before you, and I should mourn for many of them that have sinned heretofore, and repented not of the uncleanness and fornication and lasciviousness which they committed" (xii. 20, 21). We cannot but be startled by such language as this. How, we ask, after the warm words of praise in ch. vii, after saying that in everything he is of good courage concerning the Corinthians (vii. 16), can S. Paul write as he does in these final chapters? There may be considerable variety of tone to be found in the Epistle to the Galatians, and in the First Epistle to the Corinthians; but there is nothing as startling as this. Moreover, what are we to say of S. Paul's tact? As a rule, his tact is wonderful. Exquisitely sensitive himself, he is ever mindful of the sensitiveness of those whom he addresses; he feels their pulse with one hand, while he writes with the other. Yet what, we may be inclined to say, could be more tactless than his procedure in this Epistle as it stands? No doubt it is well, when stern things have to be said, to begin with generous recognition of all that is admirable in those whom we are about to blame: that is S. Paul's way. But it does not seem at all well to deal with a difficult situation gently and charitably; to appear to have said all that is in our minds, ending upon a note of love and approval; to ask for generous contributions to a cause which we had at heart; and then to blow up the dying fire, and deal with the old trouble far more severely than we have dealt with it before. Is it conceivable that S. Paul of all people would do this, while prefacing his stern language with an appeal to the gentleness and reasonableness of Christ? Nor is even this all; S. Paul may appear not only tactless, but unjust. We read his admirable words, describing the way in which the Corinthians should now deal with the man who had injured him (ii. 5–11), and bestows his own full forgiveness; we find in the seventh chapter that the penitence of the Corinthian church was so deep for the injury done to S. Paul, that the words, in which he describes it, are perhaps the finest description in all Scripture of what true penitence involves (vii. 11). How then, we ask, can he turn and rend them as he seems to do in the concluding chapters? It is not the case, as has been sometimes urged, that in the earlier part of the Epistle S. Paul addresses the now loyal majority, and in the later the disloyal minority; he addresses the whole Church throughout.

Now it is the presence of this difficulty which has led to a suggestion, brilliantly worked out by a number of writers. This is that the last four chapters are no part of this Epistle, but are a fragment saved from the letter of sorrow, of which we have already spoken. That there is no manuscript authority for such a rearrangement of the text is no doubt a serious difficulty, but not one which is in itself conclusive. There are several facts which we must here remember. We know nothing of the way in which S. Paul's Epistles were first collected, and there is evidence that our Second Epistle was not widely known as early as the First. When S. Clement of Rome wrote to the Corinthians about A.D. 95, he had the First

Epistle before him, but it is not probable that he had the Second. He speaks of "the Epistle of Blessed Paul," as if it stood alone, not only for himself, but for the Corinthians; and the Second Epistle would have been so much to his purpose in the appeal which he is making, that we can hardly suppose that he would not have used it, if he had had it before him. The probability is that, though our First Epistle, so full of teaching for the whole Church of Christ, was from the first frequently copied and widely distributed, it was not so with S. Paul's other letters to Corinth. But would they not at any rate have been carefully preserved by the Church of Corinth? We cannot be sure of this. The Epistles of S. Paul were not yet Canonical Scripture; the Bible of the early Church was the Old Testament. Moreover, all his letters were probably written upon papyrus, a very perishable material. What more likely than that the Corinthian church would carefully preserve such letters, or portions of letters, as seemed to be of permanent value, and destroy the rest? Especially would this be likely to happen, when a letter dealt with the misdoings of particular members of the Church. We do not wish to know the name of the Corinthian Christian who insulted and outraged S. Paul, nor would S. Paul himself have wished us to know it. Thus, if the four chapters are the concluding part of an Epistle, the earlier chapters of which dealt with this particular offender, we can easily understand how they might come to stand alone. The offender had been punished and was forgiven, and the Corinthian church had made all the amends possible. Would not S. Paul have said "It is finished and done with now. We do not want the story written with an iron pen, and graven in the rock for ever. Keep the second part of the letter, if you will. I was once sorry I had written it; but God blessed it—let it stand. But we will put the first part in the fire, and forget it." If S. Paul so spake, what would the Corinthians have done? On the roll, on which our Second Epistle had been copied, they would have copied also the fragment of the earlier Epistle which they wished to keep. Then, in after days, when the whole roll was again and again copied for other churches, its history might easily have been forgotten, and the Epistle read as we read it to-day. This is much more probable than that two Epistles of S. Paul accidentally lost, the one its concluding, and the other its opening portion, and were then mistaken for parts of the same Epistle. The erosions of time and chance do not respect our paragraphs and full stops with the nicety which is here required; the cuts are too clean to be other than intentional. But the story outlined above seems to be quite possible. It is very difficult to imagine how an interpolation, such as that of vi. 14–vii. 1, could take place; but an addition at the end is not unlikely, and we shall examine the modern theory without prejudice.

What then is to be said for it? The one great argument in its favour is that it gets rid of the difficulty, which so strongly presses upon us. The four chapters are not quite what the references in our Second Epistle to its predecessor would have led us to expect: neither sorrow nor love (ii. 4) seems as prominent as indignation and stern resolution. But we can easily understand how S. Paul might have regretted at one time having written them, as well as the pain which such a letter would have caused. These, however, are but details. The great point is that the separation of the two parts of the Epistle makes it no longer necessary to shew that they are consistent one with another. On this theory, the last four chapters were written under painful circumstances, and to a Church still unrepentant for grievous wrong; the first nine were written when S. Paul's sternness had produced its salutary effect, and the Corinthians had come to a different mind. Many other arguments are urged in favour of the modern theory, but they are quite unconvincing in themselves. Ultimately, our decision must be made in accordance with our answer to much broader questions. These questions are two. Attractive as the modern theory is, does it not raise greater difficulties than it solves? Is it not possible to solve the difficulties which trouble us in a more natural way?

But, before passing to these questions, it will be well to say something about the subordinate arguments, and justify the assertion that they are unconvincing. Some are concerned with the use of words in the two sections of the Epistle. It is urged, for example, that S. Paul's "confidence," his "good courage," his "glorying," are of a very different character in the one and in the other. In the one section he is confident and glories in the Corinthians themselves; in the other he is confident of his power to deal with the hostility which he will have to meet, and can glory in little but the experience which has conformed him to his Master. There is not much in this. It simply illustrates the difference in tone between the two parts of the Epistle, and that is not in dispute. More important are the instances, in which it is urged that the first nine chapters contain references to the last four, which were in fact written earlier. The best example is perhaps the way in which S. Paul in iii. 1 and v. 12 denies that he is "again commending" himself. Such words would no doubt be very natural after the great "glorying" of the eleventh and twelfth chapters. So again, in v. 13, S. Paul's words about being beside himself to God might well refer to what he had said as to the visions and revelations granted to him. We may notice also the marked correspondence between the accounts of the letter of sorrow given in ii. 3, and S. Paul's words in xiii. 10 where he explains the purpose that he has in writing. (Cf. also i. 23 with xiii. 2; ii. 9 with x. 6; iv. 2 with xii. 6; vii. 2 with xii. 17, 18.) But such facts as these may easily convey a false impression. We have to ask, not only "May these passages be regarded as cross-references?" but also "Are they unintelligible on the ordinary view?" The fact will be found to be that there is not one which on the ordinary view presents any difficulty. To take the best example, such words as "Are we beginning again to commend ourselves?" are in any case perfectly natural. In dealing with the Corinthians, S. Paul was unhappily obliged to "commend himself" frequently. He did it in our First Epistle; probably he did it in every Epistle that he wrote to them. Interesting again, but quite valueless, is a geographical argument which has been urged. In x. 16 S. Paul speaks of his hope of being able to preach the gospel "even unto the parts beyond" the Corinthians, and the Epistle to the Romans, which was written later from Corinth itself, makes it almost certain that it is Rome which is especially in S. Paul's mind (cf. Rom. i. 9–15). It is argued that S. Paul's language is quite natural, if he is writing from Ephesus, but not if he is writing from Macedonia; and that we have therefore an indication that the chapter, in which the words appear, belongs not to our Second Epistle, but to the Epistle of sorrow. We have, however, only to remember S. Paul's practice of following the great roads, and, unless prevented, taking the provinces of the Empire in order, to see that S. Paul's language is entirely natural, whether at the moment he is at Ephesus or in Macedonia. He is not thinking of the map, but of the natural order of the cities of the Empire. Just as to him Corinth was always beyond Ephesus, so Rome was always beyond Corinth. Thus not one of the subordinate arguments which are urged in favour of the modern view is at all convincing; and the same must be said of the subordinate arguments which are urged against it. Once more, the great argument in favour of the theory is that it gets rid of a serious difficulty. That must turn the scale in its favour, unless it is found to introduce equal difficulties of another kind, or we can deal with the problem in some simpler way.

It is now time to turn to the considerations which should convince us that the modern theory must be rejected. The first is this. We have seen that the Epistle of sorrow was a substitute for a personal visit, which S. Paul had intended to pay (cf. i. 23–ii. 3). But the four chapters x–xiii are not appropriate in such a letter. On the contrary S. Paul there speaks as one coming almost immediately. It is true that the chapters do not categorically assert that he is doing so, but their tone of menace implies it. In view of the current sneers at S. Paul's weakness which they reveal, it would be absurd to speak as he speaks, unless he were prepared immediately to make good his words.

But this is a trifling difficulty, compared with another. In chs. i–ix S. Paul writes with deep thankfulness for the result which his Epistle of sorrow has produced; evidently it was as great as he had dared to hope, and he expresses himself as abundantly satisfied. Yet all that has taken place, as far as we can see, is that a particular offender has been punished, and a strong revulsion of feeling taken place in S. Paul's favour. All is easy to understand, if S. Paul's letter had asked nothing more. But suppose that 2 Cor. x–xiii formed the climax and concluding portion of the letter of sorrow; how does the matter stand then? These chapters not only repeat in the strongest language those charges against the morality of the Corinthian Christians, which we find in our First Epistle; but raise the dominating issue of this part of S. Paul's career. Pharisaic Christianity is challenged to a duel to the death. Its teachers are declared to be "false apostles, deceitful workers, fashioning themselves into apostles of Christ" (xi. 13). They are charged with arrogance (x. 5), fatuous self-conceit (x. 12), impertinent intrusion into the sphere assigned by God to S. Paul (x. 13–15), and compared to Satan himself (xi. 14). Their attitude to the Corinthians is declared to be insulting (xi. 20), and the Corinthians are plainly told to compare S. Paul with them, and to make their choice. Yet when S. Paul writes his letter of thanksgiving, we can find no indication that the great issues thus raised have been faced; on the contrary, as we have seen, the old slanders against him are still rife, and the old corruption of the Gospel is still going on. None the less, S. Paul *ex hypothesi* is perfectly satisfied, and "in everything

*d*2

of good courage concerning" the Corinthians. Will it be suggested that, on the contrary, the person condemned was no other than the head of the hostile mission? If so, why is S. Paul still nursing his grievances? But, quite apart from this, the suggestion is inadmissible. The man, whom the Corinthian church condemned and punished, must have been a member of that church, not an intruder from outside. The Corinthians could no more have imposed a penalty upon an emissary of Jewish Christians living elsewhere than upon S. Paul himself. No! it is as plain as the day that S. Paul's enemies "live and are mighty," and that, if his letter demanded their repudiation, it has failed of its effect. In face of this overwhelming difficulty the modern theory breaks down; there is no road that way, and we must try to find another.

The first thing to notice is this. Though the difficulty has been stated as strongly as possible, it is in fact much exaggerated. S. Paul in chs. i–ix shews nothing like the complete satisfaction with the Corinthian church that he is said to shew, while in chs. x–xiii he is not nearly as severe towards it as he is said to be. The advocates of the modern theory base their case upon selected passages, which they in part misunderstand, without sufficient attention to the Epistle as a whole. This has to some extent been shewn already, and it will now be shewn more thoroughly. As this is done, the real background will become clear, and the integrity of the Epistle be vindicated.

But, before turning back to the Epistle, it will be well to offer some remarks about the praise which S. Paul almost always bestows upon his converts. We shall be much mistaken, if we interpret it *au pied de la lettre*. In the first place, we must allow something for the language of oriental compliment. To do so is not to charge the Apostle with insincerity. Language means what it is understood to mean; we cannot abandon conventional forms without giving a false impression. If we sign ourselves "yours truly" to complete strangers, we do not promise the devotion of a lifetime; to abandon the conventional expression of goodwill would be to mislead. Now orientals go further in the language of compliment than we do, and S. Paul is an oriental, not an Englishman. Let us take a few examples. Is it hypercritical to suggest that S. Paul's words in ii. 3—"having confidence in you all, that my joy is the joy of you all"—are not entirely consistent with the facts revealed by the context? Or consider viii. 7: "But as ye abound in everything, in faith, and utterance, and knowledge, and in all earnestness, and in your love to us, see that ye abound in this grace also." Was the Corinthian church quite as perfect and as gifted as these words would suggest? Did S. Paul think it so? English bishops do not write in this way, but orientals often do. Perhaps, if some of our commentators numbered oriental bishops among their correspondents, they would understand S. Paul the better for it. But far more important is it to remember both the reality of the change which the Gospel had made, and S. Paul's own character. Unsatisfactory as S. Paul's Corinthians were, much as their conduct fell short of the standard of Christ, the very existence of a Christian Church in such a place as Corinth was a miracle of grace. "*Ecclesia Dei in Corintho*," says Bengel, "*laetum et ingens paradoxon*"; and S. Paul's words are words of thanksgiving for what God has done. Moreover, "love believes divinities, being itself divine"; the burning love which enabled S. Paul to "endure all things," enabled him also "to believe all things, to hope all things," and not to "take account of evil." Hope, like love and faith, lies largely in the will. When S. Paul rejoices that in all things he is of good courage concerning the Corinthians, we must not suppose that all cause for anxiety has passed away. It is for the future conduct of the Corinthians to justify his words rather than for the logic of the present situation; and the more affectionately and hopefully he is able to speak, the more likely it is that the justification will be forthcoming. Once more, we must allow for S. Paul's individuality. He is not a man of equable temperament, but one subject to strong alternations of feeling. As with the great mystics, "joy unspeakable" may soon be followed by "the dark night of the soul," and all the more if the "thorn in the flesh" has once more laid him low. Thus if we put his words upon the rack, and ask whether all that he says at one moment is strictly consistent with all that he says at another, we are forgetting the conditions of our problem.

Now it is with these thoughts in our minds that we should examine the contrast which the two parts of the Epistle present. S. Paul no doubt uses warm words of praise not infrequently in the earlier part of the Epistle; but, as we have already seen, it does not require much reading between the lines to see that he is still far from satisfied. Everywhere, and not only in the final chapters, he is on his defence, and has to protest his sincerity. Everywhere we can see that his gospel and his apostleship are challenged, and that preachers of another gospel, only too acceptable to the Corinthians, are continually in his thoughts. S. Paul speaks of the sufferings, which make him the Apostle he is, in the earlier chapters just as he speaks in the later, and with the same object in view. If in the earlier chapters he dwells especially upon the way in which they identify him with his dying and risen Master, it is precisely this thought which will lend power to his later appeal. Indeed it is the character of the contrast between the earlier and later chapters which gives the clearest evidence as to their true order. Is it conceivable that S. Paul, after delivering himself of "the great invective" but a few weeks earlier, would go back and express the same thoughts in a restrained and tentative way, when no real improvement had taken place in the attitude of the Corinthians to the Jewish mission? As a preparation for the great invective already forming in his mind, nothing could be better than his earlier references to the evil. But how could he, after delivering it, write as if "willing to wound, and yet afraid to strike," and that while dwelling repeatedly upon the freedom of speech which he is able to employ? Such a theory is, in the literal sense of the word, preposterous; it puts first what must have come last.

But now let us grapple with the passage, upon which the upholders of the modern theory so largely depend, the passage which describes S. Paul's joy at the good news which Titus has brought to him (vii. 5–16). We notice first how it is introduced; nowhere shall we find clearer indications that all is not yet well. "Our mouth is open unto you, O Corinthians, our heart is enlarged. Ye are not straitened in us, but ye are straitened in your own affections. Now for a recompense in like kind (I speak as unto my children) be ye also enlarged....Open your hearts to us: we wronged no man, we corrupted no man, we took advantage of no man. I say it not to condemn you: for I have said before, that ye are in our hearts to die together and live together. Great is my boldness of speech toward you, great is my glorying on your behalf: I am filled with comfort, I overflow with joy in all our affliction" (vi. 11–13; vii. 2–4). Warm and glowing words indeed—a beautiful revelation of the heart of S. Paul! Yet how much lies behind them of unrequited affection, and of generous sacrifice still met with coldness and suspicion! But how then, it will be asked, are we to understand the paragraph which follows? The letter, which S. Paul had sent by Titus had dealt with one subject only, the outrage which the Apostle had had to endure; and it is the repentance of the Corinthians for it which is alone in view. So S. Paul distinctly says "In everything ye approved yourselves to be pure in the matter" (vii. 11). "In the matter"—we must bear in mind that limitation. Indeed *v.* 12 suggests that S. Paul's letter was such, that it might have seemed to have nothing in view but one particular outrage. What S. Paul had said to Titus was that on receipt of his letter the Corinthians would come to a better mind (*v.* 14), and what Titus so affectionately remembered (*v.* 15) was the obedience with which they had responded to S. Paul's demand for the punishment of the offender. Not a word is here said of anything else; and we misunderstand the passage, if we suppose that S. Paul is guilty of inconsistency, when both before and afterwards he blames the Corinthians for other things. No doubt, if chs. x–xiii had been written some weeks before, and had been in the hands of the Corinthians when they took action, S. Paul's strong words of approval would have to be differently interpreted: but we argue in a circle, if we first assume the modern theory in interpreting this passage, and then use the passage, thus interpreted, as the main buttress of the modern theory. In this one matter, the question of the moment, the action of the Corinthians had been all that S. Paul had desired. S. Paul says so, and regards the fact as of the best augury for the future (*v.* 16). But that is all that he says, and no presumption is created against the integrity of the Epistle.

We need not dwell further upon chs. viii and ix. No doubt they come in awkwardly; but, as we shall presently see, they could not be omitted, and no better place for them can be suggested. S. Paul writes very tactfully. Strongly as he urges his point, there is not a word which could undo the effect of the earlier chapters, or render the Corinthians unwilling to listen to his final appeal. Indeed it was all to the good that S. Paul, who was about to denounce fiercely the Jewish teachers, should shew so loyal a care for the church of Jerusalem. We pass to the final chapters. Against whom are they chiefly directed? They are addressed no doubt, not to a rebellious minority, but, like the rest of the Epistle, to the Church as a whole. But that is not the point. Against whom is the attack directed— against the Corinthians, or against the Jewish counter-mission, and its leader, these new and sinister "Apostles," who are leading the Corinthians astray? "Now I Paul myself intreat you by the meekness and gentleness of Christ, I who in your presence am lowly among you, but being absent am of good courage toward you : yea, I beseech you, that I may not when present shew courage with the confidence wherewith I count to be bold against some, which count of us as if we walked according to the flesh." Who are these "some"? They are the Jewish teachers. It is their sneer which is quoted, as the parallel passage in *v.* 10 shews. There, according to the best text, which our R.V. does not follow, substantially the same sarcasm is ascribed to the Pharisaic leader. The Corinthians are only concerned, in so far as any of them continue to support the enemies of S. Paul and of the gospel. S. Paul, like Pascal in the *Lettres Provinciales*, is attacking people other than those to whom the letter is addressed. The "strong holds" (*v.* 4), the "imaginations," the high things "exalted against the knowledge of God" (*v.* 5), are the fortresses of the Jewish argument. Battle must be joined at last; the strongholds must fall; and, when the Church as a whole has returned to its allegiance, the time will come to deal with the rebellion which still remains (*v.* 6). So in *v.* 7, S. Paul turns to his main opponent, the leader of the counter-mission. It is his words, as we have seen, that are quoted in *v.* 10. It is the fatuous self-conceit of this person and his followers which is exposed in *v.* 12; it is their intrusion into the churches won by S. Paul's labours which is denounced in *vv.* 13–18. The Corinthians are hardly mentioned, except when, in *vv.* 14, 15, S. Paul claims them for his own, and then his words are words of confidence.

But now, at the opening of ch. xi, S. Paul does turn to the Corinthians. Is there anything here inconsistent with the earlier part of the Epistle? There is not a word. The sarcasm of ch. x is instantly dropped, as S. Paul turns to his spiritual children. Humbly he speaks, and with the pathos of wounded affection, as he had spoken in the Epistle to the Galatians (cf. Gal. iv. 19, 20). Indeed we should continually compare that earlier Epistle; the danger is the same in the one case and in the other, and the method of dealing with it very similar. The Corinthians are the bride of Christ, and S. Paul the bridegroom's friend, who must bring to Him His bride in spotless purity (*vv.* 2, 3). What imagery could be more beautiful, or more full of honour to the Corinthian church? Nor is there more than a touch of sarcasm in *v.* 4. The Corinthians bear well enough with a corrupted gospel; surely then they will bear with him. It is the pathos of wounded love, that speaks again in *vv.* 7–11, as the old sore is once more opened, and S. Paul thinks of the days that he spent with the Corinthians. The fire indeed breaks out, as in *vv.* 12–15 he turns to the real enemy. But the Corinthians are unscathed by it; it is only in the next section that we find the first direct word of blame for them, and then the blame cannot be withheld. Humbly he speaks still; let them think him foolish, if they have the heart to do so. Foolish indeed he may seem to be, if his words be weighed in the balance of the sanctuary; but speak he must at last. It is their pride that is at fault, the old intellectual pride, which he had pilloried only last spring, when he wrote the First Epistle—the pride which leads to abject grovelling before the sophists and windbags who know how to dazzle them. *"Qui sont ces gens-là? Sont-ils Chrétiens?"* Will the Corinthians never understand that "the kingdom of God is not in word but in power," and that the grand proof that we belong to Christ is that we share His character and experience? So S. Paul is borne on to that great glorying in the Cross, which those who love him can scarcely trust themselves to read without tears. "Look on this picture and on that." The new teachers may be very brilliant, but where are the marks of the nails? S. Paul has them. The Jewish lash has torn him, and the Roman rods bruised him; he bears branded on his body the marks of Jesus. On the perilous seas of the heathen world,

> If blood be the price of admiralty,
> Lord God! he has paid in full.

What labour, what privation, what peril has been spared to him? Jew and Gentile, false friend and bitter enemy, have filled up the tale of sorrow and agony :

> Lone on the land, and homeless on the water,
> Pass I in patience till the work be done.

He is weak with all the weakness, burning with all the sin, of the least of his children, a living sacrifice, sweet with the fragrance of the Passion of the Lord. Do they say "Let another praise thee, and not thine own mouth"? He hears them saying it, and he has his answer ready. "I am become foolish : ye compelled me; for I ought to have been commended of you" (xii. 11). Was it for the Corinthians to blame him? Is it for us Christians of a later day, who live by his gospel, yet avoid his pain? What is there in any of this inconsistent with what has gone before?

Thus far for earth; now for heaven, as S. Paul passes from the patience of the saints to the foretastes of the great reward. Never before has he spoken of these; better that men should judge by the life they witness, and the words they hear from him. The secret of the Lord is with them that fear Him ; it is not for those who are lovers of marvels rather than lovers of God. But he must speak now. Do the Corinthians think that behind his life and witness there is nothing but "strong holds" of dialectic, human "imaginations" exactly the same in their general character as those which he is coming to destroy ? Not so. The Gentile peoples are his province ; he

> may not wander from the allotted field
> Before his work be done : but, being done,
> Let visions of the night or of the day
> Come, as they will ; and many a time they come,
> Until this earth he walks on seems not earth,
> This light that strikes his eyeballs is not light,
> This air that smites his forehead is not air
> But vision.

Yes ! he too has seen what he has seen, and heard what he has heard, "unspeakable words, which it is not lawful for a man to utter." Have they lifted him too high ? God has seen to that. That sore malady which they know so well—if it springs from Satan's hatred, it springs also from the deeper depth of the love and wisdom of God. It is his very weakness that is the condition of the supply of the strength of Christ. The greater the human weakness, the fuller the supply of the divine strength. If he glories therefore, he will glory in that. What is there in all this inconsistent with the earlier chapters ?

So the deepest and most revealing of all the Epistles draws to its close. Once more he speaks of his determination never to be a burden to them. But it is not to boast of it; it is only that he may exhibit the father's heart, gladly spending and being spent for them, thinking of their future, not of his own, and only desiring not to be loved the less, because he loves so abundantly. What will the coming visit be ? Will it be to rejoice over the living, or to mourn over the dead, humbled before God because of his identification with them ? This time he cannot hold his hand. If they still deny that Christ speaks in him, that great Christ, Who was crucified through weakness, must shew that He is living through the power of God. It is themselves that the Corinthians should test, not their Apostle and father. May there be no need for his stern discipline ! Better that his apostolic power should still be denied than that he should have to prove its reality upon those whom he loves. Then the few exquisite words of farewell, the salutation of all the saints, and his own blessing in the threefold name.

We see then how little foundation there is for the contention that the later chapters of the Epistle are inconsistent with the earlier. Yet none the less there is a change of tone, and an arrangement of the subject-matter of the Epistle which is not what we should at first have expected. It is with an attempt to explain these two facts that the Introduction shall end. The truth is that the modern commentator does not always understand how it is necessary to deal with such crises as that which arose in the church of Corinth, or the complications which they involve. Let us consider the situation, as it would have presented itself to S. Paul at Ephesus. He had to deal with three things. The first was a moral outrage which he could not pass over. The second was the collection for the church of Jerusalem. The third was the counter-mission of the Pharisaic party, and the bad spirit in the Corinthian church, for which it was so largely responsible. Not one of these things could S. Paul pass by. It was e.g. essential that the Corinthians should take their part in the collection, and at once begin to get their contribution ready. Not only were they probably of all S. Paul's churches the best able to give, but they were of all the one, the reality of whose Christianity was most likely to be suspected by the church of Jerusalem. Now it was very difficult to deal with all these matters together, and the apparent awkwardness of his arrangement of what he has to say simply reflects the awkwardness of the situation in which he finds himself. He acted with admirable wisdom; and arranged his letter, as we shall see, in the right way. When a bad spirit has expressed itself in a definite outrage, the one in command should deal with the outrage first. Those who have been guilty of it have delivered themselves into his hands. The outrage at any rate nobody can defend; it rallies all men of goodwill to his side. In dealing with it, he can count upon their support, and strike a heavy blow against the bad spirit from which it proceeds. Then, having won the necessary victory, he should consolidate his position. If he is wise, he will treat all who have supported him as being fundamentally upon his side, and express a generous confidence in them. The next step will be to invite their cooperation in the common work which lies to hand; there is nothing so helpful to unity and loyalty as common work and sacrifice. But the real enemy will have been in view throughout, as words dropped now and again will prove. Everything that has been done has tended to weaken his position, and to put him in the wrong; and it is now, and not a moment earlier, that every gun will be brought up to bombard his position. The one in command is fully aware that there is a good deal of hesitation, and not a little sympathy for the enemy, among his own friends; he will hurt some of his friends by what it will be necessary to say. But he need not directly attack them. The immediate task is to destroy the enemies' defences, while making it clear that all this is merely artillery preparation, and that he is at once coming "over the top" with the bomb and the bayonet. Military metaphors are here in place, since S. Paul uses them (x. 3-6), and they best explain the situation. S. Paul seems exactly to have followed the course described. The letter of sorrow dealt with the outrage, and nothing else; the time had not yet come to deal directly with the Jewish legalists. In our Second Epistle we see the victory consolidated in chs. i–vii, though not without thought of the attack presently to come. In chs. viii and ix the Corinthians are called to common work and sacrifice; and then, and not till then, he turns to his opponents, and overwhelms them. It is with this, and the final appeal to the Corinthians that he must end; all else would be anti-climax. S. Paul won his victory. He went to Corinth; he obtained the money for which he had asked (Rom. xv. 26); and the monument of his victory was that calm measured treatise on the law and the gospel, which he wrote at Corinth—the Epistle to the Romans. There again S. Paul writes as a master. Pharisaic Christianity never again raised its head in the West, and it was not long before it perished in the East also.

The study of the Epistle

The study of an Epistle should never begin with the reading of a commentary. The first thing necessary is to obtain an impression of the Epistle as a whole. It should be read, as we read the letters that we receive to-day, straight through—and perhaps more than once—from beginning to end. We should try to read it as if we had never seen it before, and paying no attention to the divisions into chapters and verses. Then we should ask ourselves what help we need for the better understanding of it. Probably our difficulties will be many. First—and this may be peculiarly the case with the Second Epistle to the Corinthians—we shall fail to grasp the historical situation. Secondly, we shall find ourselves unfamiliar with the writer's religious outlook, and so imperfectly understand his moral and doctrinal teaching. Thirdly, there will be many places where we shall find his language obscure ; and that, either because, as in S. Paul's case, of his faults as a writer, or because the A.V. and R.V., in aiming at a faithful translation of his words, shrink from the paraphrase which is often necessary for the understanding of his meaning. Now it is only when we feel the difficulties, and have questions to ask to which we desire an answer, that commentaries become interesting. This does not mean that no commentary should ever be read through ; almost any commentary will direct our attention to points which we have overlooked in our own reading. But questions should be ready before we begin to read it ; our desire for an answer to them will then keep our minds alert, even when the answers are not being directly given.

But is it a commentary that we chiefly need for the understanding of S. Paul ? Not necessarily. He is a most difficult writer, if we come to his Epistles without preparation ; and to our ordinary congregations much of them is unintelligible. But he is less difficult, if we know something of his religious outlook, and of the teaching which his converts had already received. What we require is (*a*) a general knowledge of the O.T., and of its religious teaching, (*b*) a knowledge of the Pharisaic Judaism, in which he was brought up, (*c*) a knowledge of the gospel which he preached, and which we can study for ourselves in the mission sermons of S. Peter and S. Paul in the Acts of the Apostles, (*d*) a knowledge in broad outline of his life and teaching, and of the main characteristics of the Gentile world of his day. Thus such books as the following are valuable :

W. O. E. Oesterley and G. H. Box. *The Religion and Worship of the Synagogue* (1911).

R. B. Rackham. *The Acts of the Apostles* (Westminster Commentaries, 1901).

F. Prat. *La Théologie de Saint Paul* (1924).

A. H. McNeile. *St Paul* (1920).

J. G. Machen. *The Origin of Paul's Religion* (1921).

W. M. Ramsay. *S. Paul the Traveller and Roman Citizen* (1897), and other works.

Kirsopp Lake. *The Earlier Epistles of S. Paul* (1911).

A fair knowledge of such books as these will make any Epistle we may wish to study comparatively easy ; and, if we have also read a good Article upon it in one of the modern Bible Dictionaries, we shall find it easier still. For the Epistles to the Corinthians, specially valuable is :

Sanday's Article in the *Encyclopaedia Biblica* on the Epistles to the Corinthians.

But, none the less, each Epistle will have its own difficulties, and it is for commentaries to solve them. Which shall we choose? The answer depends upon the questions in which we are chiefly interested. If our main interests are historical, critical, and philological, we shall find modern commentaries far more valuable than ancient. Not only has modern Textual Criticism given us a purer Greek text, but our knowledge both of the thought and life of the world of the N.T., and of the kind of Greek which its authors wrote, is continually growing. The best modern English commentary on the Second Epistle to the Corinthians is that of

A. Plummer in the *International Critical Commentary* (1915).

For those who wish to study the Epistle in Greek, and whose interests are of the kind already described, perhaps no other is absolutely necessary. But Dr Plummer's exegesis may not always satisfy us, and it is well to have other good modern commentaries at hand. Among them are those of :

J. Waite in the *Speaker's Commentary* (1881)—rather wordy, but still valuable.

J. H. Bernard in the *Expositor's Greek Testament* (1903)—much briefer.

A. Menzies (1912).

Interesting discussions of the critical and historical problems which the Epistle presents will be found also in :

J. H. Kennedy. *The Second and Third Epistles to the Corinthians* (1900).

G. H. Rendall. *The Epistles of S. Paul to the Corinthians* (1909).

J. Moffatt (a new translation of the New Testament) will often be found invaluable for making clear S. Paul's meaning, when both the A.V. and R.V. fail to do so.

If, however, our main interests are doctrinal, moral, and devotional, modern English commentaries will seldom give us what we require. The reasons are two. First, the strong point of the English mind lies in its capacity for handling facts ; our contributions to history and science are far more valuable than our contributions to philosophy and theology. Few of our critical scholars seem to be greatly interested in dogmatic theology; and fewer still in moral and ascetic. Secondly, the growth of knowledge means the growth of specialism. Even if a modern commentator is a good theologian, he will regard theology as a study which should be kept more or less separate from Biblical interpretation. He may, like Dr Plummer, give valuable references to theological books, but he will not often in his commentary handle doctrinal problems himself, and moral and ascetic problems he will let even more severely alone. Moreover, it is not common, though much commoner in England than in Germany, for a scholar to know much of the problems and difficulties of the parish priest, or to be closely in touch with the religious life of ordinary people. Now it is here that the older commentators come to our help. Theological specialism is a modern evil, not an ancient one; and to those engaged in practical work an old commentary may prove much more useful than a modern one. Let us take e.g.

S. Chrysostom's *Homilies on the Second Epistle to the Corinthians.*

S. Chrysostom is far from being an ideal commentator. He understands neither the historical background nor the characteristic outlook of S. Paul; and, although Greek is his own language, he has little exegetical insight. Primarily he is a preacher; and the sermon, as with other preachers, has often not much to do with the text. But just because he is always concerned with the difficulties and temptations of ordinary men and women, and his audiences were in some ways very like S. Paul's Corinthian converts, his interpretation, if not accurate, is always living and practical, and he appreciates S. Paul's tact and wisdom as perhaps no other commentator does.

Or again let us take

Cornelius a Lapide, *Commentarii.*

This great Jesuit commentator deals with the whole Bible; and is generally worth reading, if we are able to separate the wheat from the chaff. His commentaries are a mine of Patristic and later exegesis, good, bad, and indifferent; and he tries to provide everything that we need, though he does not always succeed.

Really valuable again are :

J. Calvin, *In Epistolas Pauli Canonicas.*
Estius, *Commentarii in omnes Beati Pauli Epistolas.*

Here we get the best Protestant and Roman Catholic exegesis of the 16th and 17th centuries. Both these writers are controversial, for they lived in an age of controversy. But they are great commentators none the less, alive to doctrinal issues; and if they do not always solve the problems which they suggest, they shew us what the problems are. Nor should we neglect either

Bengel's *Gnomon Novi Testamenti,*
or W. Kay. *The two Epistles of S. Paul to the Corinthians.*

Bengel's deep piety and wonderful terseness are well known; he is perhaps not quite at his best in this Epistle. Kay is not at all behind him in the former quality, and not much behind him in the latter.

Once more, we should remember how much excellent exegesis is to be found in modern works on Biblical theology. The great doctrinal subjects of this Epistle are those of the Atonement and of the Christian ministry, and we shall find the great books on all these subjects useful for its interpretation. Many of them contain an Index of texts, and we can see at a glance where to find the pages that are needed for our immediate purpose.

II CORINTHIANS

I. 1 PAUL, an apostle of Christ Jesus through the will of God, and Timothy [1]our brother, unto the church of God which is at Corinth, with all the saints which are in the 2 whole of Achaia: Grace to you and peace from God our Father and the Lord Jesus Christ.

3 Blessed *be* the God and Father of our Lord Jesus Christ,

---

[1] Gr. *the brother.*

I. 1, 2. ADDRESS AND SALUTATION. The words are but little altered from those of the Address and Salutation of the First Epistle. But Timothy takes the place of Sosthenes; the direction is less wide; and the description of the blessings of the Christian position is omitted. For the meaning of "Apostle," "brother," and "church," cf. the notes on 1 Cor. i. 1, 2 and Intr. pp. xv ff. Here, as in 1 Cor., the distinction between the position of S. Paul and that of his follower is very marked. The former claims apostolic position and authority from the first, and the Epistle will shew, more fully than any other writing of the N.T., exactly what this position and authority are.

1. *with all the saints...Achaia.* "The saints" is the O.T. title for the people of God (cf. Ex. xix. 6; Dan. vii. 18), and so passes on to be the title of members of that Catholic Church, into which Israel has grown. Cf. 1 Pet. ii. 9. It is not quite certain what S. Paul means by Achaia. It may be Achaia proper, the part of the Northern Peloponnesus of which Corinth was the one important city; or it may be the Roman province of Achaia which included all Southern Greece. S. Paul's language suggests

that, though there were Christians at many cities in Achaia, there was no organized church except at Corinth. Contrast Gal. i. 2.

2. *Grace to you...Christ.* "Grace" is the free favour of God; "peace" is the condition which results from its reception. Cf. the note on 1 Cor. i. 3.

3–11. The recent sufferings of the Apostle, and the divine purpose which they have served.

S. Paul generally begins his Epistles to the churches with thanksgiving for the manifestations of God's grace in them. Here, however, he begins with its manifestation in himself. The Epistle is his "Apologia pro vita sua," the most personal of all his Epistles.

3. *the God and Father...Christ.* The translation of the A.V., "Blessed be God, even the Father," is not impossible, but the R.V. is probably right. In xi. 31, Eph. i. 3, and 1 Pet. i. 3 the same ambiguity exists; but in Eph. i. 17 the meaning is clear. Our Lord Himself spoke of the Father as His God (Mk. xv. 34), and in the Johannine writings, with all their emphasis on our Lord's Divinity, we find similar language (Jn. xx. 17; Rev. iii. 12). To Chris-

4 the Father of mercies and God of all comfort; who comforteth us in all our affliction, that we may be able to comfort them that are in any affliction, through the comfort
5 wherewith we ourselves are comforted of God. For as the sufferings of Christ abound unto us, even so our comfort

tians God is the God and Father of our Lord Jesus Christ. It is in all that God was and is to Him that we learn, not only God's Fatherhood but His Godhead also. This is not to say that either was altogether unknown before the Lord came. But both Godhead and Fatherhood are personal relationships. God is God, just as God is Father, in what He does for us and in us; and it is in all that He did and does for and in Christ that His Godhead as well as His Fatherhood are most fully revealed. To take but one example, the Resurrection of Christ not only "with power declared" Him to be the Son of God, but with power declared God to be His God and Father, and the God and Father of all who become His members. If Catholic Christians to-day shrink from S. Paul's language as derogatory to the Lord's Divinity, it is because they have come wrongly to think of it as a Divinity separate from that of the Father. On the contrary, it is as eternally begotten of the Father, and abiding in the Father, that our Lord is God.

In recent years there has been much discussion of the title "Lord" as applied to Christ. This title was widely used in the heathen world of the various local gods, and was applied to the deified Roman Emperor. But it is very improbable that the Christian use of the term was influenced by this, as it appears from the first (e.g. in Ac. ii. 36), and its Aramaic form is found com-

pounded in "Maran atha" (1 Cor. xvi. 22).

the Father of mercies...comfort. For the language cf. Rom. xv. 5. It was this that God had been revealed to be in the glorification of the Lord Himself; and S. Paul's own experience of His Fatherhood and Godhead had exactly corresponded. He too, as we shall soon see, has had a death and a resurrection.

4. *who comforteth us...affliction.* Affliction and comfort are very prominent in this Epistle. Here, as so often, S. Paul does not make clear the exact scope of the plural. Christian experience has always the same broad characteristics; and what is true of any Christian is true of all, when the conditions are the same. But the following verses shew that the immediate reference does not extend beyond the Apostle and his companions, and probably he is thinking of himself alone.

that we may be able...of God. The divine comfort, in S. Paul as in Christ, has a very wide purpose. "Qui in uno genere afflictionum fuit," says Bengel, "in eo potissimum potest alios consolari; qui in omni in omni." Cf. Heb. iv. 16. "Sympathy is love perfected by experience." To this we shall return.

5. *the sufferings of Christ.* Better "of the Christ." Suffering was the path marked out by prophecy, by which the Christ was to reach His glory and redeeming power. But the Christ includes His members; and His sufferings are not all borne

6 also aboundeth through Christ. But whether we be afflicted, it is for your comfort and salvation; or whether we be comforted, it is for your comfort, which worketh in the patient enduring of the same sufferings which we also 7 suffer: and our hope for you is stedfast; knowing that, as ye are partakers of the sufferings, so also are ye of the 8 comfort. For we would not have you ignorant, brethren, concerning our affliction which befell *us* in Asia, that we were weighed down exceedingly, beyond our power, in-

by Him in separation from them. Rather, they overflow to them; and, in proportion as they share the sufferings, so the consolation which follows is shared through their union with the Glorified Christ. Cf. Mt. xx. 22, 23; Ac. ix. 4, 5; Phil. iii. 10 and Col. i. 24. S. Paul expresses this thought in his characteristic way; but it has its roots in the O.T. (cf. Ps. lxix. 9; lxxxix. 50, 51), and appears in other types of N.T. teaching in a simpler form. Cf. Heb. xi. 26; xiii. 13; 1 Pet. iv. 13. It is just those books of the N.T., which like this Epistle and the Revelation of S. John are most full of suffering, which have the greatest consoling power. Cf. Ps. xciv. 19.

6. The Greek text is here somewhat uncertain, but the general meaning is clear. The thoughts of *vv.* 4 and 5 are repeated and applied. In the life of the Apostle there is an alternation of affliction and comfort, but each has a wider purpose than the personal sanctification of the Apostle himself, namely the increase of his power to save others. But this power does not operate in any mechanical way. It makes itself felt, only as his converts in their turn share his sufferings, and patiently endure.

7. *our hope for you is stedfast.* Better "our confidence." The word

"hope," as S. Paul employs it, is without any element of uncertainty; it is the confident expectation of the fulfilment of God's promises. Rom. v. 3–5 is the best commentary on S. Paul's words here. He knows as a fact that the Corinthians are sharing both the suffering and the comfort, and he would not have it otherwise.

8. S. Paul explains why the Epistle has opened with the expression of these thoughts. He is about to tell them how desperately severe his own sufferings have lately been. Death had seemed imminent under the strain.

which befell us in Asia. i.e. the Roman province of Asia, of which Ephesus was the capital. Here, as so often in this Epistle, we see how much of S. Paul's experience S. Luke omits. S. Paul does not appear to be thinking primarily of the deep anxiety which the Corinthians had caused him; the mention of the place where the suffering took place would in this case be without point. Rather he is thinking of outward experience. We may indeed compare Ac. xix. 23–41, and the language (probably metaphorical) of 1 Cor. xv. 32. But the facts there made known to us are quite inadequate to explain the language employed here.

9 somuch that we despaired even of life: [1]yea, we ourselves
  have had the [2]answer of death within ourselves, that we
  should not trust in ourselves, but in God which raiseth the
10 dead: who delivered us out of so great a death, and will
  deliver: on whom we have [3]set our hope that he will also
11 still deliver us; ye also helping together on our behalf by
  your supplication; that, for the gift bestowed upon us by
  means of many, thanks may be given by many persons on
  our behalf.

[1] Or, *but we ourselves*   [2] Or, *sentence*   [3] Some ancient authorities
read *set our hope; and still will he deliver us.*

9. *yea, we ourselves...within ourselves.* We should translate, as A.V.
margin, "the sentence of death."
Professor Moffatt's translation gives
the sense well—"I told myself it
was the sentence of death."

*that we should not trust...raiseth
the dead.* Here as before S. Paul
looks beyond the suffering to the
divine purpose which it serves; but,
while before he dwelt upon that
purpose in relation to others, he now
dwells upon it in relation to himself.
All the greatest acts of faith, which
the Bible records, are acts of faith
in God's power to raise the dead;
and this faith S. Paul himself needed
to learn more fully by experience,
the only way in which it can be
earned adequately. To this too we
shall presently return.

10. *so great.* Better "so grievous
a death."

on whom...deliver us. This statement is not a mere repetition of the
previous one. It is true that God
will deliver, but the conditions for

the exercise of His redeeming power
must be satisfied. The conditions in
this case are two: (*a*) S. Paul's own
trust, given and sustained, that He
will do so; and (*b*) the continual
intercession of his converts. True
Christian trust is not languid optimism about the future. God has
all power and willingness to save;
but the future will be what our faith
and our prayers make it. Where they
fail, God's purpose fails. Cf. 2 Tim.
iv. 17, 18.

11. *thanks ... our behalf.* The
second half of the verse makes
a characteristic addition to the
thought. The glory of God is ever
in S. Paul's mind. First common
intercession, then common blessing,
then common thanksgiving. The
translation "by many persons" is
probably right, though "by many
faces" is a possible and attractive
translation. The faces of the Corinthians will be upturned in thanksgiving, as earlier in prayer.

S. Paul's words have not been easy to unravel; but the great truths, which
the Epistle will expound, are already appearing. S. Paul has no self-centred
religion. In the life of the Church, there is only One, who has trodden the
winepress of sorrow alone—the Lord Himself; and even He trode it for
others even more than for Himself. So it is with S. Paul. It is true that

12 For our glorying is this, the testimony of our conscience,

the experience, through which he has been called to pass, has had for its immediate object the destruction of self-trust, and the full development of trust in God who raises the dead. Man's extremity is ever God's opportunity. It is only when human strength fails, and human ingenuity can find no way out, that the servants of God are driven back upon the power and wisdom of God, and discover their never-failing adequacy. Human powers are themselves God-given, and should be employed to the uttermost; the power and wisdom of God are not intended to pauperize us, as they would do if they led us to leave undone what we are able to do. The "bright face of danger" is meant to call out our manhood; and in S. Paul, as the story of the Acts shews, it had always this effect. Thus there is no reflection upon the character of S. Paul's faith, when he says that God's dealings with him were designed to destroy self-confidence, and render him, in the words of Charles Wesley's noble hymn, "confident in self-despair." But S. Paul does not stop short at this thought. God's dealings with him, as with his Master have a much wider purpose; they perfect him, not only as a man, but as an Apostle. The Church is a great organism; and the experience of each can only be fully understood in relation to the place for which he is destined, and the tasks which thus belong to him. Here too suffering is essential. It is the men of sorrow who are the men of influence, partly because it is they who learn by experience the divine power to uphold, and partly because, as S. Paul will shew, suffering brings about a development of the divine life within, which gives a new power to bless. The higher and the more complex the ministry for which any servant of God is intended, the deeper and the more varied will be the pain through which he will be called to pass; and S. Paul will presently appeal to his sufferings as the crowning proof of the reality of his apostleship. But then this truth has another side to it. If the many are so dependent upon the experience of the one, they are bound by their continual prayers to support the one upon whom they depend. Humility may suggest that though the saint may pray for the sinner, the sinner must pray for himself. Such humility, however, ignores the corporate character of the Church. The medium of blessing to the individual is the life of the whole body, and especially of those members of the body in which it flows in the fullest stream. God blesses us through one another, because He has made us members one of another; and we support ourselves by supporting with our prayers the chosen mediums of His blessing, and in returning continual thanksgiving for the blessings which our prayers have won for them.

12–14. S. Paul's sincerity in act and word.

12. *For our glorying is this.* The point is that it is S. Paul's entire sincerity and disinterestedness which gives him the right to ask their prayers. Cf. Heb. xiii. 18. Christian intercession is an activity within the body of Christ; and it cannot have its perfect work, except where union with Christ is fully maintained. The word here translated "glorifying," and its cognate words, are peculiarly common in this Epistle. "Exulta-

that in holiness and sincerity of God, not in fleshly wisdom
but in the grace of God, we behaved ourselves in the world,

tion" is perhaps a better English
equivalent. Exultation, or glorying,
is joy in what is personal to oneself,
a form of joy legitimate and necessary to human happiness; but only
legitimate and free from pride, while
a true relation to God is maintained.
Now this S. Paul ever recognizes.
Twice (1 Cor. i. 31 : 2 Cor. x. 17) he
quotes the words of Jer. ix. 23, 24,
"He that glorieth, let him glory in
the Lord"; and, whatever his immediate ground for exultation may
be, the thought thus expressed ever
underlies what he says. Thus, like
Jeremiah, he continually repudiates
all "glorying in the flesh" (2 Cor. xi.
18), i.e. in the merely human wisdom,
power, and other advantages, which
may belong to men who are without
the true knowledge of God. On the
other hand, he will glory, in exact
accordance with Jeremiah's teaching,
in the knowledge attained by experience of God's loving-kindness
and righteousness, in all that they
have enabled him to be and to do,
and in the fruit of his work as seen
in the spiritual life of his converts.
The Corinthians seem to have com-
plained that he gloried overmuch,
and their complaints have not been
without echo in modern days. But
such complaints are ill-founded. God
is known in His action, and to glory
in Him is necessarily to glory in His
action wherever we discern it. The
extreme self-depreciation of much
Catholic devotion is morbid; while
the extreme reluctance of English
public school men to speak about
anything they may have done is
unnatural, and mainly due to the
supposed requirements of "good

form." Real humility is one with
truth. It is seldom necessary to
speak about ourselves except when,
as in S. Paul's case, the attacks
made upon us endanger the success
of our work. But, when we do speak
of ourselves, our words should faithfully reflect our real beliefs. Mock
modesty is a form of insincerity, and
often of vanity. We are vain of not
appearing vain.

in holiness and sincerity of God.
Rather "singlemindedness." The
words "of God" are probably to be
taken with both the preceding substantives. God is "the Holy One,"
ever separated from the evil of the
world: and He acts for the carrying
out of His agelong purpose of love,
and for that alone. S. Paul claims
for himself his own share in this
holiness and purity of motive.

not in fleshly...grace of God. The
grace is that which has made him,
not only a Christian, but an Apostle,
and which ever supplies both the
power and the wisdom necessary for
his apostolic work. Cf. 1 Tim. i.
12–14. Like all who fulfil the Lord's
command to be "wise as serpents"
as well as "pure as doves," S. Paul
was probably attacked on the ground
that he was "too clever"; and especially by those whose machinations
he was continually foiling. The
cleverness of the Oriental, if conse-
crated by divine grace, is a noble
quality, and not to be confounded
with the self-seeking wisdom of the
flesh. The characteristically English
dislike of it is absurd; there is
nothing Christian about muddling
through. The cause of Christ requires all the brains that we have.

13 and more abundantly to you-ward. For we write none
    other things unto you, than what ye read or even acknow-
14 ledge, and I hope ye will acknowledge unto the end: as
    also ye did acknowledge us in part, that we are your
    glorying, even as ye also are ours, in the day of our Lord
    Jesus.

more abundantly to you-ward.
Nowhere did S. Paul need the qualities that he has mentioned more
than at Corinth. It was impossible
to avoid misunderstanding with
people so suspicious, but he did all
that he could in word and deed to
allay these suspicions. His refusal
to accept maintenance from them
was one example of this; and the full
explanation of his action, which we
find in this Epistle, provides another.

13. The language of this and the
following verse is obscure to us to-
day, because of our lack of knowledge
of the exact circumstances which
S. Paul has in view; but the general
drift is clear. S. Paul means exactly
what he writes; there is no need to
read between the lines; and what
he writes the Corinthians themselves
can recognize to be true. There is
a play upon the words for "read"
and "acknowledge"; in Greek they
are very similar.

unto the end. i.e. unto the day
of our Lord Jesus Christ, which is
mentioned in the next verse.

14. *ye did acknowledge us in part.*
S. Paul probably refers to the reception accorded to the letter sent
by Titus. Cf. ii. 3; vii. 6 ff. Though
the meaning of his life is not even
yet fully understood by the Corinthians, much of the earlier suspicion
has now passed away; and the new
understanding gained of the Apostle
himself will help them to understand
the meaning of his words. A man's

life explains his words even more
than his words his life.

in the day of our Lord Jesus.
In the N.T. the O.T. phrase "the
day of the Lord" gives place to
the phrase found here. The day
of Yahweh in the O.T. is the day
of His self-manifestation, and judgment; and, except in the Similitudes
of Enoch, judgment is strictly the
prerogative of Yahweh Himself. Cf.
for the thought of later Judaism
4 Esd. v. 56; vi. 6; Ps. Sol. xv. 9,
13–14. Thus our Lord's claim to be
the final Judge is one of the most
remarkable of His claims. Cf. 1 Cor.
iv. 5. To Christians themselves the
day of the Lord Jesus Christ will
be the great day of exultation in
corporate salvation. Then only will
it be perfectly recognized what
others have been to us and we to
them. Cf. Phil. ii. 16. It should be
noticed that the Greek word for
"glorying" in *v.* 14 is different from
that employed in *v.* 12. In *v.* 14 we
might better translate "subject" or
"matter" of glorying.

15–22. From this point to the
end of ch. ii there is no real break.
S. Paul will explain his change of
plan, and the action that he has
taken till the time of his departure
from Asia into Macedonia. But his
statement is broken, partly by incidental teaching, and partly by his
desire to deal at once with an urgent
matter, the attitude of the Church
to one particular offender.

15   And in this confidence I was minded to come before unto
16 you, that ye might have a second [1]benefit; and by you to
pass into Macedonia, and again from Macedonia to come
unto you, and of you to be set forward on my journey unto
17 Judæa. When I therefore was thus minded, did I shew
fickleness? or the things that I purpose, do I purpose
according to the flesh, that with me there should be the
18 yea yea and the nay nay? But as God is faithful, our word
19 toward you is not yea and nay. For the Son of God, Jesus
Christ, who was preached among you [2]by us, *even* [2]by me

[1] Or, *grace.* Some ancient authorities read *joy.*   [2] Gr. *through.*

15. *I was minded to come before unto you.* Or "I originally wished to come to you." But the R.V. translation is probably right. S. Paul speaks of his wish rather than of his definite intention, and the Corinthians may not have known of it. The wish was evidently formed later than the despatch of the First Epistle. Cf. 1 Cor. xvi. 5, 6.

a second benefit. Or "joy." The Greek words for "grace" and "joy" are similar, and it is uncertain which S. Paul wrote. S. Paul's meaning seems to be that this new plan would have involved two visits to Corinth while the old involved but one.

17. *did I shew fickleness?* Better "levity."

according to the flesh. i.e. in a merely human way, as men do who are without the settled principle, the insight, and the sympathy, which the Spirit of God bestows, and so are ready to say Yes and No in the same breath. Levity arises from want of grasp of the seriousness of life, and of the importance of the decisions which must be made. One form of it is an obstinate adherence to a plan once formed, even though it is now unsuitable in view of the new

situation that has arisen. Fear of the charge of levity itself causes levity. The guidance of the Spirit is given to Christians, that they may come to right decisions in view of the facts before them. It does not—normally at any rate—dictate decisions, which (though right in fact) are not justified by present knowledge. Thus it belongs to real seriousness continually to review our plans as new circumstances arise. The same is true of the guidance of the Spirit given to the Church as a whole. It is given in view of the knowledge and circumstances of the time, and affords no justification for refusing to take account of later information.

18. *as God is faithful.* The words are probably an adjuration. But it is possible that S. Paul means that God's faithfulness may be recognized in his own.

19. *For the Son of God, Jesus Christ.* The order of the words in the Greek emphasizes the word "God," and the order of the titles is the order of time in the development of the Lord's Person and work. Eternally He was the Son of God; in His human life He was the man Jesus of Nazareth; by His Glorifi-

and Silvanus and Timothy, was not yea and nay, but in
20 him is yea. For how many soever be the promises of God,
in him is the yea: wherefore also through him is the Amen,
21 unto the glory of God through us. Now he that stablisheth
22 us with you ¹in Christ, and anointed us, is God; ²who also
sealed us, and gave *us* the earnest of the Spirit in our
hearts.

¹ Gr. *into*.   ² Or, *seeing that he both sealed us*

cation He has become the Christ;
and each statement is part of the
Gospel preached about Him. S. Paul
brings out the full greatness of his
Master to shew the moral impossi-
bility of levity in His service. We
find in the mention of Silas and
Timothy interesting points of contact with the Acts and with earlier
Epistles. S. Luke (Ac. xviii. 5) relates that Silas and Timothy joined
S. Paul at Corinth and the two
names recur in the salutations of
1 and 2 Thess., the two Epistles
written by S. Paul there.

was not yea...is yea. S. Paul
speaks not so much of the word of
Christ, as of His Person, Office, and
Work as proclaimed by the Gospel.
In Him God made no uncertain
affirmation of His purpose for His
people ; and, in spite of all obstacles,
it will be carried out. The next
verse explains this.

20. *For how many soever...in
him is the yea*. S. Paul looks back
over the long roll of the divine
promises, and sees in Christ and all
that He is, the reaffirmation of them
all. Cf. Rom. xv. 8. To this we shall
return.

*through him is the Amen...
through us*. The Amen is probably
the response which faith makes,
accepting the divine promises reaffirmed in Christ. Jer. xi. 5 may
well be in S. Paul's mind. Cf. Jn. iii.

33, and Rom. iv. 20. Faith "gives
glory to God" (Rom. iv. 20) as nothing else does. This Amen of faith
is truly said to come both through
Christ Himself and through those
who preach Him. Christ Himself is
the great awakener of faith, but His
appeal reaches the world through
His representatives. Cf. Rom. x. 17.

21. S. Paul proceeds to illustrate
the way in which the manifold promises of God have already begun
to find their fulfilment. It is God
Himself who has been and is the
author of the characteristic Christian
experience, thus justifying His reaffirmation of His promises in His
Son.

he that stablisheth...anointed us.
The change of tense is noticeable.
The anointing was by the gift of
the Spirit through the laying on of
hands after baptism ; the strengthening and deepening of the union
with Christ goes on continually.

22. *who also sealed us*. i.e. set
His mark upon us as His own accepted people, to be claimed at the
final consummation. Cf. Mal. iii. 17;
Jn. vi. 27 ; Eph. i. 13, 14 ; iv. 30.
It is by the gift of the Spirit that
the seal is set.

the earnest of the Spirit. The
Spirit already bestowed is the promise that the whole inheritance will
one day be ours. See the long note
below.

The passage which has just been before us remarkably exemplifies one characteristic of S. Paul—his grasp of the unity of Christian faith and action. With him the simplest actions have their roots in the deepest convictions, and he cannot even refute a charge of levity without reference to the whole Christian faith. Each step in his explanation has its own importance.

First, the Apostle's seriousness and reliability must correspond with the seriousness and reliability of the Gospel which he preaches. It is unthinkable that the preacher of the Gospel of Christ should, even in speaking of his plans, be found a "Richard yea and nay." If the message is to be taken seriously, the messenger must be taken seriously.

Secondly, the reliability of the Christian message rests upon the reliability of Christ as reaffirming all the promises of God. S. Paul has not in view those detailed fulfilments of prophecy, in which the first Christians were mainly interested. He thinks rather of the promises of that new and abiding order, which we call the kingdom or reign of God. It was these which the Lord reaffirmed, when He said that the kingdom of heaven was at hand. But the Lord did more than reaffirm these by His word; He reaffirmed them even more powerfully by His own experience. He called men to sacrifice that they might enter into the Kingdom, and by the path of uttermost sacrifice He entered into the Kingdom Himself. The Risen and Ascended Lord is Himself the proof that the Cross is indeed the way to the Kingdom, and that all who accept the divine promise, and live and suffer in dependence upon it, will in and through Him win the Kingdom also.

But, thirdly, this was not all. The Lord not only proclaimed the Kingdom, and Himself attained it; even in His earthly life it was in measure His, and His miracles were the proofs of its reality. "If I by the Spirit of God cast out devils, then is the Kingdom of God come upon you." In the Lord Himself and the little company which He gathered round Him the Kingdom of God was already embodied; and, when He had died, risen, ascended, and bestowed the Spirit, the Kingdom of God had come with power in the life of the Church. But even then there was far more to be looked for. The promises of God even now have largely to wait for their fulfilment. The highest anticipations of the prophets are not satisfied by anything that we yet see, except in the one example of the Lord Himself; and these promises He has rather reaffirmed than completely fulfilled. "Christ hath been made a minister of the circumcision for the truth of God, that he might confirm the promises given unto the fathers, and that the Gentiles might glorify God for his mercy" (Rom. xv. 8, 9). What God has already bestowed in Christ is "the earnest of the Spirit in our hearts" (i. 22). By this is meant, not so much a partial bestowal to be followed one day by a fuller one, as a bestowal of the Spirit as an earnest of the full inheritance of the Kingdom of God as a whole (Rom. viii. 14–17; Eph. i. 14). But the use of the word "earnest" is not intended to depreciate what we have already received. In the ancient world, the money paid down as an earnest of the whole sum due was a very large proportion of the whole. So it is with the gift of the Spirit.

"If Christ"—by the Spirit—"is in you, the body is dead because of sin; but the Spirit is life because of righteousness." In that the promise of all else is already contained. "But if the Spirit of him that raised up Jesus from the dead dwelleth in you, he that raised up Christ Jesus from the dead shall quicken also your mortal bodies through his Spirit that dwelleth in you (Rom. viii. 10, 11). Nor is even this all. "The creation itself also shall be delivered from the bondage of corruption into the liberty of the glory of the children of God," and only then will the anticipations of prophecy find their adequate fulfilment. Already, as S. Paul says in the passage before us, God has anointed us, made us "Christ's" in the great Christ Himself (cf. 1 Jn. ii. 20, 27), and sealed us as His own; continually He is stablishing us, in our corporate relations one to another—"us with you,"—into Christ, so that our union with Him in His glorified life may be full and abiding. All else, if we are faithful, will necessarily follow. Though as yet we may feel the Spirit's quickening touch in the life of our spirits only, it will not always be so. One day the Spirit will quicken our bodies also, and the whole creation of which they are a part.

Such then is the divine purpose; but, if it is to be fulfilled, Christ must by the preaching of the Gospel arouse in us the response of faith, and elicit from us the "Amen" by which we claim the fulfilment. All through the story of the O.T. it was the Father's good pleasure to bestow the Kingdom, but His people had been unable to enter in because of unbelief (Heb. iii. 19). The glowing ideals of the prophets had been no illusions; nor were they mistaken, when they taught that the Kingdom was at hand in their own day. If, to take but one example, the splendid picture of the life of the restored Israel, which we find in the Second Isaiah, was but little realized in the Church of Ezra and Nehemiah, it was not the fault of God. It was because among the exiles the Amen of faith was spoken by so few, and even by those few with so little confidence (cf. Jam. i. 6–8). So it still was, when all the prophecies had been reaffirmed in Christ, and in measure fulfilled. God did not purpose "according to the flesh," or say yes and no at the same time. In Christ was the yea of all the promises, the promise of the Spirit here and now, and of the full inheritance in the great days yet to be. But the Amen was as necessary as ever,—the Amen that accepted God's witness to His Son, and claimed the promise of life through baptism and the laying on of hands, and the Amen continually spoken, as baptized and confirmed Christians in reliance upon the grace bestowed set themselves to walk by the Spirit, and respond to all that He asked of them. So it ever is. The Kingdom of God is always at hand; indeed in the Catholic Church it is already with us; and in Christ is the yea of all the promises. We are not waiting for God; He is waiting for us, waiting for the Amen through Christ, which is the one way to glorify Him, and which the preachers of His gospel must call out. "If ye will not believe, surely ye shall not be established" (Is. vii. 9).

23   But I call God for a witness upon my soul, that to spare
24   you I forbare to come unto Corinth. Not that we have
lordship over your faith, but are helpers of your joy: for
by ¹faith ye stand.

II. 1 ²But I determined this for myself, that I would not
2 come again to you with sorrow. For if I make you sorry,

---

¹ Or, *your faith*   ² Some ancient authorities read *For.*

I. 23–II. 4. Return from the doctrinal digression to the explanation
of S. Paul's action. For the historical
problems cf. Introd. pp. xxxii ff.

23. *I call God...upon my soul.*
Another adjuration. Cf. *v.* 18. S. Paul
does not share the scruples of the
Society of Friends, though he was
probably aware of the Lord's teaching
in Mt. v. 33–37 to which he seems to
refer in i. 17. The word of Christians is to be as good as their oath,
and all methods of speech which go
beyond the plain Yea, Yea, and Nay,
Nay, "come of evil." Where the
relations of mutual trust between
Christians are what they ought to
be, oaths are out of place. But
where these right relations are absent, and we have to deal with those
who care little for truth in their
ordinary statements, oaths have their
value. S. Paul uses a form even
stronger than that employed in our
law-courts to-day; he invokes a curse
upon himself, if he is not speaking
the truth. Such language is entirely
legitimate. Not only is it true that
the curse of God must descend upon
falsehood; but it is our duty to welcome this truth, and not even to
desire an exception in our own case.

I forbare to come. Better "I came
no more." The first visit mentioned
in i. 15, 16 was paid, but the second
was postponed. S. Paul once more
changed his plan.

24. The word "spare" in the
previous verse was the word of
one clothed with divine power;
S. Paul adds this verse to disclaim
the despot's spirit. Probably both
he, and S. Peter in 1 Pet. v. 3, remember the Lord's words, which we
find in Luk. xxii. 25, 26. The basis
of the Christian life is faith; and
faith is nothing, if it is not the free
trust and self-surrender of the human
spirit. "Per dilectionem operatur,"
says S. Anselm; "non per dominium
cogitur." Where then a faith exists,
whose adequacy is shewn by its
fruits, the work of the true spiritual
father is not to play the despot over
the faith of his children, but to cooperate with them for the increase of
their joy. Contrast xi. 20. We shall
consider below the relation of this
truth to another, which may at first
appear to be inconsistent with it.

II. 1. *come again to you with
sorrow.* The R.V. is here unsatisfactory. The order of the words in
the Greek shews that the word
"again" is to be connected closely
with the words "with sorrow." What
S. Paul decided to avoid was a
second painful visit. Thus this verse,
rightly interpreted, proves that
S. Paul had paid a painful visit
already to Corinth, of which S. Luke
tells us nothing. Cf. Introduction,
pp. xxxv ff. The words "for myself"
are probably a tacit reference to the

who then is he that maketh me glad, but he that is made
3 sorry by me? And I wrote this very thing, lest, when I
came, I should have sorrow from them of whom I ought to
rejoice; having confidence in you all, that my joy is *the*
4 *joy* of you all. For out of much affliction and anguish of
heart I wrote unto you with many tears; not that ye
should be made sorry, but that ye might know the love
which I have more abundantly unto you.

fact that, though S. Paul did not go
to Corinth himself, he sent Titus.

2. Moffatt well brings out the
meaning. "If I pain you, then who
is to give me pleasure? None but
the very people I am paining!"
The words are a beautiful revelation
of S. Paul's heart. His converts were
among the deepest sources of his
happiness, and to give them pain
seemed an ingratitude. Cf. Prov.
x. 1.

3. *I wrote this very thing.* Or
"for this very reason I wrote." But
the R.V. is probably right. Either
the beautiful thought of *v.* 2 had
found a place in the painful letter,
or S. Paul refers to the letter as a
whole.

*lest, when I came, I should have
sorrow.* Or "that I might not by
coming have sorrow."

having confidence...joy of you all.
S. Paul's method in the painful letter
had been a profoundly wise one. He
had evidently appealed to all that
was best in the Corinthians, and to
the heart even more than to the
head. He had spoken, as the next
verse proves, of his special love to
them, and of his pride and joy in
them. He had made them recognize
that their own happiness was largely

dependent upon his own happiness
in them. There are few things that
bring greater grief than the sense
that we have destroyed the pride
and joy of others in us.

4. *more abundantly unto you.*
Either, "more abundantly than to
others," or "more abundantly, because of my present grief." The
second explanation is the better.
S. Paul's Macedonian converts seem
to have been nearest to his heart,
as their faithful affection deserved
(1 Thess. ii. 19, 20; Phil. iv. 1).
Moreover, the second explanation is
true to psychology. When the love
felt to others is largely self-regarding,
and so dependent upon the pleasure
they bestow, all that lessens the
pleasure lessens the love. But where
the love is pure and unselfish, the
case is otherwise. The sorrow and
anxiety caused by those who are
loved brings out, or even increases,
the love, even when the loved ones
are blameworthy. Cf. Gal. iv. 19, another beautiful example of S. Paul's
spirit. The mind of the Apostle is
the mind of Christ (Luk. xiii. 34); in
Him too stern denunciation ends in
tenderness; and the mind of Christ
is the mind of the Father whom He
represents. Cf. Hos. xi. 1–4, 8, 9.

The words of *v.* 24 suggest some difficulties as to the character of spiritual
authority. Two things should be clearly grasped. First, the faith, which is
the fundamental principle of the Christian life, derives its value from the

fact that it is the exercise of a personal choice, the self-surrender in trust and love of a free spirit to God as revealed in Christ. Thus lordship over faith, in the sense in which S. Paul disclaims it, is not only undesirable but impossible ; a faith which is coerced is not faith at all. Those who rely overmuch upon the authority of the Church are apt to forget this. But, secondly, it is spiritual authority, rightly understood, which both elicits faith, and sustains it after it has been elicited. Where spiritual authority does not exist, faith does not exist either ; and the absence of faith in the majority of well-meaning people to-day is largely due to the fact that they have never been brought face to face with true spiritual authority. Christians, who dislike the idea of authority in spiritual things, are as apt to forget this second fact as are other Christians to forget the first.

But what does spiritual authority mean ? It means the authority of the Spirit, the authority, i.e. of God over the free spirits whom He has created. It may be, and is, exercised by men, but only in so far as God is present in them, and exercises His authority through them. The supreme example of this authority is that of our Lord Himself, but the servants of Christ exercise it also, as our Lord Himself speaks in them (2 Cor. xiii. 3). The characteristic of this authority is that it needs no external proof ; it proves itself to the minds and hearts of those who are brought into contact with it, and are capable of recognizing it. When S. Paul spoke the word of Christ "in demonstration of the Spirit and of power" (1 Cor. ii. 4), he exercised the same authority which the Lord exercised when He said "Follow Me." Such authority as this in no way destroys or impairs our freedom ; rather it appeals to this freedom, and demands the free response of the faith which it calls out. Where this authority, though recognized, is resisted—and this is only too possible—it may be used in judgment, as well as in mercy (cf. 1 Cor. v. 3–5 ; 2 Cor. xiii. 1–4). But not even here does it overbear men ; it makes a further appeal to them by the fuller proof of its reality thus afforded. Such discipline is never employed except against moral evil ; those who are but "ignorant and erring" are dealt with very differently. But to say this is not to say that it is never to be employed against heresy ; on the contrary, it may rightly be so employed (cf. 1 Tim. i. 19, 20). But this is only when, as in the instance cited, the heresy is really the result of moral obliquity, or when falsehood is maintained by those who know it to be falsehood (Tit. iii. 10, 11). In such cases the same Spirit, who confers the authority, confers also the power of discerning spirits, by which alone it can be rightly exercised. We see then that there is no inconsistency when S. Paul, after saying that he is not lord of the Corinthians' faith, says that, if he comes, he will not spare (xiii. 2).

But how, it may be asked, can a man—or a church—attempt to exercise lordship over the faith of men ? It can be done in a variety of ways. It is done most obviously, when unbelief and heresy are treated as crimes, like theft and murder, that can be judged and punished by the civil or ecclesiastical official appointed for the purpose, however destitute he may be of the Spirit of God. It is done, scarcely less clearly, when the attempt is made to beat down the resistance of reason and conscience to the beliefs

5 But if any hath caused sorrow, he hath caused sorrow,
6 not to me, but in part (that I press not too heavily) to you
7 all. Sufficient to such a one is this punishment which was
   inflicted by [1]the many; so that contrariwise ye should
   [2]rather forgive him and comfort him, lest by any means
   such a one should be swallowed up with his overmuch

[1] Gr. *the more.*   [2] Some ancient authorities omit *rather.*

proposed to them, by threats of divine punishment, or by appeals without
rational basis to ecclesiastical or biblical authority, or by holding over men
the terror of being thought out of date. It is also done—often with the
best intentions—by what is called "creating an atmosphere," or using
psychological tricks to hypnotize men into believing what we wish them to
believe. In all these cases we are attempting to do what God Himself never
does—to overbear and destroy the very personality to which He appeals,
and by which alone the true response can be made to Him.

5-11. S. Paul turns aside to deal
with the case of an offender, against
whom he had demanded action in
his previous letter. About this
offender, and the punishment imposed upon him, we know nothing
but what we can discover from the
verses before us. Certainly he is not
to be identified with the man guilty
of incest, with whom S. Paul deals
in 1 Cor. v. For (*a*) discipline in his
case, as in that of Ananias and Sapphira, was to end in death, though
with a purpose of love beyond (1 Cor.
v. 5 ; cf. 1 Cor. xi. 30–32). (*b*) The
offence in the case before us was
plainly in some way personal to
S. Paul himself. Cf. *vv.* 5, 10, and
vii. 12, with the note there.

5. *but in part...to you all.* The
meaning seems to be that S. Paul
does not wish to press overmuch his
own personal claims. Part of the
pain has fallen on the Church.

6. *to such a one.* Either, as the
English version suggests, "to such
a person as this," or "to so-and-so"
(cf. xii. 2, 3). It was better not to
mention the name.

this punishment...the many. Probably, after the receipt of S. Paul's
letter, the presbyters of Corinth,
supported by the majority of the
church, had sentenced the man to
some form of excommunication. To
speak of a "majority vote" is to
ignore the methods of the Early
Church. The local churches were not
democracies. Cf. Ac. xv. 6, 22, 23.
The fact that S. Paul insists upon
the sufficiency of the punishment
suggests that the wish of the minority
was, not that the man should escape
punishment, but that he should be
punished more severely. This view
finds strong confirmation in vii.
6–16.

7. If the interpretation given of
the previous verse is correct, we have
here the first example of an "indul-
gence," or relaxation of the punishment imposed by the Church. Just
because such punishments are not so
much legal penalties, as efforts for
the reformation of the offender, they
should cease when their purpose has
been attained.

8 sorrow. Wherefore I beseech you to confirm *your* love
9 toward him. For to this end also did I write, that I might
know the proof of you, [1]whether ye are obedient in all
10 things. But to whom ye forgive anything, I *forgive* also:
for what I also have forgiven, if I have forgiven anything,
for your sakes *have I forgiven it* in the [2]person of Christ;
11 that no advantage may be gained over us by Satan: for
we are not ignorant of his devices.

[1] Some ancient authorities read *whereby*.   [2] Or, *presence*

8. *to confirm your love toward him.* i.e. to give him a practical assurance of your love by restoring him to Church fellowship.

9. *to this end also did I write.* Better "This was the very purpose for which I wrote." The case of this offender was a test case of the obedience of the Corinthians to their father in God, and that was why S. Paul had insisted upon action being taken. Cf. x. 6, where S. Paul recognizes that the return of the church as a whole to its allegiance was the necessary preliminary to effective dealing with individuals.

10. *To whom...I forgive also.* If the church is ready to reinstate the offender, there need be no further reference to S. Paul for instructions.

for what I...forgiven anything. There is emphasis upon the first "I." S. Paul has forgiven already, if he has had anything to forgive—as in *v.* 5 he makes light of the offence he has received—and those most jealous for his honour need not press for further punishment.

for your sakes. S. Paul's action, taken under a deep sense of his apostolic responsibility, has for its main object the welfare of the church of Corinth as a whole.

in the person of Christ. This, the translation of A.V. and R.V., gives

an excellent sense. Cf. 1 Cor. v. 3–5. Speaking, as S. Paul does, "in the name of our Lord Jesus," and "with the power of our Lord Jesus," S. Paul is so identified with his Master that the forgiveness of the one is the forgiveness of the other. All valid absolution rests upon this principle. But there is doubt, both as to whether the Greek words can mean this, and as to whether such language is likely to have been used at so early a date. If the R.V. marg. "in the presence of Christ" is preferred, the meaning of S. Paul's words is but slightly altered. S. Paul could not solemnly forgive, consciously in the presence of Christ, unless he felt that his forgiveness was in accordance with the mind of the Lord, and ratified by Him. It is just here that the value of absolution lies. The repentant sinner cannot hear the absolving word of Christ. What can be brought home to him is the forgiveness of the Church and of the minister of Christ. In the forgiveness of those whose love he can see and feel, and in the solemn absolution of Christ's minister, he will read the forgiveness of the unseen Lord.

11. *that no advantage...Satan.* The words are characteristic of S. Paul's outlook. Cf. Eph. vi. 11, 12. There are two thoughts: (*a*) The

Church is one body, and the welfare of one member is the concern of the whole. Thus, after *v.* 8, the welfare of the individual offender disappears from the foreground of S. Paul's thought, the welfare of the whole body taking its place. (*b*) The Church is engaged in personal conflict with a very astute foe, and must use an equal or greater astuteness in resisting him. The cure of souls is the art of arts, and the whole body must take its share in it. Cf. 1 Cor. xii. 24–27.

The verses just considered afford an admirable example of the nature of the Church's discipline. They should be compared with 1 Cor. v, and with the notes there. This discipline is always the same in its general character, though the methods of its application may vary. To what has been written in the earlier commentary a few points may here be added : (*a*) The action of the Church in forgiving or retaining sins rests upon the divine presence in the Church itself (cf. Jn. xx. 22, 23), and this in two ways. In the first place, all that the Church ever does is to admit men to her fellowship, or to exclude them from it. But just because the Church is the home of that divine life, which alone can deal with sin, the forgiveness of sins is bound up with effective membership in her. In the second place, it is the illumination which the Spirit brings, and the "discerning" of human spirits which it imparts, that enables the Church rightly to exercise the power of the keys, and welcome or exclude men in accordance with the mind of God. In so far then as the Church is what it ought to be, there is no contrast to be drawn between the action of the Church in forgiving sins and the action of God Himself. The Church, like the Lord in His earthly life, has "power on earth to forgive sins," because she is, through the presence of the divine life, the representative of God through whom He acts. But she has power "on earth" only. All God's dealings with men in this world have a probationary character ; His forgiveness and His grace are bestowed upon men that they may cooperate with Him for their own salvation and for that of others ; and nothing here done for them affects the fact that they "must all be made manifest before the judgment seat of Christ" (2 Cor. v. 10), and that no final judgment can be passed upon them before this takes place (cf. 1 Cor. iv. 3–5). Thus, when an ignorant bishop, in excommunicating Savonarola, used the wrong formula, and sentenced him to exclusion from the Church triumphant, Savonarola at once corrected him, and told him that excommunication had to do with the Church on earth alone. Nor is this the only limitation to be remembered. The power of the divine life within the Church, and the power of discerning spirits, vary greatly ; and with these variations the value of its fellowship and the rightness of its decisions vary also. The Church may have far less to give than she ought to have, and may act blindly and erroneously. In practice, excommunication to-day means little in any part of the Church but the refusal of the sacraments ; and that, though serious enough, will not exclude from the divine grace, if the excommunication is not in accordance with the mind of God. We have to make clear the divine method, and to convince men that Christianity is the religion of a society. But our witness must be borne in

12   Now when I came to Troas for the gospel of Christ, and
13   when a door was opened unto me in the Lord, I had no
relief for my spirit, because I found not Titus my brother :

full view both of the power of sin to interfere with the Divine purpose, and
of the actual facts of present Church life.

(b) We must remember the vast change brought about in the methods of
the Church by the flood of heathenism which entered it, when it became
the religion of the Roman Empire. It is this which explains the difference
of S. Paul's methods from those of a later day. The church of Corinth
was no democracy. When it tolerated the incestuous person of 1 Cor. v,
S. Paul passed judgment independently, and insisted upon his decision
being accepted. When the Church for the moment failed to take proper
action in the case of a gross injury done to S. Paul himself, he dealt with
the matter himself in his second letter, and again demanded "obedience"
(2 Cor. ii. 9). But it was not in the least his wish to act alone. In the one
case he certainly called upon the church to associate itself with him in the
sentence pronounced, and in the other it is probable that he did so. The
life of Christ, and therefore the authority of Christ, belong to the Church as
a whole ; and though the authority is only exercised through those members
of the body who are its appointed channels, its healthy exercise, and much
of its effectiveness, depend upon the support given by the whole body to
those members. Just as we walk, and speak, and breathe, and eat by the
proper members of our bodies, while yet no one of our members acts independently of the body to which it belongs, so it should be in the body of
Christ. In the Church of later days the exercise of discipline came to belong
to the ministry alone ; but the justification of this, as of so many similar
changes, was that the low standards of the laity rendered them incompetent
to perform their functions. In the beginning it was not so. Clearly as S. Paul
insists upon his own Apostolic authority, he asks the active interest and
cooperation of the whole body of the faithful. No act of discipline which
they do not approve is likely to be effective. Thus the protests which are
made against clerical autocracy find a real basis in the N.T. But the laity
can only recover their true position in the Church, as they become competent
in knowledge and in life to exercise their functions. It is better that the
laity should take no part in the government of the Church than that they
should govern it on the principles of the world.

12–17. The thoughts and feelings
of S. Paul on his departure for Macedonia. The digression of *vv.* 5–11
being finished, he returns to the
narrative of his journey.

12. *came to Troas.* Troas was the
port of embarkation for Macedonia,
and S. Paul hoped to find Titus
there. Had he done so, the strain
would have been relaxed, and he
would have been able to do the
evangelistic work which he had intended.

in the Lord. The force of this
characteristic expression is a little
obscure here. "In the Lord's service" is probably the meaning. Cf.
1 Thess. iii. 11.

but taking my leave of them, I went forth into Macedonia.
14 But thanks be unto God, which always leadeth us in
triumph in Christ, and maketh manifest through us the
15 savour of his knowledge in every place. For we are a sweet
savour of Christ unto God, in them that are being saved,
16 and in them that are perishing; to the one a savour from

13. *I went forth into Macedonia.*
Here Titus could sooner rejoin him;
and if Titus did not come or send
news, he could press on to Corinth
himself. The story will be resumed
at vii. 5.

14. *But thanks be unto God.*
S. Paul felt the strain of this continual
travelling; but none the less thanks
God for it, because of the divine
purpose which it serves. The order of
the words in the Greek emphasises
the word "God."

leadeth us in triumph in Christ.
S. Paul is God's captive. By the
exercise of His grace through Christ
He has turned the bitter enemy of
His gospel into its greatest champion; and now leads him from province to province of the empire, as
the great witness to His mercy. For
the thought cf. 1 Tim. i. 15, 16.

maketh manifest...in every place.
It is not likely that there is any
reference to the incense burnt at a
Roman triumph. S. Paul was a Jew,
and his language should nearly always be interpreted by its Jewish
rather than by its Gentile associations. Thus the thought is probably
of the sacrifices, or sweet savour
offerings of the O.T. Cf. Eph. v. 2.
"His knowledge" probably means
the knowledge of Christ and not
the knowledge of God. The words
which follow in *v.* 15 favour this
interpretation.

15. *we are a sweet...unto God.*
S. Paul himself is a sacrifice, but

not a new sacrifice added to that of
the Lord. It is the sufferings of the
Christ which abound unto him (i. 5);
Christ is still living His life of sacrifice in His servants; and so S. Paul
is a sweet savour unto God of Christ
Himself. In him the Father recognizes the Son, in whom He is ever
well-pleased. S. Paul, here as ever,
has his eyes fixed upon the glorified
"Christ," rather than upon the Jesus
of Calvary. He feels himself, as we
shall see more clearly in iv. 7–11,
not to be just reproducing the dying
of Jesus, but to be manifesting His
life; and thus the Christ, of whom
he is a sweet savour to God, is "the
Living One," once dead, but now
"alive for evermore" (Rev. i. 17, 18).
This will more plainly appear in the
next verse.

in them...are perishing. The
thought now becomes even deeper.
What God recognizes in S. Paul is
not Christ as separated from the
world, but Christ in the strangely
different effects which He produces
in two different classes of men, those
on the way to salvation and those on
the way to perdition. The Lord was
"set for the falling and rising up of
many in Israel; and for a sign which
is spoken against" (Luk. ii. 34), and
the same is true of His Apostle. Of
S. Paul as well as of His Master it is
true that he is come "for judgment,
that they which see not may see;
and that they which see may become
blind" (Jn. ix. 39). Both this ex-

death unto death; to the other a savour from life unto life.
17 And who is sufficient for these things? For we are not as
the many, ¹corrupting the word of God: but as of sincerity,
but as of God, in the sight of God, speak we in Christ.

¹ Or, *making merchandise of the word of God*

perience, and the understanding of
it, are as old as Isaiah, whose words
(Is. vi. 9, 10; cf. viii. 18) are so
frequently reproduced in the N.T.

16. *to the one a savour...unto
death.* To the one class the spectacle
of S. Paul's life and experience was
like the stench of a corpse. His life
seemed a living death, the last life
that they would desire to share.
Thus to them the spectacle was
only repellent, and drove them
further on the road to perdition.

to the other a savour...unto life.
To the other class, who saw more
deeply, S. Paul was a savour not of
death, but of life abounding, and
continually renewed through death.
Thus to them he was immeasurably
attractive; in desiring to share his
experience they were led to life
eternal.

And who...these things? The
clause is one of S. Paul's characteristic "asides," breaking the flow of
the thought. Cf. Rom. vii. 25. The
question here asked is answered in
iii. 4–6.

17. *For we are not as the many.*
The word "for" connects the clause
with the great statements of *vv.* 14–
16, the "aside" being ignored; and
the words "the many" contrast
S. Paul with the crowd of Jewish
and Judaizing teachers, by whom
his teaching was being undermined.
The Jew, with his pride in the law,

was always confident of his ability
to teach the Gentiles (cf. Rom. ii.
17–20).

corrupting the word of God. The
Greek word for "corrupting" suggests the dishonest methods of the
petty trader. Cf. Is. i. 22 (LXX);
Ecclus. xxvi. 29. Insistence upon
observance of the law spoilt the
Gospel, since it obscured the freedom
of God's grace.

but as of sincerity, but as of God.
Moffatt's paraphrase well brings out
the meaning: "like a man of sincerity, like a man of God." Both
points are important. We must
proclaim the message sincerely, believing it ourselves, and having no
personal aim to serve in its proclamation. We must speak with trust
in our divine mission, and confident
that God Himself speaks through
us. Cf. v. 20.

in the sight...in Christ. The
strength of S. Paul's asseverations
shews how much they were needed,
in view of the suspicion aroused
against him. He cannot but speak
with the sincerity of a true man of
God, when he speaks as conscious of
the presence of God who has sent
him, and in the power of his abiding
union with Christ. When a man is
under suspicion, protestations of
sincerity are of little avail; he must
explain the reasons which in his
case make insincerity impossible.

The profound thoughts here expressed are characteristic of this Epistle.
They underlie S. Paul's words in i. 3–7; they come to the surface here; and
they will be worked out more fully in iv. 7–18 and other passages. But they

cannot be understood, not to say practically applied, without pain; and to all they are at first unwelcome. We shall consider them (a) in relation to the Lord Himself; (b) in relation to S. Paul; and (c) in relation to the work of the Church to-day.

(a) We observe first that the offering of the Lord was the offering of life won through death, and so made available for others (Jn. xii. 23–25). Death, in the sacrificial system, had for its primary purpose the obtaining of the blood to be offered at the altar, the blood containing the life (Lev. xvii. 11). Pain and death have atoning value, not so much in themselves, as in that to which they lead. But the truth could only be partially set forth by the Jewish ceremonial, the chief reason being that the life sacrificially presented was not really communicated to the offerer. Thus our thought about the Lord's Atonement should never stop short at Calvary; it should like His own pass on to the new life won both for Himself and for His people. "Non mors, sed voluntas sponte morientis, placuit Deo," says S. Bernard; and his statement takes us to the heart of the matter, if we include in this "voluntas" not only the desire to do the Father's will, but also the desire to accomplish the redemption, which, by the mysterious law of sacrifice, could not without His death be accomplished. Modern critical writers sometimes infer from the evidence of the Synoptists that the Lord died to precipitate the coming of the kingdom which He proclaimed. This view may be fully accepted, if it is recognized that the kingdom came with power in the gift of the Holy Ghost; and that this gift was precisely that gift of new life to others, which the death of the Lord enabled Him to bestow. Now it is this offer of a new life won through death that is the centre of the Gospel. To them "that are being saved" Christ is essentially the living Christ, and the "savour of life" which proceeds from Him is the attractive force that wins them. But to "them that are perishing" it is otherwise. To the Jews especially "a Messiah crucified" (1 Cor. i. 23) was no Messiah at all. The Lord's refusal of the political rôle, which they assigned to the Messiah, had alienated them during His life; and, when His methods led Him to Calvary, for them the question was decided. Refusing to credit the message of His Resurrection, and having no interest in the spiritual salvation which was all that the Church had immediately to offer, the Jews found in Him only the savour of death, and to death it led them.

(b) We observe, secondly, that it is this sacrifice of Christ which is reproduced in S. Paul. He is not, like S. Francis, consciously engaged in the reproduction of the Lord's earthly life; though he may in fact be reproducing it. Neither the Apostles themselves nor their converts ask the question "What would Jesus do?" When the former propose to us the example of the Lord, they seem invariably to think of the example of His Passion and Death. To S. Paul especially, the earthly life of the Lord is a life that is past and over, not only for Him, but for us. But this asks more, and not less, than the simpler conception of imitation; it asks, as we shall presently see, a daily dying that we may enjoy a daily resurrection. It is this reproduction of the Lord's sacrifice which S. Paul claims for himself; and by which he has become, not just a preacher of the Gospel, but himself the embodiment of the Gospel which he preaches. Moreover the result of this embodiment is what it was in the Lord's case; it affects different men differently. To many the Apostle, who had given up all, and obtained nothing whose value they could recognize, was a savour of death. He repelled them, as death does and ought to repel. Seeing in his life only a living death, to death it led them. But to those who could look below the surface, S. Paul was a savour of life abounding. He might have continually "the sentence of death within himself" (i. 9), but the reprieve always came in time. Weak as his bodily presence might be, he bore a strain that would have broken a Greek athlete in a fortnight; "of no account" as his speech might be, a few months of his preaching had more influence than a professional rhetorician could exercise in a lifetime. The death was there, but the life out of death was there also. So those ready for the light found themselves irresistibly attracted. Death worked in him, but life in them (iv. 12).

(c) Thirdly, we consider the work of the Church to-day. To this, as to the personal experience of S. Paul, we shall return. But two things may be said immediately. First, the Church, in the fulfilment of her mission, is to exhibit—to God primarily, but to men secondarily—not just a sympathetic, kindly, and serviceable life, but a sacrificial one. Secondly, she is sent to attract, not the world as a whole, but those who are morally disposed to eternal life (Ac. xiii. 48). This does not mean that a serviceable life and a sacrificial life are to be contrasted. The sacrifice which is offered by the Church is offered to God for men; it is in doing the work which God lays upon the Church that the sacrifice is demanded; and we cannot be filled with the redemptive spirit without being "moved with compassion" as the Lord Himself was, and desiring to help whenever and wherever we can. A so-called sacrificial life which is useless is on a line with the sacrifices of the heathen world. We are, however, exposed to-day to a different danger— the danger that those, in whom the spirit of service is strong, may forget the special character of the Church's task, and substitute for it service of a lower kind. In so far as we adopt this method, we shall find ourselves altogether astray. Our Lord Himself made no successful appeal to the great body of His contemporaries, nor did the Apostles. The special task of the Church is to preach the Gospel, and that as well by the life lived as by the word spoken. This task will of itself bring sacrifice to all her members, the kind of sacrifice asked of each being determined by his special vocation. In some cases the call will be to service profitable, not only to members of the household of faith, but to others (Gal. vi. 10); and this wider service will have its appointed place in the witness of the Church to Christ (Rom. xii. 17). But such service should be undertaken primarily for its own sake, and not as an advertisement for Christianity. It is, e.g., the business of political and economic effort to produce a better social order, and not to demonstrate that the Christian "Codlin is the man," and not the Bolshevist "Short." Moreover, the value of different forms of Christian activity is not to be judged by their obvious practical results. If by the divine call Christian sacrifice in some cases takes the form of a life of prayer, such activity is not the less service to God for men, because its fruits cannot be recognized here. One result of study of the N.T. is to destroy the optimism, which supposes that, if only the Church did her duty, the world would be won. That optimism is better away. Probably it leads more often to impatience, and unfaithfulness to the Christian message, than to successful evangelistic work. If the Church in life and word were all that she ought to be, she would no doubt win many that are at present outside her borders; but she would probably lose many that are at present within them. Christ came to bring, not peace, but a sword. If the Church is faithful, the sword will divide men correctly on this side and on that, ready for the judgment; if she is unfaithful, the sword will divide men incorrectly, as it divides them to-day. But the sword will always divide. To vast numbers, as to Nietzsche, Christianity will always appear to be the religion of those who refuse to live, not of those who only die to live more abundantly.

III. 1–IV. 6. It is impossible to make any satisfactory analysis of this section, or indeed of any other till the end of ch. vii. S. Paul will tell us, in xi. 6, that though he be "rude in speech," he is "not in knowledge." In depth and beauty of thought he is here at his noblest; there is hardly a word which is not abundantly worth the trouble which it costs to understand it. But in the expression of his thought he is often extraordinarily obscure, and in the arrangement of it he is at his worst. The slender thread of narrative which began at i. 15, and has continued in spite of digressions up to ii. 13, is now altogether submerged, to reappear only at vii. 5. Never perhaps has there been another such enthusiast for the work of an Apostle. Once launched on this subject, there is no stopping him, and all sense of literary form disappears. Thought follows thought far too quickly for words to keep pace with them; a metaphor is coined to express one thought, and then is stretched to accommodate another; the language of the O.T. is applied literally, and then metaphorically, and then again metaphorically, the second metaphor being verbally inconsistent with the first. Deep principles are interwoven with references to passing sneers and slanders, the exact character of which we are not always able to determine. In all this maze we lose our way, not only as analysts, but as expositors also, unless we are already familiar with S. Paul's mind. But somehow, none the less, he beats his music out; and, as we succeed in detaching and understanding the different lines of thought, we find them perfectly consistent one with another, and of the greatest practical value. Thus no analysis will here be attempted. We shall simply take the paragraphs, as we find them in the R.V., and make our way through them as best we can.

III. 1–11. The main thoughts here expressed are those of the contrast between the old covenant and the new, and of the resulting contrast between the work of Moses and the work of the Apostles. The starting-point is the statement made in i. 17 that S. Paul is not as the many, corrupting the word of God; and behind this statement lies his indignation, not only against the corruption which Judaizing Christians are introducing into the Christian message, but also against the personal charges which they bring against

III. 1 Are we beginning again to commend ourselves? or need we, as do some, epistles of commendation to you

him, and their denial of his Apostolic position. At Corinth S. Paul is chiefly concerned with the second evil; and even when, as in the passage before us, he speaks mainly about the first, he gives his argument a personal turn so that it bears upon the former. Thus we see why Moses appears, as he does not in the Epistles to the Galatians and to the Romans, and why he seems to be so ungenerously treated. S. Paul has not before him the Moses of history, the great prophet and deliverer; the real Moses, like the Christ whom he foreshadowed, was a deliverer first, and a lawgiver only afterwards. S. Paul has before him the Moses of the Pharisees, the great Rabbi whose disciples they claimed to be (Jn. ix. 29); and whose law they were making not a tutor to bring men to Christ, but a rival to supplant Him. Indeed we may perhaps go further, and say that the contrast which S. Paul draws he has "in a figure transferred" (cf. 1 Cor. iv. 6) to himself and Moses; while the contrast really lies between himself and the Pharisaic teachers[1].

III. 1. *Are we beginning...commend ourselves?* The order of words in the Greek places the emphasis upon "ourselves," and thus gives a bad sense to the phrase. At iv. 2 it is otherwise. Self-defence is almost impossible without self-commendation. S. Paul's opponents at Corinth made the former necessary, and then blamed him for the latter. There was much in the First Epistle which exposed S. Paul to this kind of attack, especially in chs. iv and ix; and the lost letter probably contained even more. Cf. v. 12; x. 12.

need we, as do some,...or from you? Such commendatory letters were no doubt common. Cf. Ac. xviii. 27; Rom. xvi. 1; 1 Cor. xvi. 3. S. Paul's words reflect upon his opponents. They had come with commendatory letters to the Corin-

[1] The following passage from a recent book of Essays on the O.T. is of interest:

"There is more than one single tradition of Moses in the O.T.; there are at least five. There is the Moses of the Priestly Document, the most influential but the least historical of the portraits; the aged legislator...who had Aaron constantly at his side, whose chief mission was to give his people a system of ritual containing many gaps, but elaborated in other respects down to minute details. In E, his 'prophetic' character is emphasized; he works miracles as Elijah and Elisha worked them; and the Decalogue, as given in E, might be taken as the foundation of prophetic teaching. In J, Moses is a national leader; Yahweh's representative and agent rather than His spokesman—and his Decalogue, as given in J, deals with cultus rather than morals. Deuteronomy takes up E and may be said to prepare the way for P. Moses is there the great religious teacher; interested in cultus, but also in the whole national life.... Finally, there is the tradition of Moses which seems implied in the prophets.... They point back to the sojourn in the desert as a term of ideal obedience to Yahweh; and this obedience rests on morality and unwavering trust on the part of Israel, and protection and the demand for Israel's undivided worship in Yahweh Himself." W. F. Lofthouse in *The People and the Book*, pp. 225-226.

2 or from you? Ye are our epistle, written in our hearts,
3 known and read of all men; being made manifest that ye
are an epistle of Christ, ministered by us, written not with
ink, but with the Spirit of the living God; not in tables
4 of stone, but in tables *that are* hearts of flesh. And such
5 confidence have we through Christ to God-ward: not that

thian Church, and may have received a similar letter from it to be used elsewhere. The letters brought to Corinth may have been either from the Pharisaic Christians of Jerusalem, or from the churches of Galatia, which they had already visited, and where they had been only too successful.

2. *Ye are our epistle...read of all men.* The Epistle of Polycarp seems to refer to this verse in xi. 3, and in ii. 2 to iv. 14. These references are the earliest we have to this Epistle. The simple thought, with which S. Paul begins, is that the Corinthian church itself is his best commendation, the best proof of the reality of his apostleship. Cf. 1 Cor. ix. 1, 2, and (for the last words of the verse) 1 Thess. i. 8–10. There is a play upon the Greek words for "known and read" as in Ac. viii. 30. But S. Paul's affection leads him to confuse the metaphor by the addition "written in our hearts"; and in the next verse a different turn is given to it. So Queen Mary said that "Calais" would be found written upon her heart. It is sorrow rather than joy which thus works for continual remembrance.

3. *being made manifest...epistle of Christ.* The manifestation is still to the world. S. Paul means that Christ Himself is the author of the commendatory letter—the life of the Corinthian church—which introduces S. Paul to new fields of evan-

gelization. Cf. x. 15, 16, where the thought of the Lord as the true commender immediately follows.

ministered by us. S. Paul is perhaps the courier, rather than the amanuensis. The same word is used similarly in viii. 19, 20, and the corresponding substantives are used of S. Paul's work in ministering the new covenant (*vv.* 6, 7).

written not with ink...living God. The amanuensis is the Holy Spirit, the author of the spiritual life of the Corinthian church. The contrast is the greater, because the ink used in S. Paul's day was easily washed off.

not in tables of stone...hearts of flesh. The thought of writing on the human heart appears in Prov. iii. 3; vii. 3; Jer. xxxi. 33; and the contrast between the stony heart and the heart of flesh in Ez. xi. 19; xxxvi. 26. But it is Jer. xxxi. 33 that S. Paul had chiefly in mind, with its contrast between the new covenant and the old. It is this contrast which he is about to explain; and so, in speaking of the Corinthian church as a witness to the world of the reality of his Apostleship, he notes that the power of the new covenant is already manifested in their experience.

4. *such confidence...to God-ward.* i.e. looking up to God, on whom we rely. The confidence is that to which expression has been given in the final verses of the last chapter. Cf. especially *v.* 14. It is confidence, no

we are sufficient of ourselves, to account anything as from
6 ourselves; but our sufficiency is from God; who also made
us sufficient as ministers of a new [1]covenant; not of the
letter, but of the spirit: for the letter killeth, but the spirit
7 giveth life. But if the ministration of death, [2]written, *and*

---

[1] Or, *testament*   [2] Gr. *in letters.*

---

doubt, as S. Paul's usage of the word suggests, in God's acceptance of him in his sacrificial life (cf. Eph. iii. 12); but as ii. 16 shews, the thought of the sufficiency bestowed upon him for his work is the dominant thought. We have thus a transition to what follows.

5. *not that we are sufficient...as from ourselves.* In one sense, S. Paul was the author of all the best work done at Corinth (1 Cor. iv. 15); but he was not the ultimate source from which it proceeded. For the two sides of the truth cf. 1 Cor. xv. 10.

6. *who also made...a new covenant.* Better perhaps, "a fresh covenant" in contrast with the old, now superseded. The word "also" adds emphasis. A far greater "sufficiency" is needed to be a minister of the new covenant than to be a minister of the old, as S. Paul will shew. The word used in the N.T. for "covenant" has no satisfactory English equivalent. It means an "unilateral enactment," a disposition of property, or an establishment of relations between one and another, which depends upon a single will. The rendering "covenant" is unsatisfactory, because it suggests a bargain made by two or more, who meet upon equal terms; while the word "testament" is even more unsatisfactory, since it suggests only the disposition of property, and implies the death of the testator. Thus it is best to retain the word "covenant," while remembering that

it must be for God alone to settle the terms of the relations between Himself and us.

not of the letter, but of the spirit. The old relationship to God rested upon obedience to a code of laws; the new rests upon the gift of the Spirit.

for the letter killeth...life. Better "the letter puts to death." The words explain why the sufficiency divinely bestowed upon S. Paul was that he might be a minister, not of the old covenant, but of a new one. The contrast will be explained below.

7. *if the ministration of death... came with glory.* The ministration of death is the gift of the law by Moses on his descent from Mt Sinai. Cf. Ex. xxxiv. 29–35, especially *v.* 30. This law was "in letters" (R.V. margin), and letters alone; no power of the Spirit was granted that it might be kept. It was "engraven on stones," and not on the hearts and wills of those who received it. Thus the ministration of the law was the ministration of death. It threatened death, if it was not obeyed; and there was neither the power nor the will to obey. The law might have a glorious inauguration in the glory of the countenance of its minister; but it brought a curse, and not a blessing. The law in itself was unto life, but in its result it was unto death. "Lex data est ut gratia quaereretur; gratia data est ut lex impleretur" (S. Augustine). So also

engraven on stones, came [1]with glory, so that the children
of Israel could not look stedfastly upon the face of Moses
for the glory of his face; which *glory* [2]was passing away:
8 how shall not rather the ministration of the spirit be with
9 glory? [3]For if the ministration of condemnation is glory,
much rather doth the ministration of righteousness exceed
10 in glory. For verily that which hath been made glorious
hath not been made glorious in this respect, by reason of
11 the glory that surpasseth. For if that which [4]passeth away
was [5]with glory, much more that which remaineth *is* in
glory.

[1] Gr. *in*.　　[2] Or, *was being done away*　　[3] Many ancient authorities
read *For if to the ministration of condemnation there is glory*.　　[4] Or, *is being
done away*　　[5] Gr. *through*.

S. Chrysostom excellently: "The law
laid hold on one that gathered sticks
on a sabbath day and stoned him.
This is the meaning of 'the letter
killeth.' The Gospel takes hold on
thousands of homicides and robbers, and baptizing them delivereth
them from their former vices. This
is the meaning of 'the Spirit giveth
life.' The former maketh its captive
dead from being alive, the latter
rendereth the man it hath convicted
alive from being dead." Cf. Gal. iii.
10.

for the glory of his face. The
reason, why the children of Israel
could not gaze upon the face of
Moses, was not the dazzling character
of the glory, but the terror which it
inspired. So it is with the law.

which glory was passing away.
Better, as in R.V. margin, "was being
done away." The passive sense will
be needed in *v.* 14, where the R.V.
translates "is done away"; and
therefore the passive sense should
be given to the word in *vv.* 7, 11,
and 13. Moreover, the passive sense

is the more consistent with Hebrew
ways of thinking. The Hebrews did
not think of mechanical processes,
but of the direct action of God in
all that took place.

9. As has been explained above,
the law brought condemnation, because men were unable to keep it.
The Spirit, which S. Paul ministers,
brings a declaration of righteousness,
the opposite of condemnation.

10. *that which hath been made
glorious.* i.e. the countenance of
Moses. The thought of the verse is
simple, though awkwardly expressed.
The lesser glory disappears in the
greater as the stars become invisible
when the sun rises.

11. *much more...in glory.* The
distinction between being "with
glory" and being "in glory," is the
distinction between the glory of a
temporary investiture, and the glory
of an abiding character. The permanence of the new covenant raises
it above the old, and not only the
greatness of the blessings which it
brings. Cf. 1 Cor. xiii. 10.

There is no break at this point; but it will be well at once to consider the contrast here drawn between the letter and the Spirit. We notice:

(*a*) That the contrast has nothing in common with that which we ourselves draw between the letter and the spirit. We contrast the "letter of the law" with its underlying "spirit." We know e.g. that when the Lord said, "Whosoever smiteth thee on thy right cheek, turn to him the other also" (Mat. v. 39), He was not commanding a particular motion of the head, but the meekness which He Himself exhibited, when, being smitten, He said, "If I have spoken evil, bear witness of the evil: but if well, why smitest thou me?" (Jn. xviii. 23). But S. Paul's contrast is wholly different. He does indeed mean by the "letter" a legal code; but he does not mean by the "Spirit" the principle underlying it. He means the Holy Spirit, which the Lord has won for His people, and poured out upon them (Ac. ii. 33). Indeed it is doubtful whether the word "Spirit" is ever used impersonally in the N.T., Gal. vi. 1 probably affording no real example of this use.

(*b*) Wide as is the application of S. Paul's teaching, he has his opponents at Corinth primarily in view. He himself is above all things a minister of the Spirit. Wherever his Gospel is believed, and men are baptized into the Church, and the Apostle's hands laid upon them, the Spirit is bestowed. The ministers of the letter, in their turn, are as real and recognizable as S. Paul himself. They are Jewish teachers, Christians in the sense that they believe Jesus to be the Christ, and are expecting His return in glory, but pressing upon Gentile converts the observance of the Mosaic law. Whence these men came, and what authority they claimed, it is impossible to say with certainty. The earliest reference to such teachers is found in Ac. xv. 1–5. Here it is possible, but not likely, that a distinction is to be drawn between the legalists of *v.* 1 and those of *v.* 5. There was, no doubt, a difference between the observance of the law inculcated by the Pharisees and the less rigid observance common among many Jews of the Dispersion; but there seems to be no evidence that the difference was of importance in the case of the Gentile Christians. S. Paul (Gal. v. 3) held that to accept circumcision bound men to the observance of the whole law; and it is difficult to see how this could be denied in theory, whatever concessions might be made in practice. The Jews of the first century read the O.T. quite uncritically. Moses in their eyes was the minister to men of the whole law as we read it to-day. The same law, which forbade murder and adultery, forbade also the eating of rabbits; who could venture to say that the former prohibitions were binding upon the people of God, and the latter not? Now the Jewish teachers, who opposed S. Paul both in Galatia and at Corinth, evidently pressed the observance of the law on some ground upon S. Paul's Gentile converts. What is not so clear is whether at Corinth they repudiated the decisions of the Conference of Jerusalem; or whether, while accepting them, they none the less pressed the observance of the law on other grounds than its necessity for salvation. There was a great deal that was morally deplorable to be found in the church of Corinth, and it would have been plausible to argue that the law was the only cure for it. But S. Paul argues, here as elsewhere, as if the law were being put forward as the means of salvation, and probably this is what his opponents did actually maintain. They were in fact as characteristically ministers of the letter, as S. Paul was a minister of the Spirit. To him the question at issue was one of two different religions; and the Corinthians had to choose between them.

Now in order to understand this far-reaching contrast, we must first understand the common ground occupied by S. Paul and his opponents. The great hope of the people of God was the setting up of that divine kingdom, which the prophets of Israel, the Baptist, and the Lord had alike proclaimed. God, the God of Israel, would by His own immediate action, or through the Messiah whom He would send, overthrow all the enemies of His people, and uplift the latter to universal sovereignty (1 Cor. vi. 3). Wherever the enemies of God's people might be found, whether in the unseen forces of evil (Eph. vi. 12), or in the kingdoms of the world, or in the unfaithful Israelites who had made terms with the world, God would vindicate His people against them all. In the expectation of this far-reaching vindication, or justification, at the hand of God, S. Paul and his opponents were of one mind. They were also of one mind in holding that before God would thus vindicate His people, they must be a "righteous" people; His claims upon them must have been satisfied. The public vindication in the eyes of the world would itself be a declaration of their righteousness. "Therefore is the enemy eager to destroy all that call upon the Lord. For he knoweth that upon the day on which Israel shall repent, the kingdom of the enemy shall be brought to an end" (*Testaments of the Twelve Patriarchs*, Test. Dan. vi).

But how was this righteousness to be obtained? The Jews held that what was necessary was the fulfilment of the law. The law was the means by which God had revealed Himself to His people. It had existed with God from all eternity, and would never pass away. Everything needed for salvation was to be found in it. It gave life to those who practised it in this world and in the world to come (cf. Pirke Aboth vi. 7, and Ps. Sol. xiv. 2-3). Thus to minister the law to men was to minister the greatest of blessings, since it was there that the claims of God were revealed, upon which His salvation and blessing depended. Nor was this view necessarily abandoned when Jews became convinced that Jesus was the Messiah, and that He would return from Heaven to set up the divine kingdom. That He, and no other, was to be the instrument of the vindication in no way affected the condition upon which it would be given (cf. Ac. iii. 19-21); and it could plausibly be maintained that, in insisting upon the observance of the law, the Jewish Christians were but echoing the teaching of the Lord Himself (Mt. v. 17-20; xxiii. 2, 3). To an appeal to the Gentiles there could be no objection; the Pharisees themselves were most anxious to make proselytes (Mt. xxiii. 15). Only they must be real proselytes; they must be incorporated by circumcision into the people of God, and join them in their effort to attain that "righteousness of the law," upon which the coming vindication depended. Indeed even Jews who refused to accept Jesus as the Messiah would not necessarily object to the work of Christian evangelists. As long as Christians were simply a sect of the Jews, bound by the law like all others, Gentile converts to Christianity were Gentile converts to Judaism also. S. Paul had only to preach circumcision as well as Christ, and the stumbling-block of the Cross would be done away (Gal. v. 11).

Now it is here that S. Paul joins issue, and upon two grounds. In the first place to seek for righteousness by obedience to the law is to seek for it by a method foredoomed to failure. There is no road that way. The people of God have never succeeded in obeying the law, and they never will succeed. The law has inevitably brought "condemnation," not "righteousness"—the continued declaration in act by God that He regards His people as unrighteous, and so refuses to vindicate them. Moses, regarded as the Pharisees regarded him, had been no minister of life; he had been the minister of death, for death was the penalty of disobedience to the law, and disobedience was inevitable. The letter "puts to death"—judicially—by the punishment it imposes. The law had no doubt its use; and S. Paul has much to say about this in other Epistles. But a means of righteousness, of salvation, and of life it cannot be; any covenant, or established relation between God and His people, which depends upon obedience to the law, can bring no satisfaction and possess no permanence. In the second place, righteousness, life, a relation to God satisfying and permanent, can be, and are in fact attained in a new and different way. God's real claim upon us is for faith, for belief in His message, and response to His call. What God asks is repentance, and belief in Jesus as the Christ, to be followed by incorporation through baptism into Him and the company of His people. When men believe, and are baptized, the guilt of past sin is removed, and the Spirit is bestowed; and when the Lord returns, and the great vindication of God's people takes place, it is those whom God finds thus attached to His Son, who will have their share in it (Gal. v. 5). Indeed the gift of the Spirit is itself a preliminary vindication, bringing with it, as all may see, the new life of the Kingdom, and is thus itself the earnest of the final inheritance. The Spirit, righteousness, and life go together (cf. Rom. viii. 11), as the letter, condemnation, and death go together; and S. Paul is the minister of the one group, his opponents of the other. It is true—and S. Paul elsewhere insists upon this—that the gift of the Spirit is the great source of Christian conduct and character. But that is not the point here. S. Paul is here concerned with righteousness not as contrasted with wickedness, but as contrasted with condemnation, present and to come. If here, as elsewhere in his writings, he seems not clearly to distinguish between righteousness and God's declaration of it, that is only to be expected. To the Jew, morality and religion are one; those only are righteous, whom God declares to be so.

But now a twofold difficulty arises. In the first place, if, as S. Paul teaches, faith, incorporation into Christ, and the gift of the Spirit, are all that is necessary, what is wanting to these Jewish Christians? Might they not each, as baptized believers in Jesus Christ, have asked "What lack I yet"? In the second place, if baptism brings the Spirit, and the Spirit righteousness and life, how comes it that so many of S. Paul's Gentile converts are so profoundly unsatisfactory? To the first question, we shall

12   Having therefore such a hope, we use great boldness of
13 speech, and *are* not as Moses, *who* put a veil upon his
face, that the children of Israel should not look stedfastly

return at a later stage, when we have heard the charges which S. Paul will
bring against his adversaries. At this point it may suffice to say that the
value of the confession of Jesus as the Christ, and of the baptism, in which
faith finds its expression, depend upon the meaning which is attached to
the title. What is important is not the title that we give to the Lord, but
the faith that we repose in Him, and the practical attitude which we adopt
towards Him. If e.g. we continue to look for our acceptance with God not
to Him and to His Spirit but to obedience to the old legal code, we can
have no proper conception of His place in the purpose of God ; we deny
His Christship in fact, though we may maintain it in word.

> Christ ! I am Christ's ! and let the name suffice you,
>   Ay, for me too He greatly hath sufficed.

If the name does not suffice us, if we must reinsure against the judgment
by meticulous obedience to the law, we can never have understood or
"believed in the name."

To the second question, reply is the more necessary, since scholars of
great authority regard S. Paul's theology as refuted by experience. Every
one who has received the Spirit ought *ex hypothesi* to be a perfect Christian,
completely the master of his lower impulses, and completely fulfilling the
divine claim (Rom. viii. 3, 4). The answer is that this statement is true or
false, according as we attach to the word "ought" a moral or a logical
meaning. Without doubt those who are the members of Christ, and have
drunk of His Spirit, ought to control their lower impulses ; they ought
because they can. No temptation assails them but "such as man can bear."
"God is faithful, who will not suffer you to be tempted above that ye are
able" (1 Cor. x. 13). But to say that they ought is not to say that they will.
The Spirit is given us to deliver us from our slavery to sin, and to take the
place of the law as the guide to action. But because as Christians we "live
by the Spirit," it does not follow that "by the Spirit" we shall "also walk"
(Gal. v. 25); it is precisely this that we must be exhorted to do, and set
ourselves to do. We may grieve, and resist the Holy Spirit of God ; and if
we continue to do this, neither He, nor the Lord from whom He comes, will
guarantee our acceptance at the final judgment (v. 10). A union with Christ
and His people, which makes through our own fault no moral difference to
our conduct, will make no difference to our final destiny.

12. *Having...such a hope.* Christian hope has no element of uncertainty. It is the confident expectation that God will fulfil His promises. Here what is in view is the gift of the Spirit, and all that results from it.

boldness of speech. e.g. in the claims for our ministry.

13. *the children of Israel...passing away.* Better as R.V. margin, "unto the end of that which was being done away." Cf. *v.* 7. This seems to be the right interpretation

14 ¹on the end of that which ²was passing away: but their
³minds were hardened: for until this very day at the
reading of the old ⁴covenant the same veil ⁵remaineth
15 unlifted; which *veil* is done away in Christ. But unto this
day, whensoever Moses is read, a veil lieth upon their
16 heart. But whensoever ⁶it shall turn to the Lord, the veil
17 is taken away. Now the Lord is the Spirit: and where the

---

¹ Or, *unto*   ² Or, *was being done away*   ³ Gr. *thoughts.*
⁴ Or, *testament*   ⁵ Or, *remaineth, it not being revealed that it is done away*
⁶ Or, a man *shall turn*

---

of Ex. xxxiv. 33–35. The glory faded, until renewed by fresh communion with God. The Judaizing teachers, S. Paul suggests, conceal the fact that the glory of the law is a glory which fades. The law is but preparatory; it is not God's means of salvation.

14. *but...hardened.* Or "made dull." Cf. Rom. xi. 25. The thought, as the following words shew, is not simply of the story in Exodus, but of the abiding lack of spiritual perception in the Jews.

for until this...remaineth unlifted. The point is that the Jews still fail to recognize the transitory character of the legal system, and of its glory: S. Paul is not here thinking of the application of the O.T. to Christ and His kingdom. The phrase "the old covenant" here first appears.

which veil...in Christ. Or "because it is in Christ that it is done away." What reveals the transitoriness of the old is the coming of the new. It is Christ and the Spirit, Who by Their saving power beggar the glory of the law. Cf. *v.* 10. It is needless to explain to Christians that the glory of the law fades; they see it for themselves, when the Spirit has been given to them. The

exact construction of the Greek of this verse is not certain (cf. R.V. margin), but the general sense is clear.

15. The thought is substantially the same as in the previous verse, but the application of the metaphor is altered, the veil being transferred from the law itself to the heart of the Jewish people. S. Paul is preparing for the new application to be made of Ex. xxxiv. 34 in the next verse.

16. The words are quoted from Ex. xxxiv. 34, and refer to Moses. Thus we should translate "whensoever he," not "it" (i.e. the heart of Israel), or "a man." The ultimate salvation of the Jews as a whole is perhaps in the apostle's mind. Cf. Rom. xi. 23, 26.

17. *Now the Lord is the Spirit.* i.e. "the Lord" in Exodus is, as S. Paul applies the language, the Spirit which he ministers to men. When men turn to that Spirit, which in baptism they receive, they at once recognize the transitory character of the legal system.

and where...there is liberty. The alteration of one letter in the Greek would give the reading "where the Spirit is Lord." But the ordinary reading is probably right. The Holy Spirit is the Spirit Who comes from

18 Spirit of the Lord is, *there* is liberty. But we all, with unveiled face [1] reflecting as a mirror the glory of the Lord, are transformed into the same image from glory to glory, even as from [2] the Lord the Spirit.

[1] Or, *beholding as in a mirror*

[2] Or, *the Spirit* which is *the Lord*

the glorified Lord. Cf. Ac. ii. 33; xvi. 7. The transition from the thought of the Spirit to that of the Lord, from Whom He comes, is required for the next verse.

The great saying "Where the Spirit of the Lord is, there is liberty" is one which has many applications. Cf. e.g. Jn. viii. 34–36; Rom. viii. 2; Gal. v. 1, 18. The freedom particularly in view here is probably, as the context suggests, freedom from the burden of the Mosaic law. The Spirit frees us from the law (*a*) by more than taking its place as the director of our action, and (*b*) by breaking the chains of sin, and so enabling us to fulfil the law of love, in which all God's moral claims are included. Cf. Rom. viii. 1–4, 9, 12–14; Gal. v. 16.

18. *But we all.* Communion with God, and its transforming power, are for all Christians, and not just for one, as in the story of Exodus. Having turned to the Spirit, the veil is removed, and we can see God revealed in Christ. The last thought will be brought out early in ch. iv.

reflecting…glory of the Lord. As so often, the general meaning is clear, but the exact force of the language uncertain. "Mirroring" is probably right. R.V. text suggests the reflecting of the glory back to the source of the glory; and R.V. margin is inconsistent with the closeness of the communion of which S. Paul is thinking. We cannot draw from iv. 4 the thought that the

Gospel is a mirror. At first the Glory of Christ in us is but a reflection, but the Spirit fixes the reflection, and makes it permanent. Cf. Rom. viii. 29; 1 Jn. iii. 2. S. Chrysostom interprets rather differently: "Just as if pure silver be turned towards the sun's rays, it will itself also shoot forth rays, not from its own natural property merely, but also from the solar lustre; so also doth the soul being cleansed, and made brighter than silver, receive a ray from the glory of the Spirit, and glance it back."

the same image. The glorified Lord (iv. 4) is Himself "the image of God," but He should not be the only one.

from glory to glory. The thought is either (*a*) that the transformation proceeds from the divine glory, and brings glory to us, or (*b*) that the glory instead of fading grows from more to more. Cf. Jn. i. 16; Rom. i. 17. Estius quotes S. Augustine: "De gloria recreationis in gloriam justificationis: de gloria fidei in gloriam speciei; de gloria qua filii Dei sumus, in gloriam qua similes ei erimus, quoniam videbimus eum sicuti est."

even as from the Lord the Spirit. S. Paul looks back to the interpretation of Ex. xxxiv. 34, which he has already given. The transformation is a characteristic example of the Spirit's divine activity. The alternative translation in R.V. margin yields the same sense.

G.

3

S. Paul is often declared by modern writers to have identified in *v.* 17 our Lord with the Spirit. Examples of some such confusion are to be found in a few early Christian writers[1], but to regard S. Paul as guilty of it is preposterous. Not only are the Epistles preceding and following the one before us peculiarly full and clear about the doctrine of the Spirit (cf. e.g. 1 Cor. ii and xii; Rom. viii), but the distinction between the Lord and the Spirit is peculiarly plain in this very Epistle (cf. xi. 4, and above all xiii. 13, the clearest Trinitarian passage in S. Paul's writings). Indeed this extraordinary suggestion makes S. Paul contradict himself in *v.* 17; the Spirit, Who is the Spirit of the Lord, cannot be identical with the Lord Himself. There is no difference between S. Paul's language here and that which we find elsewhere in his writings; here as elsewhere he recognizes both the unity and the diversity of the action of Father, Son, and Holy Spirit. If we find his language here unusually puzzling, there are three reasons for this.

In the first place, the ancients did not possess our device of inverted commas, and much obscurity in the N.T. is due to this. Let us insert them here at the right places, and the obscurity will largely disappear :—But unto this day, whensoever Moses is read, a veil lieth upon their heart. "But whensoever he turneth to the Lord, the veil is taken away." Now "the Lord" is the Spirit. In the phrase which puzzles us, the words "the Lord" are repeated from the passage quoted from Exodus; and S. Paul applies them to the Holy Spirit, for a reason which we shall presently see.

Secondly, our thought tends to be tri-theistic. We tend, not only to distinguish the three "Persons" of the Blessed Trinity, but to separate them One from Another; while by S. Paul, as by all Catholic theologians, the unity of the divine action is taken for granted. The Father is revealed to us by Christ, and His life communicated to us through Christ by the Spirit; to turn to One is necessarily to turn to All. To arise and go to our Father (Luk. xv. 18), to turn to the Lord Jesus Christ (Ac. ix. 36), to yield ourselves to the Spirit (2 Cor. iii. 16), are but different ways of describing the same activity of faith; and, when we come to mirror the glory of the

---

[1] Great caution should be exercised in charging early Christian writers with confusion here for two reasons: (*a*) The language of the N.T. and of early Christian writers is not the technical language of later theology, but the simple language of Christian experience; and it is Hebrew rather than Greek thought which lies behind it. The Hebrews think of God as He is practically known in His redeeming activity. Thus though the language of the N.T. implies an "economic" Trinity—i.e. a Trinity revealed in Christian experience—no doctrine of an "essential" Trinity in the divine Being is ever formulated. The one may imply the other, but we must not expect early Christians to write with the precision of the Athanasian Creed. (*b*) The usage of the word "Spirit" is not yet fixed. To the Hebrews "Spirit" was the characteristic of the divine nature, as "flesh" of the human (cf. Is. xxxi. 3), and we find the same conception in the N.T. (cf. Jn. iii. 6; iv. 24). Thus though "divinity" or "deity" as abstract terms can be rendered into Greek (Rom. i. 20; Col. ii. 9), the concrete divine nature of the Lord is best described as "Spirit." So it is apparently in Rom. i. 4; Heb. ix. 14; and perhaps in Jn. vi. 63.

IV. 1 Therefore seeing we have this ministry, even as

Lord, the glory is "the glory of God in the face of Jesus Christ" (iv. 6) communicated to us by the Spirit's power. Though to those familiar with Plotinus and other mystics the language of iii. 18 may suggest the mystic's rapture, nothing of the sort is in S. Paul's mind; he is thinking of normal Christian experience. Indeed, had we been able to question him as to the way in which he understood the O.T. narrative to which he refers, we should probably have found that he read Christian theology into it. He would not have supposed that Moses gazed directly upon the face of God (cf. Col. i. 15; 1 Tim. i. 17; vi. 16); but that God was manifested in His "glory" or Shekinah, or in that Angel of Yahweh, who is often in the O.T. all but identified with Yahweh Himself, and whom S. Paul, like the early writers of the Church, identifies with our Lord as pre-existent (1 Cor. x. 9). So, again, he would probably have supposed that the glory of the face of Moses, transitory though it was, was the work of the Spirit of Yahweh. His language is thus entirely natural and correct, even from the standpoint of the later developed theology.

But, thirdly, it is important to notice why S. Paul interprets here "the Lord" as the Spirit, and says that it is He Who works the transformation in us all. It is the divine power of the Spirit, as contrasted with the importance of the law, which is the very point that he desires to bring out. For the Corinthian Christians, instead of turning to "the Lord the Spirit," Whom S. Paul ministered to them, were being persuaded to turn away from Him to a supposed means of salvation destitute of His transforming power. S. Paul's controversy with the Judaizing teachers was not primarily about the lordship of Christ; they would have said that they too had turned to "the Lord" Jesus, and accepted His claims. The controversy was about the Spirit, as "the Lord, and giver of life"—the Nicene language is probably drawn from this passage, as the Church rightly interpreted it—and about the Spirit as the means of salvation.

It should be noticed that the interpretation given above is far the most strongly supported by the Greek Fathers, probably the best judges on such a question of interpretation as this. If anyone thinks that, in view of *vv.* 14 and 18, and iv. 4, we must in *vv.* 16 and 17 interpret "the Lord" as referring to Christ, it will still be impossible to suppose that S. Paul identifies Him with the Holy Spirit. We shall rather suppose that S. Paul means that, so close is the unity of the Lord with the Spirit, that to turn to the One is to turn to the Other. But true as this thought is, the words of the text would indeed be a strange way of expressing it.

IV. 1-6. There is no break at this point. S. Paul proceeds to explain, more fully than in iii. 12, 13, how the glory of his ministry determines the character of his action. Cf. 1 Th. ii. 1-12.

1. *this ministry.* The word "this" is emphatic. S. Paul thinks of the power of the Spirit to bring life and righteousness, to bestow liberty, and to transform into the likeness of Christ.

2 we obtained mercy, we faint not: but we have renounced
the hidden things of shame, not walking in craftiness, nor
handling the word of God deceitfully; but by the manifestation of the truth commending ourselves to every man's
3 conscience in the sight of God. But and if our gospel is
4 veiled, it is veiled in them that are perishing: in whom the

we obtained mercy. Cf. 1 Cor. vii.
25; 1 Tim. i. 12–16. The special
mercy of God to S. Paul was seen
not only in his call to be a Christian,
but in his call to be an Apostle.
Cf. Ex. xxxiii. 19 (quoted in Rom.
ix. 15), a text which may be in
S. Paul's mind.

faint not. i.e. relax our efforts, as
the next verse shews. The choice
lay between bearing the whole burden, and making things easier for
himself by adulterating the Gospel
to suit Jewish prejudices. Cf. Gal.
v. 11 ; vi. 12.

2. *the hidden things of shame.*
S. Paul has no need of the conceal-
ment which Moses had to practise,
or of that crafty adaptation of the
Gospel to Jewish prejudices which
his opponents found necessary.
S. Paul from the first has never
been ashamed of the Gospel of Christ,
as offering salvation on equal terms
to Jew and Gentile. Cf. Ac. xiii. 46 ;
Rom. i. 16 ; both passages recall Ps.
cxix. 46.

but by the manifestation…of God.
We may translate either as the R.V.
does, or "unto every kind of conscience," or "to the whole conscience."
But the R.V. is simplest and best.
S. Paul speaks ever as "in the great
Taskmaster's eye," and so makes
clear the whole Gospel message,
however unpalatable it may be. But
the conscience of man, unlike his
desires and prejudices, has an af-
finity with the Gospel, and approves

its faithful proclamation. This point
is of great importance. Too often
we confuse the real witness of our
hearers' consciences with what they
pretend to be their witness ; and so,
in taking account of the latter, fail
in our appeal to the former. Englishmen, who have a strong Puritan
tradition behind them, are less willing than Continentals to admit that
they are acting against their convictions. They do not as a rule admit
the reality of a duty, unless they
intend to perform it ; or the force of
an argument, unless they intend to
yield to it. Thus they particularly
often conceal what the witness of
their consciences is.

3. *But and if our gospel is veiled.*
The R.V.'s strange array of conjunc-
tions seems intended to mark the
fact (made clear in the Greek) that
S. Paul admits that his Gospel is
often veiled. It is very likely that
his opponents charged his teaching
with obscurity; but S. Paul looks
back to iii. 14. The veil lay on the
hearts of the Jews when the law was
read to them, and even more heavily
when the Gospel was preached to
them. S. Paul replies that, in the
case of the Gospel, there is no obscurity except for those without the
prepared heart.

4. *the god of this world.* Or "age."
Cf. Jn. xii. 31; xiv. 30; xvi. 11; 1 Jn.
v. 19. S. Paul's description of Satan
is even more startling than that
given in these passages. We should

god of this ¹world hath blinded the ²minds of the unbelieving, ³that the ⁴light of the gospel of the glory of
Christ, who is the image of God, should not dawn *upon*
5 *them.* For we preach not ourselves, but Christ Jesus as
Lord, and ourselves as your ⁵servants ⁶for Jesus' sake.

¹ Or, *age* 　　　² Gr. *thoughts.* 　　　³ Or, *that they should not see the
light...image of God* 　　　⁴ Gr. *illumination.* 　　　⁵ Gr. *bondservants.*
⁶ Some ancient authorities read *through Jesus.*

compare Luk. iv. 6, and Rev. xiii.
2–4. To understand such language,
we should remember that to the
Hebrews the dominant thought of
God was that of His relation to those
who accepted His rule, and not that
of His metaphysical relation to the
world. Cf. Mk. xii. 26; Heb. xi. 16.
Thus to say that Satan is the god
of this world in no way involves a
dualistic conception of the universe.
It is simply to say that it is in fact
Satan's will, and not God's, which is
being done; and that it is the power
of lawless violence and lying (Jn.
viii. 44) to which men are looking,
and not to the power of righteousness and love. In that sense, Satan
is the god of our own "age of the
world" (Eph. ii. 2), as of that which
S. Paul knew. It is true that the
world does not recognize the violence and lying to which it trusts
as centred in a personal power; but
it worships the devil none the less.

hath blinded the minds. S. Paul
is not offering an excuse for dullness
and unbelief, but explaining that it
is no discredit to the Gospel, if its
light does not penetrate everywhere.
Satan only blinds the minds of those
who have become his worshippers.
Cf. 2 Thess. ii. 9, 10.

the gospel of the glory of Christ.
The central point in S. Paul's Gospel
is the present glory of Jesus the
Messiah. Cf. Ac. ii. 36. It is He

Who is the source of that gift of the
Spirit, which both makes the Church
the present embodiment of God's
kingdom, and secures its final consummation.

the image of God. Cf. Col. i. 15;
Heb. i. 3; and for the meaning of
"image" Heb. x. 1. The image is
the most complete representation
possible (Jn. xiv. 9). S. Paul here
thinks chiefly of the ascended and
glorified Christ, of love triumphant
and redemption through sacrifice.
The truth about God which is con-
veyed in Christ crucified and glorified is all the truth about Him which
we are here able to grasp, and the
illumination of the Gospel which
proclaims this glory the only adequate illumination.

5. *not ourselves...as your servants.* Cf. 1 Cor. ix. 19. The second
proclamation is involved in the first.
No one can proclaim Christ as Lord
without proclaiming that he himself
is simply His bondservant, and so
the bondservant of all who are, or
may become, His. Cf. 1 Cor. iv. 1;
ix. 19; and contrast xi. 20 of this
Epistle. S. Paul's claims for himself,
both as to his position in the Church,
and as to his moral faithfulness,
are remarkable. Probably he was
charged with making exaggerated
claims. But it is always as the instrument of Christ for the salvation
of His people that the claims are

6 Seeing it is God, that said, Light shall shine out of darkness, who shined in our hearts, to give the ¹light of the
knowledge of the glory of God in the face of Jesus
Christ.

¹ Gr. *illumination*.

made. The more that in this connexion he exalts himself, the more
he exalts the Corinthians, for whose
sake God has made him what he is.
Just in so far as the rightful claims
of the Christian ministry are denied,
the laity are deprived of their true
honour.

6. *Seeing it is God.* It is the
greatness of Him, from Whom
S. Paul's call to Apostleship came,
and His purpose in calling him,
which determine the character of
his preaching.

Light shall shine out of darkness.
The exact words here quoted are not
found in the O.T. They recall Is. ix.
2, and Ps. cxii. 4. But it is probable
that S. Paul is thinking of the first

utterance of God in the O.T., the
"Let there be light" of Gen. i. 3. To
him the light had come with equal
suddenness on the Damascus road.
But the light came that it might
be passed on to others. Cf. Ac. xxvi.
16–18 ; Gal. i. 15, 16. When the call
came to the Apostle of the Gentiles,
"darkness was upon the face" of
the heathen world, though "the
spirit of God moved upon" it.

*the glory of God in the face of
Jesus Christ.* "Ipse Lux nostra,"
says Bengel, "luminis non solum
autor, sed etiam fons et sol." The
meaning is the same as in *v.* 4 : the
glory given to the Lord is the glory
of God Himself ; in seeing the One
we see the Other.

Attention to these six verses might save Christian preachers from many
mistakes.

In the first place, it is often forgotten that the one way of appealing to
the universal conscience is to set forth the Christian Gospel just as it is, and
not to attempt to adapt it to the conscience of one particular audience. It
is quite true that we must appeal to the conscience; and that, if we do not,
we shall speak in vain. But it is a great mistake to pay too much attention
to what we suppose to be the particular demands which the conscience of
a particular audience is making. The duties, on which men are most
disposed to insist, are the duties of others to themselves; and it is therefore easy to suppose that we shall best win their conscience to our side by
special emphasis upon these duties, e.g. that we shall best appeal to the
artisan classes by insisting upon social reform in their interest, and dwelling
continually upon the new world which practical Christianity would bring
here and now. An other-worldly message seems to us unlikely to appeal to
our particular audience ; and so, "walking in" a well-intentioned "craftiness," we handle "the word of God deceitfully." No real success will come
in that way. The Gospel of God, just because it is God's, appeals to the
universal conscience, though it may seem not to do so ; and we must not
be "ashamed of" it. If our audience seems not to like it, that is precisely
because the awakening of the conscience is unpleasant to us all. In a word,

the Gospel must be preached faithfully, the popular and unpopular elements having each its due place given to it.

In the second place, we must not suppose that everything can be made clear and attractive to men, whatever their moral condition may be. Simplicity of language, and sympathy with our audience, will carry us far; but it will always remain true that "every one that doeth ill hateth the light, and cometh not to the light, lest his works should be reproved" (Jn. iii. 20). "Why do ye not understand my speech?" says our Lord. "Even because ye cannot hear my word" (Jn. viii. 43). His language was unintelligible, because men were without moral sympathy with His message. The Lord does not expect us to overcome a difficulty, which He Himself did not overcome. The simplicity of the Gospel lies in the simplicity of the moral issues which it raises, and not in the ease with which its teaching can be explained to the careless and the hardened. It is addressed to men conscious of their sin, and desirous to be rid of it, to the heart and the will quite as much as to the mind; and it is accepted largely because we know ourselves to require it, and feel that what comes home to us with such power must be the very truth of God. Though the Lord sends us to preach the Gospel to the whole world, He does not expect us to convert the whole world. Rather His message is to be a sword dividing men on the right hand and on the left, ready for His judgment. (Cf. Mt. x. 34–36.) Thus, when the charge is made that our Gospel is unintelligible, and makes no appeal, we shall not be unduly cast down. If our failure is due to lack of clear thought and speech, we are indeed to blame. But if it is due to the fact that the complainers are as yet as incapable of perceiving spiritual truth as a blind man of perceiving colour, we are not to blame; and we must certainly not "corrupt the word of God" in hope of being more effective. If our word is really His, we forward His purpose when we speak, whether men hear, or whether they forbear.

In the third place, S. Paul makes peculiarly clear in this passage what the centre of the Gospel is. It is "the glory of Christ," and not only the Cross of Christ. The Cross appears in the Gospel as the path to the glory, and as, in a true sense, the first stage of the glory. When S. Paul determined to know nothing among the Corinthians "save Jesus Christ, and him crucified" (1 Cor. ii. 2), he did not determine to make the Cross alone the centre of his Gospel. The centre was "Jesus Christ," Jesus, i.e. glorified, and made Lord and Christ by the Resurrection and Ascension (Ac. ii. 36); by adding "and him crucified" S. Paul indicates that, in spite of the prejudice of the Jews against a "Messiah crucified," he made it entirely clear that the Cross had been the path by which the glory had been reached. The mission sermons of S. Peter and S. Paul in the Acts will illustrate the description of the Gospel which the latter gives. The proclamation is not just of death, but of new life won through death; and that by the Christ Himself first, and then by His members through Him. In Christ, in all that the Father has made Him, in all that He is to us as the Bestower of the transforming Spirit, and the Saviour of His Body the Church, the glory of God has shone out as never before, and He has set up a ladder of light, by which it reaches to us. At the top there is God Himself, "dwelling in light

7   But we have this treasure in earthen vessels, that the
exceeding greatness of the power may be of God, and not
8 from ourselves ; *we are* pressed on every side, yet not

unapproachable, whom no man hath seen, nor can see" (1 Tim. vi. 16); we
cannot see God there. Just below there is "the glory of God"—the shining
out in action of what He is. Lower still there is "the knowledge of the
glory of God"; and, again lower, the "light" which it brings (iv. 6). Though
the glory of God shines out even in the visible world (Ps. xix. 1; Rom. i. 20),
it can only be fully grasped by us, and fully illuminate us "in the face of
Jesus Christ." The great title "Christ" is here all-important. No doubt the
glory of God shone out in the Lord even in His earthly life (Jn. ii. 11); and
it is natural that S. John, the eye-witness of that life (1 Jn. i. 1–3), should
dwell upon this, as S. Paul does not. But we should not interpret the great
words of Jn. xiv. 9, without remembering that the whole discourse, of which
they form a part, looks forward as well as backward (cf. Jn. xiii. 31, 32). It
is in the face of Jesus glorified that we see the glory of God best, because
in Him God has reconciled the world unto Himself by the path of loving
sacrifice, and through Him has bestowed upon us the Holy Spirit (cf. 1 Jn. iv.
10–13). God had to deal first with the sin of the world; but in dealing
with it He dealt with its darkness also, for God is best known through His
redemptive activity under the new covenant, as He was under the old.

7–18. The purpose of God in human weakness, illustrated by S. Paul's
experience.

7. *this treasure.* i.e. the Spirit of
illumination and life, which S. Paul
ministers.

in earthen vessels. The thought
of the bodies of clay (Gen. ii. 7; Job
iv. 19 etc.), which are our instruments of service and of sacrifice, is
common in the O.T. S. Paul perhaps
remembers the Lord's words in Ac.
ix. 15.

of God, and not from ourselves.
Better "God's, and not from us."
Though God creates the ministry,
inspires it, and uses it, the power
by which its work is done is all His
own. Cf. Introd. p. xx. The weakness of the instrument prevents mistake as to the source of the power
both in those through whom it is
exercised, and in those who experience it. For the former, cf. xii. 7–10;
and for the latter, 1 Cor. ii. 3–5;

iii. 9. But there is a deeper thought,
as the words to follow will shew. It
is only when the human power fails,
that the divine can be fully manifested; death is the way to life
abounding in the members of Christ,
as in Christ Himself.

8. *we are pressed.* The words
"we are" would be better away, as
there is no new sentence. In *vv.* 8–10,
the first word or clause in each contrast brings out the human weakness,
and the second the more than com-
pensating divine strength. Ceaseless
pressure brings ever-enduring influence; the apparent hopelessness of
the situation leads to the divine
solution of the difficulty; the persecution manifests the divine power to
deliver; the temporary defeats shew
the divine power to save in spite of
them. All this had been illustrated

9 straitened; perplexed, yet not unto despair; pursued, yet
10 not ¹forsaken; smitten down, yet not destroyed; always
    bearing about in the body the ²dying of Jesus, that the
11 life also of Jesus may be manifested in our body. For
    we which live are alway delivered unto death for Jesus'
    sake, that the life also of Jesus may be manifested in our
12 mortal flesh. So then death worketh in us, but life in you.
13 But having the same spirit of faith, according to that
    which is written, I believed, and therefore did I speak;

---

¹ Or, *left behind*   ² Gr. *putting to death.*

---

in S. Paul's recent experience at
Ephesus, and in his trouble with the
Corinthians themselves.

10. *the dying of Jesus.* Better,
with R.V. marg., "the putting to
death of Jesus." The Lord's experience is being reproduced in S. Paul;
his life is a continual Passion. Cf.
Rom. viii. 36; 1 Cor. xv. 31. And it is
this in order that the life of the Risen
Jesus may be manifested in his body.
Cf. Gal. vi. 14; Phil. iii. 10. The
words "bearing about" may look
back to ii. 14.

11. *alway.* The word is emphatic.
The death is not died once for all.
Similar as this verse is to the last,
new thoughts appear in it: (*a*) S. Paul,
like the Lord, is continually being
betrayed to death. When e.g. his
fellow-countrymen brought him before Roman tribunals, the experience
of the Lord was in him repeated.
(*b*) It is for Jesus' sake—because of
Jesus—that he suffers. It is only
suffering of this kind, which is so
abundantly blessed. (*c*) There is a
new stress upon the "mortal flesh"
as the scene of the manifestation of
the divine power. A merely spiritual
resurrection would not manifest the
life of the Risen Lord in the same
way.

12. *but life in you.* The thought

advances a further stage. The glory
of Christ had two manifestations, one
in His own glorified body, and the
other in His gift of the Holy Ghost.
So it is with S. Paul. The life of the
Risen Christ is manifested not only
by the marvellous power of endurance which his body exhibits, but in
the divine life communicated to the
Corinthians. Those who profit by
his sufferings should be the last to
despise his weakness.

13. *But having.* Better "And
having." S. Paul turns to a new
thought, but not to a contrasted one.
It is through his speech, his Gospel
preaching, that the divine life is
communicated to those who hear
him. S. Paul gave the Spirit, because
the depth of his experience of the
grace of Christ enabled him to speak
the word of God with overwhelming
conviction and power, so that men
were brought to faith and baptism.

spirit of faith. The word "Spirit"
should probably have its capital
letter. It is not a question of a
particular disposition. The same
Spirit which speaks in the words of
the Psalm inspires and sustains
S. Paul's own faith.

according to...written. Ps. cxvi.
10. The Psalmist's experience resembled S. Paul's. But the context

14 we also believe, and therefore also we speak; knowing
    that he which raised up [1]the Lord Jesus shall raise up us
15 also with Jesus, and shall present us with you. For all
    things *are* for your sakes, that the grace, being multiplied
    through [2]the many, may cause the thanksgiving to abound
    unto the glory of God.
16   Wherefore we faint not; but though our outward man
    is decaying, yet our inward man is renewed day by day.
17 For our light affliction, which is for the moment, worketh
    for us more and more exceedingly an eternal weight of

[1] Some ancient authorities omit *the Lord*.   [2] Gr. *the more*.

suggests that S. Paul understands his words as the utterance of the Lord Himself, in Whose person he prophetically speaks. It is a Psalm of the Resurrection, as the divine answer to the Lord's prayer to be "saved out of death" (Heb. v. 7). Thus in *vv.* 3, 4 we are to see the Agony of Gethsemane, and in *vv.* 5–9 the joy of Easter, and the Lord's perpetual service in "the land of the living." It is confidence in the communicated life of the Risen Christ which enables S. Paul to continue His witness.

14. *raise up...Jesus.* It is not clear whether the thought is still of the daily supply of the risen life, or of the resurrection of the body. Both proceed from the same divine activity; and S. Paul, as we shall shortly see, hoped to escape death by the return of the Lord. The next words in any case look on to the end.

present us with you. Cf. xi. 2 and 1 Cor. xv. 24. The whole Church will at last be presented to God in its perfection (Eph. v. 27).

15. *all things.* i.e. the whole work of God, as it is seen in the suffering of the Apostle, and the continual manifestation of the life of the Resurrection within him.

being multiplied through the many. Cf. *v.* 12, i. 11, and ix. 14. The grace bestowed upon S. Paul is multiplied through its extension by his work to others, and so leads on to multiplied thanksgiving.

unto the glory of God. Always the final end to be attained.

16. *Wherefore we faint not.* A return to the thought of *v.* 1.

is decaying. Better "is continually being destroyed." Cf. *v.* 10.

our inward man. i.e. the abiding personality, the deepest self, where the work of the Spirit begins (cf. Rom. viii. 10), though one day the body will have its share in the transformation. For the thought, cf. Rom. xii. 2; Eph. iii. 16; iv. 23; Col. iii. 10; and iii. 18 of this Epistle.

17. *For our light...moment.* Moffatt well "the slight trouble of the passing hour." The R.V. lays a stress upon the short duration of the trouble, which is not found in the Greek. Language is tasked to the uttermost to express the contrast. The affliction, which seems so heavy, is really light; the glory which seems so unpalpable, is a weight hardly to be borne; and all "in a surpassing manner to a surpassing result." It is the suffering which brings the glory

18 glory; while we look not at the things which are seen, but
at the things which are not seen : for the things which are
seen are temporal; but the things which are not seen are
eternal.

by bringing about the continual
supply of the Resurrection power.
Cf. Rom. viii. 17, 18.

18. *the things which are not
seen.* The Kingdom of God, with
all the glory which it will bring.

S. Paul thinks of blessings which we
do not yet see, but not of blessings
incapable of being seen. It is by
keeping the eye of faith fixed upon
these, that the present affliction
seems light.

There is perhaps in S. Paul's Epistles no passage deeper than this, or
more directly practical; it may be largely because we do not understand
and act upon its teaching that our tasks are so badly performed. We do not
indeed suppose that the work of God can be done by human power, or forget
to pray "Come, Holy Ghost"; but we do forget that the presence of the
Spirit of the Ascended Christ is one thing, and His manifestation another;
and that it is only as we share in that Cross of Christ, by which the Spirit
was won for us, that the manifestation can be given. There was a time,
when "the Spirit was not yet given, because Jesus was not yet glorified"
(Jn. vii. 39); there was a time also, when Jesus was indeed glorified, but
the Church was still tarrying in Jerusalem until it should be "clothed with
power from on high" (Luk. xxiv. 49); but both have now passed away, never
to return. The Church has already received "the earnest of the Spirit," and
looks for no further endowment until her earthly task is over. No doubt
the divine gift is one to be continually renewed (1 Th. iv. 8); even though
we lose it by sin, we may recover it by the grace of God after repentance;
while by deeper self-surrender and more earnest prayer we may win it in
greater abundance (cf. Ac. iv. 29–31). But all this must not be allowed to
obscure the fact that the Spirit is already ours, and the life of the Risen
Christ which the Spirit brings; what we require is that practical manifestation of their presence, which can only come as in spite of our weakness
we face the whole task laid upon us, and so receive and bear the Cross.
That is what the Lord's own experience suggests, and what S. Paul teaches
us here. It is when the human powers fail, that the divine power comes
fully into action.

How did the Cross, and through the Cross the Resurrection, come to the
Lord Himself? They came to Him, because in all His human weakness He
set Himself to carry out the task which the Father had given Him. The
ordinary troubles of the world did not fall upon Him, as far as we know,
with any peculiar severity. Apparently He never knew illness or any
crushing bereavement; certainly He never knew the disappointment of
earthly hopes, since He had none for the world to disappoint. Nor was it
ever His way to lay suffering upon Himself. He did not seek for the Cross;
He sought the accomplishment of the Father's will; and the Cross was the
consequence of doing so. All that the Lord had He sacrificed, when it was

asked of Him; and what we see in Gethsemane is the breakdown of the human powers under the strain which they had to bear. "The spirit indeed is willing, but the flesh is weak" are words true of the Lord as well as of the Apostles (Mt. xxvii. 41). It is just as true, to quote some later words of this Epistle, that He "was crucified through weakness" as that He now lives "through the power of God" (xiii. 4). But the manifestation of "the exceeding greatness" of the power was only possible because the sacrifice asked had been completely made. If the Lord Ascended was able to bestow the Spirit, as in His earthly life He had not been, it was because fruitfulness can only come by sacrifice. It is the grain, which falls into the earth and dies, which reproduces itself a hundredfold in other grains that are like it (Jn. xii. 24).

Now it is this experience which S. Paul reproduces, as we have already seen (ii. 15, 16). S. Paul himself, as far as we know, never sought after suffering. He took his part no doubt in the fasts of the Apostolic Church; but, if we interpret his words in 1 Cor. ix. 27 of self-imposed austerities, we almost certainly misinterpret them. The context suggests that he is there speaking of his apostolic labours. He buffeted his body, and brought it into subjection, by the severity of the labours which he thus imposed upon it. The Cross came to him, as to the Lord, because in spite of his weakness he faced the whole task laid upon him, and set himself to accomplish it. What an iron frame, what a convincing eloquence, would have seemed to be required to justify such a call as his! And what was he? A man frequently assailed by an illness far from calculated to attract others to him (Gal. iv. 13, 14; 2 Cor. xii. 7), a man whose speech was contemptible, if judged by the standards of his day. That his powers should fail was inevitable. But it was as he said. As the human powers failed, the divine power was manifested even in his "mortal flesh" and imperfect intellectual equipment. So far from his weaknesses hindering the divine power, it was precisely because of them that it was so wonderfully manifested. The daily dying brought with it the daily resurrection, and the continual communication of life to other men.

So it is with the work of the Church. Both the Cross and the Resurrection must come by facing the whole task—physical, intellectual, and spiritual—and setting ourselves just as we are to accomplish it. In a perfect world, our tasks might be exactly adapted to our powers; they might but call out, develope, and perfect these powers, and make for unbroken health of body and of mind. But in a world of sin that cannot be. The penalty of sin is not work, but overwork (Gen. iii. 17–19); and so the Cross comes. It is not God's intention that we should be in ourselves adequate to our tasks, but that we should be inadequate—not strong enough, or clever enough, or possessed of sufficient knowledge, to have, humanly speaking, any chance of accomplishing them. If we will only accept the tasks which we think adapted to our powers, we shall not respond to His call. God can make us sufficient; indeed He has already done so (iii. 5); but only by a gift of the Spirit, which remains latent until the human strength fails (xii. 10). If God has given us our task, we must do it now, and do it as we are. The Church is always in a crisis, and always will be. Difficulties, limitations, insoluble

V. 1 For we know that if the earthly house of our [1]taber-

[1] Or, *bodily frame*

problems, want of men and money, a menacing outlook, endless misunderstandings and misrepresentations—we have not just to do our work in spite of these things; they are precisely the conditions requisite for the doing of it, and the proofs that we are at grips with our real task. If we are "pressed," it means that we are pressing others, for all pressure is reciprocal; so far from its "straitening" us, it means that our influence is growing wider. If we are "perplexed" by our intellectual and practical problems, it means that we are facing them; those who refuse to face them suffer from no perplexity. If we are "persecuted," it means that we are being taken seriously: false prophets—"dumb dogs" that "cannot bark, dreaming, lying down, loving to slumber" (Is. lvi. 10)—may win the world's contempt, but not its active hostility. If we are "smitten down," it means that the world at its own weapons is the stronger. The Lord has sent us to make a frontal attack upon the enemy; thank God, we have not missed our way; this is where the enemy is; and, though we fall, we shall arise (Mic. vii. 8). If we suffer, we shall exercise an influence; if we refuse to suffer, or resent suffering, we shall have next to none. And the reason is, not just that suffering arouses attention and human sympathy; but that "death" must "work" in us, if "life" is to "work" in those to whom we go. That risen life of Christ which the Spirit brings is not given to pauperize us, to injure our manhood by enabling us to do more easily and comfortably what with a little more effort we could do by ourselves. It is given us that we may accomplish tasks, under which our human powers must fail; and, if we desire its manifestation, we must so act as to require it. That is "the King's Highway of the Holy Cross." Always with more work than we can do, with harder problems than we can solve, with more opposition than we can meet; never seeing how the work is going to be done, and yet, when the time comes, doing it. So we become to God "a sweet savour of Christ"; and, since all must be tested by the message of the Gospel, whether we prove to be "a savour of life unto life," or "of death unto death," we do God's work, and accomplish His will.

V. Again there is no break in the thought. The body of the future is one of the abiding realities, upon which the eyes of Christians are fixed; and it is the one just now particularly in view. S. Paul will shew how unimportant is the destruction of the outward man (iv. 16).

1. *we know.* S. Paul refers to what he has already taught the Corinthians; he is not, as apparently in 1 Thess. iv. 15, giving a new revelation. Thus we shall expect the teaching here given to be consistent with that of 1 Cor. xv.

if the earthly...tabernacle. Both the present body, and that for which we look, are regarded as houses, or dwelling-places, of the abiding personalities, to which they belong; but they differ in their character, and their capacity for continuance. The present body is "earthly"; its life is lived upon the earth, and it

nacle be dissolved, we have a building from God, a house not
2 made with hands, eternal, in the heavens. For verily in this
we groan, longing to be clothed upon with our habitation

is adapted to our present existence
there. It is a tent, or tabernacle,
for those who have "here no continuing city" (Heb. xiii. 14), or a
frame (R.V. marg.) weighing us down
(Wisd. ix. 15). If the last passage is
in S. Paul's mind, we have here a
link with Greek thought, for Wisd.
ix. 15 is reminiscent of Plato, *Phaedo*,
81 c. The body of the future will
come to us more directly from God
(cf. Luk. xx. 36; 1 Cor. xv. 38); it
will be a permanent "building," as
contrasted with a tent. It will be
"not made with hands," i.e. a spiritual
or supernatural body—the Greek
adjective here used has no longer
always its strict meaning, as we see
in Col. ii. 11, and Heb. ix. 11; it
will be a body to abide eternally in
the heavens. It is noticeable that
the charge was brought against the
Lord, that He had said that He
would destroy the temple made with
hands, and in three days build another "not made with hands" (Mk.
xiv. 58). If S. Paul knew of this
charge, and interpreted the words
used by the Lord, as S. John interprets them (Jn. ii. 19–21), he
would naturally speak of the bodies
to be one day borne by ourselves as
"not made with hands." His whole
conception of these bodies is drawn
from the revelation of the Risen
Lord given to himself and to his
fellow Apostles. Cf. the longer note
below.

be dissolved. Better "be destroyed." S. Paul's suffering may
end in death. Again we have a word
used in Mk. xiv. 58. "For like as
we, when purposing to take houses

down, allow not the inmates to stay,
that they may escape the dust and
noise; but causing them to remove
a little while, when we have built up
the tenement securely, admit them
freely; so also doth God." S. Chrysostom.

we have. The present tense does
not necessitate the adoption of the
view of some expositors, that S. Paul
thinks of the body of the future as
already existing. S. Paul means that
we have it in anticipation. Cf. 2 Tim.
iv. 8, where also the present tense
is used. Moffatt renders "I get a
home from God." For a full discussion of the meaning of this verse,
see below.

2. *For verily...groan.* The connexion of thought is not quite certain. Have we an additional reason
for keeping the eyes fixed upon the
abiding realities (iv. 18), or a reason
for knowing that a spiritual body
awaits us? Probably the latter. In
view of the glory of God's final kingdom we cannot believe that the
body as it now is will be there our
dwelling-place. Cf. 1 Cor. xv. 50,
and *v.* 4 of this chapter.

longing to be clothed upon with.
This strange expression seems to
shew that S. Paul expected the
spiritual body to be the result of
a re-clothing given to the present
one. Cf. *v.* 4, and the word used of
S. Peter's garment in Jn. xxi. 7. In
1 Cor. xv. 53, 54 the language is
similar, and exactly describes what
took place at the Resurrection of
the Lord. S. Paul is not here thinking of the resurrection of the dead,
but of the transformation of living

3 which is from heaven: if so be that being clothed we shall
4 not be found naked. For indeed we that are in this [1]taber-
nacle do groan, [2]being burdened; not for that we would
be unclothed, but that we would be clothed upon, that
5 what is mortal may be swallowed up of life. Now he that

[1] Or, *bodily frame*   [2] Or, *being burdened, in that we would not be unclothed, but would be clothed upon*

Christians; indeed death is not yet definitely in view at all. The bodies of living Christians, when the Lord returns, will not be laid aside; but they will, like the body of the Lord on the Easter morning, be wholly transformed by the incorruption and immortality which they will put on. There is not the slightest suggestion of a new spiritual body to be bestowed at death. See further below.

3. *if so be that...found naked.* S. Paul's obscurity is here at its worst, and the R.V. does nothing to relieve it. The arrangement of the Greek particles at the beginning of the clause is an uncommon one; and much turns upon the answer to the question whether the word "if" introduces a supposition which is doubtful, or one which can safely be made. Now the same arrangement of particles is found in Gal. iii. 4; and there the supposition clearly is doubtful. We may translate then "If so be that clothed, not naked, we shall be found." S. Paul explains that his words in the previous verse refer to the experience of Christians, who will be still clothed with their earthly bodies when the Lord returns, and not to that of those who will then be discarnate spirits. In the case of the latter, the word translated "clothed upon" would not have been appropriate. This interpretation gives an excellent sense, and complete consistency to S. Paul's

language. We are "clothed," when we still retain our earthly bodies; we are "unclothed" or "naked," when we have laid them aside at death; we are "clothed upon," when the Lord's return finds us still with our earthly bodies, and they put on incorruption and immortality. The question of the resurrection of those who have already died does not come directly into view.

4. *do groan...burdened.* In reading these words emphasis should be placed on the word "burdened," to make it clear that *v.* 4 is an explanation of *v.* 2.

not for that we would be unclothed. i.e. the longing is not to get rid of the present body, but to obtain the better one. The Platonic view that the body is the prison of the soul is totally contrary to Biblical thought; and S. Paul may wish to combat it. To the Hebrews, the thought of being disembodied was most cheerless. Cf. Job vii. 9; Ps. vi. 5; lxxxviii. 4, 5; Is. xxxviii. 18, 19. Indeed, it probably is so to almost all men. All our activities are bound up with the body, and therefore all the personal life that we know.

what is mortal...life. The words of Is. xxv. 8, quoted in 1 Cor. xv. 54, are in S. Paul's mind. His language here, as in 1 Cor. xv. 53, is magnificent and impressive; but language to which it is impossible to attach a

wrought us for this very thing is God, who gave unto us
6 the earnest of the Spirit. Being therefore always of good
courage, and knowing that, whilst we are at home in the
7 body, we are absent from the Lord (for we walk by faith,
8 not by ¹sight); we are of good courage, I say, and are
willing rather to be absent from the body, and to be at
9 home with the Lord. Wherefore also we ²make it our aim,

¹ Gr. *appearance*.   ² Gr. *are ambitious*.

very definite meaning or an imaginative picture. To this we shall
return.

5. *he that wrought us.* This
strange phrase reproduces the
strange phrase of the original. There
has been a new creation, as we shall
see in *v.* 17.

the earnest of the Spirit. Cf. i. 22,
and the note there. Though the
Spirit as yet does little but transform
the inner man, at the final consummation He will transform the body
also; and God has had this in view
from the first. Cf. Rom. viii. 22 ff.
S. Paul is still thinking primarily of
Christians, who will be alive at the
Lord's return.

6. *always of good courage.* i.e. as
to the future. That is assured, whatever may now happen to the body.

at home in the body. A deplorable
translation. The present body is
quite unworthy of the name of home.
We should translate "dwelling" or
(with Moffatt) "residing in the
body."

absent from the Lord. Close as is
our union with Him, He dwells in a
different sphere from ours, and we
cannot see Him. S. Paul at once
explains his meaning, lest it should
be misunderstood.

7. *by faith, not by sight.* Literally
"not by visible form," or "by that
which is seen." For the N.T. usage
of the word cf. Luk. iii. 22; ix. 29;

Jn. v. 37; and for S. Paul's meaning
1 Cor. xiii. 12. Faith, as Estius says,
is "imperfecta et aenigmatica visio."
To live by it is the characteristic
attainment of the Christian, and his
necessary discipline; but love asks
for something more satisfying. We
should notice that the characteristically Christian antithesis is that of
faith and sight; not that either of
faith and reason, or of faith and
knowledge. Such words as those of
Tennyson:

We have but faith: we cannot know;
For knowledge is of things we see;

are as alien from N.T. thought as
from sound philosophy. Faith, as
Dr Inge says, is "the logic of the
whole personality," and thus a means
of knowledge. Cf. the final note on
1 Cor. xiii, and the Collect for the
Epiphany.

8. *are willing rather.* Here death
seems to come clearly into view.
Though it is not the discarnate state
that S. Paul desires, the fuller vision
of the Lord will more than compen-
sate for it. His view is that, even as
discarnate, He will have the vision
of Christ (cf. Phil. i. 23), as he has it
not here.

at home with the Lord. "Pere-
grinator patriam habet" says Bengel.
But the thought of home is no more
found in the Greek here than in
v. 6; and it is doubtful whether

whether at home or absent, to be well-pleasing unto him.
10 For we must all be made manifest before the judgement-
seat of Christ; that each one may receive the things *done*
¹in the body, according to what he hath done, whether *it
be* good or bad.

¹ Gr. *through.*

S. Paul would think of anything short of the final Kingdom of God as home.

9. *make it our aim.* Better perhaps (with Moffatt) "we are eager." For the word, cf. Rom. xv. 20; 1 Th. iv. 11. The idea of seeking after honour, which originally belonged to the Greek word, seems to be almost lost in the N.T.

whether at home or absent. The language is not clear, as both expressions have been used of two different conditions. The point is that the Lord's approval is equally precious, wherever we may be.

10. *must all be made manifest.* All, whether in the body, or no longer in the body, must appear just as they are. In the N.T. judgment is always regarded as taking place at the final consummation, and not before. Cf. i. 14 and note there. The thought of a particular judgment passed upon each soul at death is not found in the N.T. The life of the world is a vast and continuous whole, and there can be no adequate manifestation of the value and meaning of any life, until its issues are seen in the final consummation, to which its own tiny contribution has been made. To say this is not to forget the parable of the rich man and Lazarus; or to deny the profound truth of Newman's thought in the *Dream of Gerontius,* that the vision of the Lord must bring to each the knowledge of how we stand with Him.

the things done in the body. The reference here is to the actions themselves, and not to the results produced by them, as in Eph. vi. 8 The Greek verbs differ in the two cases. The R.V. marg. "through the body" gives the more accurate translation. The body is the instrument of all activity, even that of thought and contemplation. Our works follow us (Rev. xiv. 13), but we cannot, strictly speaking, be said to receive them back; and, though S. Paul at first says this, he corrects himself. It is however true to say that we must receive what we are. "Sow acts, and you reap a habit; sow a habit, and you reap a character; sow a character, and you reap a destiny."

whether it be good or bad. The singular takes the place of the plural. Action must be judged as a whole.

These ten verses are among the most difficult in S. Paul's Epistles, and they have been variously interpreted. They afford an admirable example of the importance of attending, nor merely to the words at the moment before us, but to the mind of S. Paul as a whole.

We observe first that, in looking forward into the future, the standpoint of the Apostolic Church was very different from our own. Modern Catholic Christians expect in due course to die, and at the final consummation to rise from the dead. Between death and resurrection, they think, a vast interval of time may be interposed; and thus they are greatly interested in all questions which have to do with the intermediate state. To them the question of the body of the future is the question of the body to be theirs at the resurrection, when their present bodies have long mouldered away; and, if they give a thought to those Christians who may be alive when the end comes, they regard them as unimportant exceptions to the general rule. But with the early Christians all this was otherwise. They expected the Lord to return soon; they did not expect to die, and had no thought of preparing for death; they had little interest in the intermediate state; and, when they looked forward to the future, they thought not so much of resurrection, as of the transformation of their present bodies into bodies worthy of the divine kingdom. To their minds, the death of a Christian was a little startling; and, when it took place, it aroused serious misgivings. Cf. Commentary on 1 Corinthians, pp. 137, 138. Now, in interpreting the N.T., this difference of standpoint must continually be remembered. Such parables as those of Mt. xxv would not to the early Christians suggest any thought of resurrection; nor would such words as those of Phil. iii. 21. So it is in the passage before us. There is not a word of resurrection. S. Paul recognizes it as a possibility that he, like others, may die before the Lord's return; but that is all. Those who are to stand before the judgment-seat of Christ are in his view for the most part Christians who have never died, and it is with them that he is primarily concerned. He has dealt with the question of the resurrection of the dead in the First Epistle, and does not here recur to it.

Secondly, we must remember that the source of S. Paul's teaching is almost certainly the revelation contained in that transformation of the body of the Lord, which took place on the Easter morning. We are not likely to obtain much help in understanding his language from such Jewish sources as the Book of Enoch and the Ascension of Isaiah, and still less from the Iranian teaching, which Reitzenstein supposes to lie behind them. Even if S. Paul had read these books, their conceptions of the future would have seemed to him valueless compared with what he and his fellow Apostles had learned from the revelation of the Risen Lord. Christ is "the firstfruits" of redeemed humanity, and the rest of the redeemed will resemble him. Cf. 1 Cor. xv. 42–54 and Phil. iii. 21. The Lord's Resurrection did not consist in the laying aside of the body which He took of Mary, and the assumption of one entirely new and spiritual, but in the transformation of the body in which His work on earth had been done. What was "mortal" was "swallowed up of life"; and so it will be with those alive at His coming.

Thirdly, we must remember here, as so often, that S. Paul is "rude in speech, but not in knowledge." He is a most authoritative teacher, entirely sure of his inspiration and of the truth of what he says. In the whole of his writings, there is no example of a change of "view," or of a retractation of what he has once said[1]. On the other hand he is often as a writer careless

---

[1] There is e.g. no change to be discovered even in S. Paul's view of the nearness of the Second Advent. In 2 Cor. he is less confident that he will be alive to see it than in 1 Cor.; and in Phil. he is less confident still. But the change

and obscure, and particularly so in this Epistle, which he wrote after a period of terrible strain. Thus the *prima facie* meaning of his words is often not the true one. With him, if the choice lies between the supposition that he has contradicted himself, and the supposition that he has expressed himself very badly, the latter should always be adopted.

Now it is with all this in our minds that we must grapple with the difficulties of these verses. We shall expect to find S. Paul thinking primarily of the transformation of living Christians, though of course not ignoring the possibility of death; we shall expect what he says to be consistent with all that he has said in earlier Epistles, and will say in later ones; and we shall expect the chief source of his teaching to be the revelation of the Risen Lord.

With regard to the first point, there is no foundation for the view that S. Paul looks for a spiritual body to be his at the moment after death. This view has been advocated in two different forms. According to the one, the spiritual body already exists "in the heavens" waiting for us; according to the other, it is being gradually formed within us by the power of the Spirit. To a modern reader, unfamiliar with early Christian thought, the idea of a spiritual body waiting for us in the sky is undoubtedly the idea which S. Paul's words in *v.* 1 at first suggest. But, quite apart from the overwhelming objections to be urged presently, this explanation does not suit the context. The word "eternal," or "everlasting," in *v.* 1 looks back to the same word in iv. 17 and 18. The body of the future is not a garment already prepared in the "eternal tabernacles" of Luk. xvi. 9; its glory is being fashioned day by day by the patience and courage of those who will bear it. Thus the second form of the view which we are considering is the better suited to the context, and may be thought to find support in *v.* 5. But this form also is untenable, and Martensen, the great Danish theologian who maintains it, has had few followers. S. Paul undoubtedly regards the Holy Spirit as dwelling in our bodies, ready to transform them at the right time (Rom. viii. 11), but that is a different thing; and we cannot suppose that, if S. Paul had held Martensen's view, he would have thought of the intermediate state, as one in which he would be "unclothed." The truth is that in *v.* 1, S. Paul's eyes are fixed, as those of the early Christians always were, not on the moment of death, but on the moment of the Lord's return. He has already said (iv. 16) that his outward man is continually being destroyed, and he now recognizes that the process may end in death; but he looks beyond it to the Lord's return, and all that it will bring. Even *vv.* 8 and 9 may possibly not directly contemplate death, though, in view of Phil. i. 23, the view taken in the notes appears the more probable.

We turn to the question of S. Paul's consistency with himself. We need not concern ourselves with 1 Thess. iv. 13–18, as in that passage S. Paul says

---

is due to a change, not in his thought about the Second Advent, but to a change in his own circumstances and prospects of long life. Between the writing of the two Epistles to the Corinthians, he has been very near to death; and, when he writes to the Philippians, he is looking forward to possible martyrdom.

nothing about the character of the body of the future. The question which arises is that of the consistency of the teaching of the verses before us with that of 1 Cor. xv. Now so far from there being any want of consistency, the very reason of S. Paul's obscurity in these verses is probably in part that he means them to be interpreted by the First Epistle. The Second Epistle was written but a few months after the First, and the teaching of the First Epistle about the body of the future is the chief doctrinal teaching to be found in it. There the doctrine of the transformation of living Christians is taught with authority as one of the secrets revealed to the Church (1 Cor. xv. 51, 52). It is to this teaching that S. Paul may refer, when in 2 Cor. v. 1 he begins with the words "For we know." Had S. Paul intended to go back upon what he had said, he would have been obliged to say so very plainly. Instead of this the old language reappears. The words "earthly," "mortal," "swallowed up," all come from the earlier statement; the words "from heaven," used of the body of the future, recall the same words used of the Lord in 1 Cor. xv. 47; and the statement that the new body will be "from God" recalls 1 Cor. xv. 38. The word "swallowed up" is particularly significant. It is a strange word and comes from Is. xxv. 8. Why does S. Paul not quote Isaiah's words? Probably because he has already quoted them in 1 Cor. xv. 54, and presupposes that they are known. Thus no Corinthian Christian familiar with the First Epistle would misunderstand the teaching of the Second. All would understand S. Paul to have in view Christians still living at the Lord's return, and interpret his words by 1 Cor. xv. 52–54.

But this is not all. Shortly after writing the Second Epistle, S. Paul wrote the Epistle to the Romans, and some years later the Epistle to the Philippians; and in both he teaches the same doctrine of the transformation of the present body which we find in the First Epistle to the Corinthians. Cf. Rom. viii. 10, 11, 23 and Phil. iii. 21. In neither case is there any direct reference to the resurrection; the early Christian standpoint is maintained in both. In Rom. viii. 11, e.g. the quickening of the mortal body is the quickening of the still living body which the previous verse has declared to be spiritually dead; while in Phil. iii. 21 the meaning is even clearer. In both these Epistles S. Paul's doctrine is not that at death we lay aside the old body, and assume a new spiritual one; but that the old body is re-fashioned and conformed to the body of the glorified Lord. Are we seriously asked to believe that S. Paul, after teaching one doctrine with peculiar solemnity in the First Epistle to the Corinthians, taught a totally different one to the same Church only a few months afterwards, and then went back to his original "view"? That would indeed be to speak the "yea, yea" and the "nay, nay" at the same time. Many modern writers not only do not believe in S. Paul's inspiration, but forget his own belief in it, and that of his converts. When we are merely investigating questions of scholarship, or speculating about the unseen, there is no reason why we should not change our minds every six months; but, if we claim to be inspired teachers, nothing of the kind is possible.

Thirdly, can we say that S. Paul's one source of information was the revelation of the Risen Lord? He tells us of no other; nor, when we rightly interpret him, do we find him saying anything which the Risen Lord did not reveal. His language may suggest to us at first the momentary coexistence of two bodies, the earthly and the spiritual, the latter being put on over the former. But it is only his literary awkwardness which leads us so to understand him, as the final words of *v.* 4 shew (cf. 1 Cor. xv. 53, 54). Alike in *v.* 2, in *v.* 4, and in 1 Cor. xv. 53, 54, the subject of the change is a concrete reality—this bodily frame, this corruptible thing, this mortal thing; but what is put on, and changes it, is not a similar concrete reality, but incorruption, immortality, life; and the body to which S. Paul looks forward only comes into being, when what is mortal has been swallowed up of life. The Apostles of course believed the message of the empty tomb; that the old body of the Lord had somewhere been "cast as rubbish to the void" never occurred to their minds. But just as little did they suppose that a new body had descended from heaven and been put on by Him over the old, for they had seen His Hands and His Side after He had risen. S. Paul's words describe what he believed about Christ the firstfruits as accurately as what he believed about those who would be Christ's at His coming; and if, lofty and uplifting as they are, they do not in the least explain the mystery which such a change involves, that is unavoidable. The change in question is a change from one order of being to another, and not a change within this present order. A change, which we could explain, would be proved by the explanation to be wholly within the order that we know.

A few words may be added as to our own attitude to S. Paul's teaching. "Do we," it will be said, "any longer believe in any return of Christ, or end of the world, or transformation of material things?" Such conceptions are no doubt profoundly difficult for the imagination, since the imagination can only work with the data provided by past experience; and when we speak of things as difficult for the mind, we very often mean difficult for the imagination, or (in other words) that we cannot picture them, and gain that assistance to faith which a definite picture provides. But this failure of the imagination is not important. Intellectually, S. Paul's teaching presents hardly more difficulty to-day than when first he gave it. A world, which is to possess a meaning, must necessarily have an end; since it is only in view of the end attained that we can fully understand what has gone before. Similarly, a world, in which we look forward to judgment, must necessarily have an end; since no final judgment can be passed upon action, until its final issues are seen. Just as reasonable, if rightly understood, is the Christian belief in the Second Advent of Christ. If, as Christians believe, "all things have been created through him, and unto him" (Col. i. 16); if He is Himself the centre of history and the revelation of its moral and spiritual goal; the end, when manifested, must be the manifestation of Him, and nothing can be judged apart from Him. "Behold, he cometh with the clouds; and every eye shall see him, and they which pierced him" (Rev. i. 7): that, of course, is a symbolic picture. But can we find any words which will take us nearer to the reality? Christianity is the religion of truth embodied in visible fact; and, just as the truth of the destined union of Deity with humanity finds its embodiment at Bethlehem, and the truth of atonement through sacrifice its embodiment at Calvary, so the truth of judgment to come must in turn find its embodiment, though we ourselves may as yet foresee what it will be as little as we foresaw the manger and the Cross. Here, as so often, to abandon a part of the faith, in deference to the supposed demands of the modern mind, does not make what remains easier of acceptance to those who care more for intellectual coherence than for modernity, but a great deal more difficult. Modern knowledge will substantially alter our outlook here in two ways only. First, we shall recognize that, when we speak of "the end of the world," we mean the end of our own world, the world of which human life is "the roof and crown," and for which Christ died. And, secondly, we shall recognize that, though the confident expectation of the Lord's immediate return was natural to the Christians of the first century, it is not so to us. The present age of the Spirit is the final age of the world's history; and the first Christians, who thought that all the previous ages were contained in about four thousand years, naturally expected it to be short. We, on the other hand, who know the vast periods of time which lie behind us, equally naturally expect it to be long.

Finally, what of that transformation of the present body, of which S. Paul has been speaking? He does not, let us observe, regard it as an isolated "miracle." Just as Christ is "the firstfruits" of redeemed humanity, so redeemed humanity is the firstfruits of creation (cf. Jas. i. 18), and its transformation is but an illustration of the "working whereby" the Lord "is able even to subject all things unto himself" (Phil. iii. 21). "The creation itself also shall be delivered from the bondage of corruption into the liberty of the glory of the children of God" (Rom. viii. 21). That sense of the world's unity, which is characteristic of the modern outlook, is in perfect harmony with the mind of S. Paul. Of course, as has already been pointed out, such changes from one order to another can no more be pictured or understood in the case of ourselves and the world, than in the case of the Risen Lord; to explain such changes would be to deny their reality. But by faith to accept them seems to be the one way in which the survival of personality can be intelligible. Personality, as we think of it to-day, is bound up with our characteristic activity in an environment, with which we can deal, and in which our personality can be manifested. The Greeks might conceive of an immortality of the soul as a thinking subject apart from the body, which is our instrument of activity and self-expression, but not the Hebrews or (let us add) the English. There are times, when we are very tired, or very lazy, or very much occupied with ourselves; and then perhaps we may be satisfied as personal beings to "cease upon the midnight with no pain," or "turn again home" to some "boundless deep" of thought and aesthetic appreciation. But would this be the survival of personality? Personality demands, with a greater thinker, though not a greater poet, than those whose words have just been quoted, "some adventure brave and new"; and for that we require the fullness of a transformed humanity, active, and expressing itself in a transformed environment, to which it corresponds. What is mortal must be swallowed up by life, and not by death. For a time it may be very desirable that we should be "unclothed," and find ourselves, as Martensen says, in "a kingdom of calm thought and self-fathoming, a kingdom of remembrance...in such a sense...that the soul now enters into its own inmost recesses"; and the less we have "gone into retreat" here,

11   Knowing therefore the fear of the Lord, we persuade
     men, but we are made manifest unto God; and I hope that
12   we are made manifest also in your consciences. We are not
     again commending ourselves unto you, but *speak* as giving
     you occasion of glorying on our behalf, that ye may have

the more we may need to do so, when our earthly life is over. But that
surely can only be for a time, for thought is of little worth except as a
preparation for action; and when we have garnered the harvest of the past,
it must be "seed for the sower" as well as "bread to the eater." "This
modern doctrine of immortality," says Martensen again, "is only a poor
reflection of the Christian doctrine of eternal joy, a remnant which is re-
tained after dissolving and evaporizing the Christian doctrine." And if the
modern Sadducees, like the ancient, say that what we believe is impossible,
we shall give the classical answer, "Ye do err, not knowing the Scriptures,
nor the power of God" (Mt. xxii. 29). For Scripture ever speaks to us, not
of death out of life, but of life out of death, for the whole Church of God,
and for every faithful member of it in the fullness of his manhood; and there
is "nothing too hard for the Lord."

11–21. Still there is no break in
the thought. S. Paul continues that
defence of his conduct as an Apostle,
which at iv. 6 was interrupted. But
his passionate devotion to the Gospel
leads him to speak of its content, as
well as of his own conduct in de-
claring it.

11. *Knowing...fear of the Lord.*
Just as in the N.T. the "day of our
Lord Jesus" takes the place of the
O.T. "day of Yahweh" (i. 14), so
the "fear of the Lord" Jesus takes
the place of the O.T. "fear of Yahweh." S. Paul is "constrained" by the
fear of Christ, as well as by the
thought of that love of His, of which
he will speak in *v.* 14; and his fear
is both for himself and for those to
whom he speaks. The effort sometimes made to-day to represent the
character of Christ, and of the Father,
as devoid of elements which should
inspire fear finds no justification in
any N.T. writing. Christian poetry
and art, as well as theology, have
given a great place to Christ as Judge.

The tenderness and the awfulness of
the "Dies Irae" are equally true to
the N.T. teaching.

we persuade men...unto God.
S. Paul's opponents no doubt said
that he was only too persuasive;
and charged him, as he in his turn
charged them, with corrupting the
Gospel and making things too easy.
His answer is that, though in view
of the approaching judgment, he does
indeed persuade men to repentance
and faith, God knows his absolute
sincerity, and he hopes that by this
time the Corinthians know it also.

12. *not again...unto you.* In the
Corinthian church itself the victory
has been won. But the Jewish mission
is still active, and S. Paul's supporters
must be given their "brief," and told
what to say on their Apostle's behalf.
The emphasis in this verse falls upon
the word "ourselves"; and the contrast lies between self-praise and defence of the cause of God, since so
often the cause of God and the cause
of the man who represents it to

wherewith to answer them that glory in appearance, and
13 not in heart. For whether we [1]are beside ourselves, it is
unto God; or whether we are of sober mind, it is unto you.
14 For the love of Christ constraineth us; because we thus
15 judge, that one died for all, therefore all died; and he died
for all, that they which live should no longer live unto
themselves, but unto him who for their sakes died and
16 rose again. Wherefore we henceforth know no man after

[1] Or, *were*

the world are inseparable. For the
meaning of "glorying," cf. note on i. 12.

in appearance...in heart. "Appearance" includes all the advantages
which can be enjoyed without faithfulness to God and to His cause. The
"heart" is the seat of moral purpose,
and includes the will. For the claims
of S. Paul's opponents, cf. pp. xl ff. ;
xlix.

13. The past tense of R.V. marg.
is to be adopted, but we do not know
the ground of the charge that S. Paul
in the past had been beside himself.
The reference may be to his conversion, to his visions, to his apostolic
zeal, or to his painful letter. The last
explanation is the most probable.
This "madness" was directly "for"
or "unto" God; and there is a natural
contrast between it and the sobriety
of tone thus far adopted for the
benefit of his converts in the present
letter.

14. *For the love...us.* The love of
Christ is always the Apostle's overmastering motive, whatever tone he
may at the moment adopt. The
context shews that he speaks here
not of his own love for Christ, but of
Christ's love for His people. It is
not S. Paul's way to speak of man's
love of God, though 2 Th. iii. 5 may
afford one exception.

because we thus judge...all died.

It is the view that S. Paul takes of
the meaning and purpose of the
Lord's death, which makes it to
him the revelation of the love of
Christ. It is a serious blunder to
draw too great a contrast between
the death of Christ as a fact and our
understanding of it. This death,
apart from our interpretation, though
it may reveal the Lord's perfect self-surrender to the Father's will, is no
revelation of His love to ourselves.
The doctrinal teaching here found
will be considered below.

15. *they which live.* i.e. they who
live with the new supernatural life
won by this death. In the last clause
of this verse the words "for their
sakes" should probably be connected
with the words "rose again" as well
as with the word "died." As the
death of Christ carries with it the
death of all, so His rising carries
with it the rising of all. The immediate point is that S. Paul, as in
v. 13 he has shewn, is not living for
himself.

16. *henceforth.* i.e. from the date
of our rising to new life in Christ.

know...flesh. Both here and in the
next clause, the words "after the
flesh" probably go with the verb
"know," and not with the object of
the knowledge. But the sense is the
same in either view of the construc-

the flesh: even though we have known Christ after the
17 flesh, yet now we know *him so* no more. Wherefore if

tion. S. Paul refuses to pay attention
to the position of any man regarded
just as a member of the present
world. The position of S. James, the
Lord's brother, is perhaps in view.
Cf. Gal. ii. 12, which suggests that
S. Paul's opponents may have claim-
ed—probably without justification
(Ac. xv. 24, 25)—the authority of
S. James for their action.

even though...no more. The Christ,
for Whom S. Paul lives, is always the
glorified Christ, rather than the
"Jesus of History." With no one of
the writers of the N.T. is our Lord
but a great figure of the past : all
alike think of Him as a present living
Person, Whose relation both to God
and to men is peculiar to Himself.
It is this twofold relation which explains His power to reconcile. But
how are we to interpret the words
"even though we have known Christ
after the flesh"? We notice (*a*) that,
as the absence of the definite article
in the Greek shews, "Christ" is here
a proper name, and not a title. Thus
S. Paul is not looking back to a time
when those of whom he speaks took
a carnal, or merely nationalist, view
of the work of the Messiah ; though
his own view before his conversion
probably rose no higher than that of
his countrymen. To know Christ
after the flesh must mean to know
Him in His human characteristics
only. But (*b*) S. Paul is here speaking
for all those "which live" (*v.* 15)
with the new life which is theirs in
Christ, and not for himself alone.
Many of these, beside the Twelve,
would at first have known the Lord
simply as a man. Whether S. Paul
had ever seen the Lord during His

earthly life we do not know. As a
pupil of Gamaliel, he must have been
at Jerusalem before the Lord's ministry ; and he was there not long after
it. But he was not a member of the
Sanhedrin when the Lord was condemned. Had it been otherwise, his
penitence for the past would have
chiefly attached itself, not to his
persecution of the Church, but to his
condemnation of the Lord Himself.
Cf. Ac. xxvi. 9, 10 ; 1 Cor. xv. 9.
Probably, as the question of Ac. ix. 5
suggests, he never knew Christ after
the flesh. But, though he had not
known the Lord in His earthly life,
and seldom mentions the details of
that life, the warm personal quality
of his love for the Lord proves how
strong was his grip of the "Jesus of
History." What needs to be explained by those who reject S. Paul's faith
is this :—How was it that those who
had known Jesus "after the flesh"
came almost at once to believe both
that He had come down from heaven,
and that He was now reigning there ?

17. *Wherefore.* The conclusion
follows from the doctrine enunciated
in *vv.* 14, 15. Those who not only
claim to belong to Christ (x. 7), but
are "in Christ" as His members,
share His experience. In Christ
Himself—by His Death and Resurrection—a new creation took place.
All that belonged to the conditions
of His earthly life—subjection to the
law (Gal. iv. 4), the burden of His
people's sin and suffering (Mt. viii.
17), the limitations of earthly existence (Luk. xii. 50)—passed away from
Him for ever ; all things, even the
body which He had taken of Mary,
became new. So it is with those who

any man is in Christ, [1]*he is* a new creature: the old things
18 are passed away; behold, they are become new. But all
things are of God, who reconciled us to himself through

[1] Or, there is *a new creation*

are identified with Christ by faith
and baptism. In them too there is a
new creation. They too are no longer
under the law and the curse which it
brings (Gal. iii. 13), or under the guilt
and power of sin (Rom. vi. 6; Gal. v. 24).
Life in the Church, the ante-chamber
of the Kingdom of God, is wholly
different in its power and blessedness
from life outside it. Though, as S. Paul
has already made clear, we do not
yet find the transforming power of
the Spirit either in the body, or in
the outward conditions of our life,
the inner life is being transformed,
and one day both the body and the
outward scene will be transformed
also. Cf. Is. lxv. 17; Rom. viii. 18–
25. S. Chrysostom gives a wider application to the thought: "Instead of
the Jerusalem below, we have received that mother city which is
above; and instead of a material
temple, have seen a spiritual temple;
instead of tables of stone, fleshy ones;
instead of circumcision, baptism; instead of the manna, the Lord's body;
instead of water from a rock, blood
from His side; instead of Moses or
Aaron's rod, the Cross; instead of
the promised land, the kingdom of
heaven; instead of a thousand priests,
one High Priest; instead of a Lamb
without reason, a Spiritual Lamb."

18. *all things are of God.* The
great reconciliation is the free gift
of God, and not purchased by obedience to the law; the apostolic ministry is a divine creation, and needs no
human authorization. The action of
the Father on our behalf is in the

N.T. contrasted with our own action
for ourselves, and not with that of
the Lord. Thus, though the teaching
of the N.T. always traces redemption
back beyond the Lord to the Father
(cf. Jn. iii. 16; Rom. v. 8), and it is
important in view of some popular
errors about the atonement to insist
upon this, S. Paul is not insisting
upon it here.

*who reconciled us…through
Christ.* S. Paul's thought moves upon
O.T. lines. Sacrifice is effectual, because it is of divine appointment.
It is not that man recognizes the
barrier which his sin creates, and
devises a sacrificial system to remove
it. It is God Who recognizes the
barrier, and provides for its removal.
The initiative is taken by Him, and
the cost borne by Him. Cf. Lev. xvii.
11; 2 Sam. xiv. 14; Rom. viii. 32.
This is S. Paul's point here. It is
frequently said that the N.T. speaks
always of our being reconciled to
God, and not of His being reconciled
to us; and it is true that it is our
attitude to God which needs changing, rather than His to us. But
reconciliation is always mutual; God
must deal with us as we deal with
Him; and the language of Scripture
speaks both of the wrath of God, and
of sinners as being enemies of God
(Rom. xi. 28; Jam. iv. 4). Cf. Sanday
and Headlam's Additional Note (after
Rom. iii. 26) on "The Death of Christ
considered as a Sacrifice," as against
Westcott's attempt to empty the
word "propitiation" of its natural
meaning.

19 Christ, and gave unto us the ministry of reconciliation; to
wit, that God was in Christ reconciling the world unto
himself, not reckoning unto them their trespasses, and
having ¹ committed unto us the word of reconciliation.

20   We are ambassadors therefore on behalf of Christ, as
though God were intreating by us : we beseech *you* on
21 behalf of Christ, be ye reconciled to God. Him who knew

¹ Or, *placed in us*

gave unto us...reconciliation.
Awkward as it is to change the
meaning of the word "us" so sud-
denly, S. Paul is almost certainly
guilty of the awkwardness; otherwise
we should be obliged to regard the
previous clause as referring to the
Apostles alone. He speaks of the
Apostles, who by the Word and
Sacraments minister to others the
reconciliation which God Himself
has accomplished. The Greek words
for "the ministry" cannot, like the
English, be used in a concrete sense
of the ministers as a body.

19. *to wit, that.* i.e. these are the
truths which the Apostles have God's
commission to declare. The doctrine
of the divine call of the Christian ministry is itself part of the Gospel. The
love of God is shewn, not only by the
reconciliation which He has provided,
but also by the call of men to minister
it. It is thus a great mistake to regard the doctrine of the ministry as
unimportant.

God was...himself. The words "in
Christ" should be joined closely to
the word "reconciling." The point
brought out is not the presence of
the Father in Christ, but His employment of Christ as the means of
reconciling a world to Himself. The
reconciliation was accomplished on
its divine, if not on its human side,
before the Gospel was preached.

not reckoning. The reconciliation

was itself a refusal to reckon to men
their sins.

*and having committed...recon-
ciliation.* The reconciliation was
committed to Christ; the Gospel
which offers it to the Apostles.

20. *We are ambassadors.* Christ
is the one great ambassador of God,
through Whom He intreats us; the
Apostles are the representatives of
Christ, through Whom He acts. An
ambassador is the authorized representative of his sovereign, to whom
much is committed; he is far more
than a messenger or herald.

as though...by us. A very bad
translation, since it suggests that
God does not in fact intreat by His
ambassadors. Better "God, as it
were, intreating by us," or "seeing
that it is God who intreats by us."

be ye reconciled to God. On the
divine side the reconciling work is
already accomplished; on the human
it is not. The reconciliation must be
known, welcomed, accepted, and
acted upon.

21. *Him who knew no sin.* i.e.
Who had no personal experience of
it. The assertion of our Lord's entire
sinlessness belongs to all types of
N.T. teaching; the title of "the
righteous One," which was given to
Him, is itself an assertion of it. Cf.
Heb. iv. 15; Jam. v. 6; 1 Pet. ii. 22;
1 Jn. iii. 5; Ac. vii. 52; xxii. 14. The
miracle of the Lord's moral perfection

no sin he made *to be* sin on our behalf; that we might become the righteousness of God in him.

was part of the primitive Gospel; and the claim thus made for the Lord is most remarkable, in view of current Jewish teaching as to the universality of sin. Cf. 1 Kgs. viii. 46; Eccl. vii. 20; Ecclus. viii. 5. Difficulty is sometimes felt in this connexion about the Lord's acceptance of baptism. But Luk. iii. 21 probably presupposes the same explanation as that implied in Mt. iii. 15. The Christ, the new Head of the people of God, is united with them in all the experience through which God calls them to pass. What God asks of them, He asks also of Him.

made to be sin. A most difficult expression, which finds no complete parallel elsewhere, though cf. Gal. iii. 13. It will be best to begin by attempting to clear up a few obscurities, leaving the fuller exposition of the Apostle's meaning for the fuller discussion to follow. (*a*) The word here translated "sin" is rightly so translated; we cannot interpret it as "sin-offering," as it may occasionally be interpreted in the Septuagint, since there is an obvious contrast here between "sin" and "righteousness." (*b*) The R.V. rightly refuses to follow the A.V. in using the same word "made" in the translation of two different Greek verbs. God "made" the Lord "to be sin" by treating Him as if He were sin, and delivering Him up to that death which sin itself must in us all undergo. For this use of "make," we may (with Dr Bernard) compare Jn. v. 18; viii. 53; x. 33. Just as the Lord, according to the Jews, "made" Himself God by the way in which He spoke, so the Father "made" Christ

to be sin by the way in which He acted towards Him. We have to do, i.e. not with a fact, but with a representation. What God desired was the death of sin (cf. 1 Pet. ii. 24), and the death of the Lord was the way to its attainment. God smote sin in smiting the Lord (Is. liii. 4, 5). He was "numbered with the transgressors," though He did not belong to them. The form of the Greek negative employed in the phrase "Him who knew no sin" marks not merely that the Lord was without sin, but that God recognized His freedom from it. The contrasted— not parallel—expression, "that we might become the righteousness of God," marks not a representation, but a fact. We actually do become "righteousness," though Christ did not actually become sin. (*c*) There is again a contrast between "on our behalf" and "in him." The Lord in His Death acted for us, as for those not yet identified with Himself. We, on the contrary, "become the righteousness of God," not just because of what He did, but "in him." The change takes place only when we become His members by faith and baptism. The whole verse is an exhortation to make our reconciliation with God a reality, as its connexion with *v.* 20 shews.

the righteousness of God. This strange expression is to be explained by that teaching of the Second Isaiah, which lies behind S. Paul's doctrine of God's justification, or vindication, of His people. Cf. (in this order) Is. li. 5, 6; xlvi. 13; xlv. 24, 25; liv. 17; Jer. xxiii. 6. God's own righteousness is His faithfulness to His promise to vindicate. The righteousness of God's people is that freedom from the guilt of sin, which God's vindication of them publicly declares. The same saving activity on the part of God manifests and declares both God's own righteousness and the present righteousness of His people. Cf. Rom. iii. 26; Phil. iii. 9. Just as by raising the Lord from the dead the Father declared both His own righteousness, and the righteousness of Christ; so by bestowing the Holy Spirit on those who believe and are baptized God declares and manifests both His own righteousness and theirs. What we receive is not only righteousness, but "the righteousness of God," a righteousness freely bestowed by God, and not attained by our own obedience to the law. If S. Paul says, not "attain righteousness," but "become righteousness," that is probably in part to provide a corresponding phrase to "made to be sin," and in part to mark the fact of the close identification of our own personal life with that of the Lord. He Himself is the grand example of acceptability to God publicly declared; and, in becoming His members, we share it.

The foregoing verses contain some of S. Paul's most striking sayings on the subject of the Atonement; they are, as Dr Denney has said, "the *locus classicus* on the death of Christ in S. Paul's writings." But we must not expect to find in them a complete expression of his mind. He is here primarily concerned with the reality and importance of his own mission: and, though no doubt in his pastoral earnestness he says more about the work of the Lord than is necessary for his immediate purpose (cf. Phil. ii. 4–11), his doctrinal statements are not much more than incidental, and presuppose fuller teaching already given. Thus we cannot hope to understand these verses without a grasp of S. Paul's theology as a whole; and we must not be surprised if we cannot always be certain of his precise meaning. Here it must suffice to attempt an answer to three questions. First, how does he understand that corporate relation of the Lord to His people, which is presupposed when he says, "One died for all, therefore all died"? Secondly, how does he think of the redeeming power of the Lord's Death and Resurrection? Thirdly, what is our own part in our salvation? How is it consistent both to say that God has reconciled us (*v.* 18), and to beseech us to be reconciled to God (*v.* 20)?

First then, how does S. Paul understand that solidarity of the Lord with His people, which is to him so important? An explanation of his outlook may be sought in what is called his "mysticism," i.e. in his peculiar experience of identification with the Lord (cf. e.g. Gal. ii. 20). This explanation is far from satisfying. In what sense it is true to say that S. Paul was a mystic, we may consider when we reach ch. xii. But in any case mystical experience affords no foundation for fundamental doctrine. Rather, it is the mystic's fundamental belief which leads to his quest; and which interprets his experience to him, when it has been gained. The same, or a similar experience, may be reached by a Christian, and by an Indian pantheist; but each will interpret it in accordance with his own convictions. Spiritual experience gives fuller meaning to doctrinal belief, rather than itself creates it. Moreover, there is no reason to suppose that the teaching here found was peculiar to S. Paul, or originated by him. The solidarity of the Lord with His people is prominent in the Fourth Gospel (cf. especially Jn. xv. 1–6); it is presupposed in such earlier language as that of Mt. x. 40–42; xxv. 35–40; and in the words of the Risen Lord at S. Paul's own conversion (Ac. ix. 4, 5). In a word, it goes back to the mind of the Lord, and to His identification of Himself both with the Christ and with the Second Isaiah's "Servant of Yahweh." But all this in its turn requires explanation, and it is in the O.T. that we must look for it.

We notice then that a corporate outlook is characteristic of O.T. thought. S. Paul's belief e.g. that "in Adam all die" was common to him and to many of the Jews of his day, and he had taught it to the Corinthians (1 Cor. xv. 22). The father includes within himself all who will spring from him (cf. Is. li. 1, 2; Heb. vii. 9, 10), and his action affects them both for good and for evil. To the Jews it was Abraham, who was the great example of this principle. It was he who by his faith and obedience had won the divine acceptance and blessing for all his seed (Gen. xxii. 16–18); indeed it might have been said that "as through" Adam's "disobedience the many were made sinners, even so through the obedience of" Abraham the many had been "made righteous." No doubt such teaching was capable of abuse; warnings against its actual abuse have not to wait for the Baptist (Mt. iii. 8, 9), but are found in the O.T. itself (Is. lxiii. 16; Ez. xxxiii. 24–26); but, rightly understood, it was true and valuable. Heredity is a great fact; personal influence and example, noble family and national traditions, are greater facts still, and have much to do with making us what we are, and preparing us for our God-given tasks. Moreover, it was always God's purpose to manifest Himself to the world through the glory of His people's corporate life (Jer. xiii. 11): and thus His blessings were corporate blessings, in which the individual shared by membership in the body—by being "in Abraham" either by descent from him or by incorporation into his family. Of course, it is made clear in the O.T. itself that in God's acceptance of the seed of Abraham for Abraham's sake, the following of Abraham is presupposed; if the influence of Abraham fails of its intended effect, the acceptance of his seed must fail with it (Gen. xviii. 19). Though the Jews are "beloved for the fathers' sake" (Rom. xi. 28), no one can ultimately inherit Abraham's blessing who does not reproduce his faith and obedience. When S. Paul says that "they are not all Israel which are of Israel : neither, because they are Abraham's seed, are they all children," and claims that Gentiles may be true children of Abraham (Rom. iv. 16–18; Gal. iii. 7–16), he but reproduces the O.T. witness (Rom. ix. 27–29; x. 16–21). But to insist upon the moral and spiritual demands which sonship to Abraham demands is not at all to substitute the individual for the corporate outlook. Not even the most spiritual of the prophets ever supposed that Gentiles could inherit Abraham's blessing without being incorporated into Abraham's seed; though God could raise up children to Abraham from the stones of the desert (Mt. iii. 9), children of Abraham they would none the less have to become. As Ruth well knew, "Thy people shall be my people, and thy God my God" were resolutions which went necessarily together: *extra ecclesiam nulla salus* is good O.T. doctrine, if by "*salus*" we understand the covenanted salvation of the people of God.

Now it is this corporate outlook which we must bear in mind, if we would understand that solidarity of Christ with His people, upon which S. Paul's view of the Atonement depends. To him the true seed of Abraham to which the promises belong, is Christ (Gal. iii. 16)—Christ, i.e. not just as an individual, but as including His members (cf. 1 Cor. xii. 12). S. Paul, as he says in this chapter, does not think of Christ "after the flesh," but in view of His relation to the Father, and to the Church, which is His Body; and the same is true of our Lord's own thought about Himself. His tremendous self-assertion is the necessary self-assertion of One Who knows Himself to be the representative of God upon earth, the predestined Head and Centre of the divine kingdom of human souls. Such a Christship as this makes all that our Lord is and does to be of far greater concern to His future members than anything which Abraham was and did could be to his descendants, just because the relationship in the former case is so much deeper than it is in the latter; and from this it follows that the one relationship must supersede the other, and union with Christ, and not with Abraham, become the *sine qua non* for membership in the Church of God. Indeed, in view of much of our Lord's language, we may well ask whether He did not Himself see His identification with His people foreshadowed in the O.T. The Lord claims to be the Son of Man of Dan. vii. 13, the stone rejected by the builders of Ps. cxviii. 22, the Vine of Ps. lxxx. 8, and the Suffering Servant of Is. liii; and probably in every case the original reference is to Israel as a nation. Even in the Synoptic Gospels, though the Lord fully recognizes the special position of the seed of Abraham (Luk. xiii. 16; xix. 9), and during His earthly life confines His ministry to it (Mt. xv. 24), it becomes plain that Israel after the flesh is to pass away, and that the Church must be rebuilt upon the faithful "remnant" which accepts Him as the Christ and attaches itself to Him (Mt. xvi. 18; cf. xxi. 43). We see then that S. Paul's doctrine of union with Christ is not based upon any mystical experience peculiar to himself, though doubtless his experience immensely deepened its hold upon him. What he believes is just what all Christians who understood the O.T. and the teaching of the Lord were bound to believe.

Secondly, how does S. Paul think of the redeeming power of the Lord's Death and Resurrection? How do they reconcile us with God, and bring about a new creation? Here again, the example of Abraham may help us. Abraham won God's acceptance for his seed by winning it first for himself; and he won it for himself through the faith, by which he believed the promise of life out of death (Gen. xv. 4-6, explained by Rom. iv. 18-22), and the obedience by which—again believing the promise of life out of death—he surrendered his only son to death (Gen. xxii. 16-18, explained by Heb. xi. 17-19). So it was with the Lord Himself. He too believed a promise of life out of death, that promise of life out of death for the Messiah and Servant of Yahweh which He found in the Scriptures (Luk. xxiv. 26, 27, etc.), and surrendered Himself to death at the Father's call, in sure confidence in "him that was able to save him out of death" (Heb. v. 7). So He became

God's "righteous servant" (Is. liii. 11); and, like Abraham, was justified through His faith. This divine justification, or vindication of the Lord, was an open and practical vindication. It took place by the Lord's Resurrection and Ascension (Jn. xvi. 10; Ac. ii. 23, 24, etc.; 1 Tim. iii. 16); in the Lord Himself there was a new creation; the old things passed away, and became new; and in that new life to which His Death has brought Him, He is able to bestow the gift of the Holy Ghost (Ac. ii. 33), and so reproduce Himself in thousands whom He enables to be like Him (Jn. xii. 24, 25). Now it is into the inheritance of the Lord's acceptability to God, and of God's public declaration of it, that the members of Christ enter, as the seed of Abraham entered into the inheritance of those of Abraham. The Lord died and rose "for our sakes" (v. 15) or "on our behalf" (v. 21); since, though our representative, He was as yet wholly distinct from us; we were not, and could not yet be, His members. But, though we were not His members then, we are by faith and baptism His members now; and so "in Him"— the preposition is noticeable—we "become" far more fully identified with His righteousness than He was with our sin. Thus we are reconciled to God, and God declares our righteousness openly and practically by the gift of the Holy Ghost, raising up our souls even now to new life in union with the Ascended Lord, and promising one day the resurrection of the body also (cf. Rom. viii. 10, 11; Eph. ii. 4–6). The Lord bore our sin by bearing death, its crowning and most characteristic penalty; as far as outward suffering and inward anguish were concerned, He was "made sin," as no one else has ever been. But, as S. Paul's words shew (cf. note on v. 21), God recognized His sinlessness all the time, and it was His sinlessness which gave to His death its power to win new life for Himself and for us (Mk. x. 45). We, on the other hand, do not bear Christ's righteousness, only as He bore our sin. Through our union with Christ by the Spirit we "become" it, or are perfectly identified with it. Cf. 1 Cor. i. 30.

Thirdly, what is our own part in our salvation? How can S. Paul both say that God has reconciled us (v. 18), and beseech us to be reconciled (v. 20)? Here we must take account not only of the corporate outlook characteristic of Biblical theology, but of the moral considerations which must always qualify it. If much "Protestant" interpretation of S. Paul forgets his corporate outlook, there is much teaching, both "Catholic" and "Protestant," which forgets the moral considerations. S. Paul holds fast both to the one side of the truth and to the other.

About the corporate outlook little more need be said. Redemption belongs to the Church; the "many," for whom the Lord gave His life, are the many members of the people of God (cf. Mk. x. 45 with Is. liii. 11). If He died for the world, and is "the propitiation for the whole world" (1 Jn. ii. 2), that is because the Church is open to the whole world, and all may enter if they will. Into this "elect people of God" we must enter by baptism, if we would share the redemption which belongs to it; and baptism implies faith in Jesus as the Christ, either attained before baptism, or (in the case of infants) expected, as soon as it is possible, as the condition of the operation of baptismal grace. We have only to compare the teaching here given with that given a few months later in Rom. vi. 1–11 to see how essential to

S. Paul's theology is his sacramental doctrine. Justification is through faith alone; we are "sons of God, through faith, in Christ Jesus" (Gal. iii. 26). But faith is a principle of action, and must take shape, as in Abraham's case it did, in the action to which it calls us. The same sacrament which is necessary to incorporate us into the Church, is necessary to incorporate us into Christ Himself, for Christ and His people are one; and the Apostles would have recognized no reality in any faith in Christ Jesus which left its possessors willingly unbaptized (cf. Ac. ii. 37–39). Indeed so fully does S. Paul identify faith with the baptism to which it leads, that he can write "Ye are all sons of God, through faith, in Christ Jesus. For as many of you as were baptized into Christ did put on Christ." We may dislike the sacramental teaching of the Apostles, but there can surely be no question about what it is. As the old and excellent distinction puts it, God is free to dispense with the sacraments, and to bestow His grace as He wills (cf. Ac. x. 44–47); but we are not free to reject them, if we desire the grace of God.

But S. Paul was not thinking of baptism, when he wrote v. 20, but of what baptism must continually demand of all who have received it; and it is all-important to notice what this is. "Catholics" have been only too prone to rest upon sacraments, and "Protestants" to "rest upon the finished work" of Christ, without considering what both demand for their saving operation. "One died for all," S. Paul says, not that we might "rest" either in His finished work, or in our sacramental incorporation into Him, but "that they which live should no longer live unto themselves, but unto him who for their sakes died and rose again." "They which live" with the new supernatural life, which the Spirit brings, have in Christ the power to die to sin and to live unto God; and what they have the power to do they must do in deed and in truth. They too must believe in "God, who quickeneth the dead, and calleth the things that are not, as though they were"; they must look to the promise of life made in the Lord's Resurrection; not waver through unbelief, but wax strong through faith, giving glory to God, and being fully assured that in them, though "as good as dead," what God has promised He is able also to perform (Rom. iv. 17–25); and then, trusting in God's upholding power, they must live unto Christ as fully and loyally as He lives unto God. "Baptism doth represent unto us our profession: which is to follow the example of our Saviour Christ, and to be made like unto him; that, as he died, and rose again for us, so should we, who are baptized, die from sin, and rise again unto righteousness." Just as at the beginning of the Christian life there is no true faith, which does not take shape in baptism, so in its long development, there is no true faith which does not take shape in obedience to the ever-growing demands which Christ makes upon us. Without this there can be no abiding reconciliation. Just as those only are effectively sons of Abraham who follow Abraham's faith, so those only are effectively members of Christ who reproduce His self-surrender, and (like S. Paul) die daily in order daily to rise. Just in so far as we willingly stop short of the death, we stop short of the life to which it leads. If it is true that "if any man is in Christ, there is a new creation; the old things are passed away: behold, they are become

VI. 1 And working together *with him* we intreat also that
2 ye receive not the grace of God in vain (for he saith,
　　　At an acceptable time I hearkened unto thee,
　　　And in a day of salvation did I succour thee:

new"; the converse must also be true. If there is plainly no new creation,
and the old things remain as they were, there can be no being in Christ.
God's work of reconciliation through Christ is so perfect, that it will never
need to be done again; but our work in availing ourselves of it is so imperfect, that it needs with most of us to be done repeatedly. Thus there is
no inconsistency when S. Paul follows up his Gospel that God has reconciled
us to Himself through Christ by the earnest exhortation "Be ye reconciled
to God." "In Christ" we must be sacramentally, for all our power to do
God's will comes from Him. But "in Christ" we must also be morally; for
to be able to do God's will, if we do it not, will but increase our condemnation[1].

VI. There is no break in the thought; but S. Paul turns more directly
to his own work, and to the experience which renders it possible. After a
few words of exhortation, he allows the Atonement to fall into the background.

1. *working together with him.*
The last two words, though not
found in the Greek, are rightly
supplied in view of v. 18–20 and the
close parallel found in 1 Cor. iii. 9.
The subject of the sentence is probably the Apostles; but, as in all
these chapters, S. Paul thinks chiefly
of himself.

receive not...in vain. i.e. to no
profit. The grace of God here in
view is that love of God which has
taken shape both in His work of
reconciliation through Christ, and in
the provision made for its proclamation and application to the world.
Cf. the last verses of the preceding
chapter. Nothing will come of this
love, if the human response is either
refused from the first, or at a later
stage ceases to be given. It was the
latter which was threatened at
Corinth, and in part owing to the
Judaizing influence. Gal. ii. 21 and
v. 2 explain S. Paul's meaning.

2. This verse is parenthetical, and
breaks the construction. The quotation comes from one of the Songs of

---

[1] An interesting parallel to S. Paul's teaching is found in the thought of
ancient Egypt, as well as in that of Israel. "In Egypt the future life is at first
reserved for royalty, but the reward must be earned. When the king dies 'the
sky weeps for thee, the earth trembles for thee, clouds darken the sky, the stars
rain down.' His death was an almost cosmic event, and naturally, since all
prosperity was bound up in his person. But he does not reach his heaven by
virtue of his rank; there are certain ethical requirements. And these requirements, demanded of *the* man, the king, and then of the great men, the nobles,
are ultimately for every man." S. A. Cook in *The People and the Book*, pp. 65,
66. If for the king we put Christ, for the nobles the Apostles, and for the people
the members of the Church, the thought will almost reproduce S. Paul's.

behold, now is the acceptable time; behold, now is the day
3 of salvation): giving no occasion of stumbling in anything,
4 that our ministration be not blamed ; but in everything
commending ourselves, as ministers of God, in much
5 patience, in afflictions, in necessities, in distresses, in

the Servant (Is. xlix. 8), and the
context there should be carefully
examined. The words are spoken to
the despised and persecuted Servant
of Yahweh, and assure him that his
prayer has been heard, that the
divine salvation has been granted,
that the scattered people of God will
through him be gathered, and the
divine salvation extended to all
nations of the world. Thus S. Paul
probably interprets the words of the
glorified Christ, "heard for his godly
fear" and saved out of death (Heb.
v. 7), His perfect acceptance with
the Father being established by the
Resurrection. But the Christ, as
v. 14–21 has made clear, is not just
an individual. His own acceptance
and salvation carry with them those
of His members; and the whole
period between the first Whitsun-
day and the final coming is a period
during which the divine righteousness and salvation are offered to men,
as they never have been before. It
should be observed that, though it
is fully in accordance with the
teaching of Scripture to contrast the
time when the grace of God is still
being offered with the time when it
will be too late for repentance,
S. Paul does not insist upon that
contrast here. His contrast is at
least as much between the present
and the past, as between the present
and the future. For the thought cf.
Luk. iv. 18 ff., the great example of
the Lord's preaching to the multi-
tude. S. Paul's thought is perfectly
continuous with that of the Lord,

though his Gospel is fuller, now that
the work of redemption has been
accomplished.

3. The construction of *v*. 1 is now
resumed. *that our ministration...
blamed.* The R.V. correction of the
A.V. is here important. The ministration is that described in ch. iii.
6 ff., and further explained in the
final verses of ch. v. The Gospel of
the Spirit and of reconciliation
through Christ must not be dis-
credited by any inconsistency of life
in those who minister it. Cf. i. 17–
20 and the notes there. If the reputation of the clergy is a matter of
importance, it is chiefly for the sake
of the message which they are sent
to deliver.

4. *commending ourselves, as
ministers of God.* The comma should
not be ignored in reading this verse.
The Greek shews that S. Paul means
not "proving ourselves to be ministers of God," but "commending ourselves, as ministers of God should
do." How they should commend
themselves, he at once proceeds to
shew.

in much patience. Rather "endurance." The words which follow
shew the great variety of forms
which endurance had in his case to
take. Probably there is no conscious
logical arrangement; but we may
perhaps say that "afflictions, necessities, distresses" belong to the common lot, and do not suggest any
special hostility on the part of the
world ; that "stripes, imprisonments,
tumults" come directly from the

stripes, in imprisonments, in tumults, in labours, in watch-
6 ings, in fastings; in pureness, in knowledge, in longsuffering, in kindness, in the [1]Holy Ghost, in love unfeigned,
7 in the word of truth, in the power of God; [2]by the armour
8 of righteousness on the right hand and on the left, by
glory and dishonour, by evil report and good report; as

[1] Or, *Holy Spirit:* and so throughout this book.   [2] Gr. *through.*

world's hostility; and that "labours, watchings, fastings" are things voluntarily undergone for the Gospel's sake. The sufferings of S. Paul will be considered in greater detail when we reach ch. xi.

5. *in watchings, in fastings.* The place of these in the sentence, next to "labours," and separated from "necessities" and "distresses," suggests that voluntary watchings and fastings are in view. S. Paul had often to forego sleep in order to labour and to pray (cf. Mk. i. 35 and Ac. xx. 34); and, like the saints both before and after the Lord's coming, to give power to his prayers for the people of God by joining fasting with it. Cf. xi. 27, where hunger and fasting are distinguished.

6. *in pureness.* Here in the simple sense of purity of life. In xi. 3 the word has a metaphorical sense.

in knowledge. It may seem strange to find knowledge mentioned at this point, where S. Paul is speaking of moral qualities. But he is writing throughout in view of the charges made against him, and attacks upon his competence went hand in hand with attacks upon his character.

in longsuffering, in kindness. It was necessary to remind the Corinthians of his general bearing towards them, as his last letter had been very severe.

7. *in the word of truth, in*

the power of God. Cf. 1 Cor. ii. 4.

the armour...on the left. The best commentary is found in Eph. vi. 10–17; 1 Th. v. 8; and in the O.T. passages there in view. Cf. Is. lix. 17; Wisd. v. 17 f. The word "armour" is much too narrow; S. Paul thinks of the equipment of the soldier as a whole. The right hand would hold the sword or spear, and the left the shield. The context in this passage shews that S. Paul is far from thinking only of defence, and that "the sword of the Spirit, which is the word of God," is particularly in view. Moreover, in interpreting the word "righteousness," we must not forget either Is. lix. 17 or 2 Cor. v. 21. God's righteousness is His faithfulness to His promise to redeem His people, and vindicate them before the world, and it has been manifested by the redeeming work of Christ, culminating in the gift of the Spirit. It is of this divine righteousness that S. Paul is the minister to the world; and his equipment of sword and shield is the equipment belonging to this righteousness.

8. *by glory...good report.* The first two words may refer to the action taken against or for S. Paul, and the last two to the language used about him. At Corinth he had had more than words of which to complain.

9 deceivers, and *yet* true; as unknown, and *yet* well known;
  as dying, and behold, we live; as chastened, and not killed;
10 as sorrowful, yet alway rejoicing; as poor, yet making
  many rich; as having nothing, and *yet* possessing all things.
11 Our mouth is open unto you, O Corinthians, our heart is
12 enlarged. Ye are not straitened in us, but ye are straitened

9. In this verse the actual charges made against S. Paul probably appear. He was charged both with being a deceiver, and with being an unknown and unauthorized adventurer, with no standing in the Church. His answer is that the truth of his message had been abundantly demonstrated by its spiritual power; and that, though he may once have been unknown, he is becoming ever better and better known.

as dying...not killed. Cf. ch. iv. 10, 11, and the notes there. S. Paul here quotes the language of Ps. cxviii. 17, 18, the whole psalm being, as he must have felt, wonderfully descriptive of his late experience. For the thought of chastening cf. i. 8, 9.

10. *as sorrowful, yet alway rejoicing.* Better "as grieved." It is possible to be grieved by particular acts of cruelty and injustice without the abiding joy of the Christian life being affected. The grief is occasional and incidental while the joy is an abiding possession. The translation of both A.V. and R.V. is unduly paradoxical.

as poor...possessing all things. The contrast between poverty and the enrichment of others is more striking than the simpler contrast which we expect, and which is found at the end of the verse. One great reason why the world despises poverty is that the man without money appears to the world to be a man from whom nothing can be expected. In the case of apostolic poverty the very opposite is true; the earthly poverty and the spiritual wealth are inseparable. Cf. Ac. iii. 6, and the well-known story of S. Thomas Aquinas and the Pope of his day. The word here used for "possessing" is a strong one; it seems to imply a secure possession. Cf. 1 Cor. iii. 21–23, and notes there.

11–13. The appeal now becomes more personal. S. Paul turns directly to the Corinthians, pointing out that the freedom of his speech is matched by his all-embracing love. The reserve and the restraint, the littleness and the suspicion, are upon their side, and not upon his. What they need is "minds big enough for trifles to look small in."

11. *our heart is enlarged.* The language of Ps. cxix. 32 is reproduced. In dealing with man, as well as with God, it is self-centredness, the restriction of the outlook to personal ambitions and interests, which prevents right thought, affection, speech and action. Eloquence is far more a moral characteristic than we generally regard it as being. Awkward and stumbling speech is in part the result of thinking of ourselves, and not of the needs of our hearers.

12. *straitened.* The English slang metaphor "to be stuffy" well expresses the meaning. S. Paul thinks

13 in your own affections. Now for a recompense in like kind (I speak as unto *my* children), be ye also enlarged.

of the want of space in the minds of the Corinthians; we think rather of the want of fresh air.

13. For the tenderness cf. 1 Cor. iv. 14. But S. Paul's wisdom is as marked as his tenderness. Littleness, reserve, and suspicion are never overcome by standing upon our guard. They are overcome when those who exhibit them find their reserve and suspicion dissolved by the real affection with which we speak, and the frankness with which we put all our own cards upon the table. Frank criticism, even when mistaken, has none of the alienating power of aloofness and reserve. The dislike of other nations for the English, and their abiding suspiciousness of us, is largely explicable in this way. The Englishman is desperately anxious not to "give himself away"; but, while he refuses to give himself, nothing else that he gives is likely to be acceptable.

VI. 14–VII. 1. This passage is frequently regarded as an interpolation—a Pauline fragment embedded in an Epistle to which it does not belong; and the suggestion has been made that it really belongs to the very early Epistle, to which reference is made in 1 Cor. v. 9–11, and explains S. Paul's language there. For this view there is something to be said. The passage certainly appears to us on our first reading of it to be out of place; and ch. vii. 2 follows naturally after ch. vi. 13. But this view introduces more difficulties than it solves. For (*a*) the preservation of such a fragment as this, apart from the rest of the Epistle to which it belongs, is not very probable; nor is it likely that it would have been inserted here. The more out of place the passage at first seems to be, the less probable its insertion is. A loose leaf would have been recognized as such; and its contents, if inserted at all, inserted at the end of the Epistle, or in a more appropriate place, e.g. after ch. xii. 21. (*b*) S. Paul is far from being a logical writer, and this Epistle is the least logical in its arrangement of all that he wrote. He is quite without the Greek sense of form; and we do not make a passage more Pauline by improving according to our own taste the arrangement of the material. (*c*) We know far too little of the exact situation at Corinth, when S. Paul wrote, to be able to judge whether S. Paul's words are appropriate here or not. The right course is to form our conception of the situation from what S. Paul says, not to correct what he says by our conception of the situation. He is conducting a war upon two fronts, the Corinthians being exposed both to the influence of Judaizing teachers, and to that of the heathen atmosphere of the city; and the hostility of the Corinthians to him probably arose even more from his condemnation of their license than from his condemnation of their legalism. It is of the former that his first Epistle is full, and his condemnation of Corinthian license will appear again in ch. xii. 21.

14 Be not unequally yoked with unbelievers : for what
fellowship have righteousness and iniquity ? or what com-
15 munion hath light with darkness? And what concord
hath Christ with ¹ Belial? or what portion hath a believer
16 with an unbeliever ? And what agreement hath a ² temple
of God with idols ? for we are a ² temple of the living God;

¹ Gr. *Beliar.*   ² Or, *sanctuary*

14. *Be not...unbelievers.* Better
"do not become." Voluntary associations are in view. It is not improbable that S. Paul has Deut. xxii. 10
in mind, since he gives a "moral," as
contrasted with a "literal," sense to
such words as are there found. Cf.
1 Cor. ix. 9, 10, and the Additional
Note there on S. Paul's Interpretation
of the O.T. S. Paul's refusal to per-
mit the marriage of a Christian with
an unbeliever in 1 Cor. vii. 39 illustrates his meaning, but he is not here
thinking only of marriage.

for what fellowship? Of the four
questions found in this and the following verse, all but the third suggest a
sharing in common benefits. "Righteousness," the fulfilment of the claims
which God makes upon us, is here
contrasted with "lawlessness" (not
"iniquity"), the habitual rejection
of these claims. "Light" and "darkness" are righteousness and lawlessness regarded from a different angle,
that of illumination rather than of
law. There is a close parallel here
with the language of the Testaments
of the Twelve Patriarchs, Lev. xix. 1.
The law of God does not lay commands upon us, the purpose of
which we are not able to see. Cf.
Jn. xv. 15.

15. Belial or Beliar is the head
of the infernal kingdom, as Christ of
the heavenly. He is perhaps to be
identified with the Antichrist of

2 Thess. ii. 8 ff., and may even be regarded as the devil incarnate. The
purpose of the Christ is to establish
the Kingdom of God ; the purpose
of Antichrist to establish his own.
Cf. Jn. v. 43, where probably the
reference is to Antichrist.

16. *agreement...idols?* The exact force of the Greek is hard to
express in English ; but the A.V.
translation, "the temple," is less misleading than that of the R.V., "a
temple." There are not many temples
of God, but one only, the Catholic
Church ; but both the local church,
and the individual Christian have a
share in its sanctity. They are, in
what may be called an adjectival
sense, "temple of God." Cf. 1 Cor.
iii. 16, and note. The word here used
for "temple" means the inner shrine,
as distinguished from the whole
temple enclosure ; and S. Paul thinks
of unfaithful Christians as setting
up idols in the sanctuary. Cf. 2 Chron.
xxxiii. 7, and the outrage of Caligula,
to which reference is probably made
in Mk. xiii. 14. The purpose of the
Church is to be the dwelling-place of
God among men, the word "we"
being here emphatic. It is not in
accordance with Christian thought
to speak of any material building
as God's "house" or "temple." The
dwelling-place of God is His Church
or people, and the reverence often
given to buildings ought to be given

even as God said, I will dwell in them, and walk in them;
and I will be their God, and they shall be my people.
17 Wherefore
Come ye out from among them, and be ye separate,
saith the Lord,
And touch no unclean thing;
And I will receive you,
18   And will be to you a Father,
And ye shall be to me sons and daughters,
saith the Lord Almighty. **VII.** 1 Having therefore these
promises, beloved, let us cleanse ourselves from all defilement of flesh and spirit, perfecting holiness in the fear of
God.

to the Church. Cf. Commentary on
1 Cor. Additional Note on iii. 16.

I will...walk in them. Cf. Lev.
xxvi. 11, 12. There was originally
nothing of mysticism about the
thought of the divine indwelling.
The tabernacle or temple was the
house of God, as the palace was the
king's house. God, having thus a
home, could live and move freely
among His people, manifesting His
presence by His beneficent activity.

and I will be their...my people.
From Ez. xxxvii. 27. Cf. Jer. xxxii.
38. Again the language suggests a
free and living activity on the part
of God. To be the God of a people
is far more than to be the object of
their worship ; it is to be their Pro-
tector, Champion, Leader, and Provider.

17, 18. S. Paul combines the language of many O.T. prophecies. Cf.
Is. xliii. 6 ; lii. 11 ; Jer. li. 45 ; Hos.

i. 10; Am. iv. 13 (LXX). In *v.* 18 the
old promise of divine adoption made
to Solomon (2 Sam. vii. 14), and applied to the expected Messiah (Ps.
ii. 7), is extended in Christ to all His
members. The Lord all-sovereign
calls them to be His children. The
Greek word for "almighty" refers to
the active exercise of rule, and not
only to fullness of power.

VII. 1. *defilement of flesh and
spirit.* The danger from the Gentiles
was chiefly to the flesh, and from the
Jews to the spirit. S. Paul, it should
be observed, neither regards the flesh
as necessarily evil, nor the spirit as
necessarily good.

perfecting holiness. "Coepisse non
satis est," says Bengel, "finis coronat
opus."

in the fear of God. His presence
with His people is ever a source of
danger, if His holiness is forgotten.

The foregoing section is of great importance for all who would understand
the right attitude of Christians to the world to-day; since, in dealing with
the Corinthians, S. Paul is dealing with those whose position was similar to
our own. When the Church is proscribed and persecuted by the world, there
is no problem; the world itself effects the separation. When the Church is
accepted by the world, as it was in the Middle Ages, the problem is com-

paratively simple. All our neighbours are our fellow-Christians; and there is no question of separating ourselves from them unless they come under the Church's censure. But the position of the Corinthian Christians closely resembled ours. They were not persecuted by the heathen around them. All kinds of religions flourished at Corinth, and few felt much concern about the religion of their neighbours. Civic business and social life were equally open to all. The First Epistle to the Corinthians, e.g., makes it clear, not only that Christians were asked out to dinner by their heathen neighbours, but that they were even invited to banquets held in heathen temples (cf. 1 Cor. viii. 10; x. 27-31); and thus the question what their relation to the world was to be had to be decided by themselves, just as it must be by Christians to-day.

Now the great characteristic of S. Paul's handling of the problem in this passage is that he approaches it, not primarily from the side of morality, but from that of religion. The first consideration is the relation of the Church to God. The Church is the "shrine of the living God." It stands in a peculiar relation to Him as His "people," and He stands in a peculiar relation to it as its God, dwelling therein through Christ by the Spirit, and acting therein, in mercy or in judgment, as His action is required (*v.* 16). Nor is this all. Each individual Christian should claim his personal share in this profound relationship to "the Lord All-Sovereign." The sons and daughters of the Church are to become in the fullest sense the sons and daughters of God, and He is to become in the fullest sense their Father (*v.* 18). But then this plainly demands a progressive sanctification resting both upon the great hope just described, and upon the fear inspired by the divine holiness (ch. vii. 1); and it is in view of all this that the attitude to be adopted to the world must be considered. Plainly, as S. Paul recognizes (1 Cor. v. 10), we cannot go out of the world. Not only have Christians like others their living to get; but they have duties to perform to the State, which protects their persons and property, and a debt to discharge to the whole society of which they form a part. They must, however, recognize that the Church is a society within the nation or State which is meant to be clearly distinguishable from it (cf. 1 Cor. x. 32); and in many ways to be contrasted with it. To become a Christian must mean in some degree to come out from the world, and to remain out; to refuse to touch a great deal which the world takes as a matter of course, but which is in fact defiling (*v.* 17); and, if this is not grasped, idols are introduced into the temple, and the personal relationship to God, to which Christians are called, cannot be realized.

What then shall we do? The chief way of responding to our position is to refuse to form close associations with any but our fellow-Christians. It is one thing to cooperate with non-Christians for political and civic purposes, and to play games with them; it is quite another to marry an unbeliever, or to enter into a business partnership with him. Christians have their own convictions about marriage and about business; and cooperation for the common end is in both cases impossible with those who do not share them. There is a passage in R. L. Stevenson's *Virginibus Puerisque*, in which he brings out with much humour the importance, if a marriage is to be success-

2   ¹Open your hearts to us: we wronged no man, we cor-

¹ Gr. *Make room for us.*

ful, of a fundamental similarity of outlook in husband and wife; and identity of moral and religious outlook is particularly important.   Christians regard marriage, not primarily from the standpoint of physical satisfaction or of personal happiness—that is the standpoint of Beliar—but from that of the Kingdom of God, and of the Christ, Who is working for its establishment. The bringing into the world of children to be brought up in the Kingdom and to serve the Kingdom; the permanence of the home, which is the first interest of children; the training of character in husband and wife by moral self-restraint and mutual self-adaptation; these things bulk far more largely in their minds than individual happiness or personal freedom.   But those who have no belief in the Christian Gospel, and no hope beyond the present life, cannot be expected to accept the Christian views of marriage; freedom of divorce, and artificial birth-control, are to them simple matters of commonsense; and "if the case of the man is so with his wife" as Christians say, "it is not expedient to marry" (Mt. xix. 10).   So with business. Christians regard it primarily from the point of view of social service; the making of money, like personal happiness in married life, is secondary; and, though honesty may be the best policy, they have not to consider whether it is or is not.   But unbelievers, in the face of modern competition, cannot be expected to regard the matter in this way. They are "not in business for their health," either physical or moral, or for the health of the com- munity; and the scruples of Christians in a world such as this seem to them midsummer madness.   Both in marriage and in business it is not only the unequally-yoked Christian who is to be pitied, but the unequally-yoked unbeliever also.   Thus S. Paul's command not to form such unions is plain commonsense.   Even good Christians are as yet but very imperfect Christians; and just because their way is the difficult way, and the world's the easy way, it is not the Christian but the world's standpoint that will almost certainly prevail, if such associations are formed. S. Paul's stand- point, as the First Epistle to the Corinthians shews, is not that of the Plymouth Brethren.   But in England to-day the flogging of Puritanism is the flogging of a dead horse: the real evil is forgetfulness of the nature and purpose of the Church, and the degradation of Christianity to the position of a cult, which, like the many cults of ancient Corinth, is merely a satis- faction of the religious impulse, without influence upon either individual or social conduct.

VII. 2–16.   The warning of vi. 14–vii. 1 being concluded, S. Paul returns to the point reached at vi. 13; but he soon passes from remonstrance to praise, as he comes to deal with the reception which Titus had received at Corinth.   There is hardly a more characteristic passage to be found in his writings; but his words need close attention if their teaching is to be appreciated.

2. *Open your hearts to us.* An excellent paraphrase, though not a literal translation (cf. R.V. margin).

we wronged...advantage of no man. S. Paul speaks of his im- mediate followers, as well as of him-

3 rupted no man, we took advantage of no man. I say it not
to condemn *you*: for I have said before, that ye are in our
4 hearts to die together and live together. Great is my boldness of speech toward you, great is my glorying on your
behalf: I am filled with comfort, I overflow with joy in all
our affliction.

5   For even when we were come into Macedonia, our
flesh had no relief, but *we were* afflicted on every side;
6 without *were* fightings, within *were* fears. Nevertheless he
that comforteth the lowly, *even* God, comforted us by the
7 ¹coming of Titus; and not by his ¹coming only, but also
by the comfort wherewith he was comforted in you, while
he told us your longing, your mourning, your zeal for me;
8 so that I rejoiced yet more. For though I made you sorry

¹ Gr. *presence.*

self. Cf. ch. xii. 17, 18. In saying
that he corrupted no man, he may
refer to the charge that his anti-
legal teaching was antinomian.

3. *to condemn you.* The word is
a strong one. His rebukes are not
of the kind that involve the severing
of relations. That this is his meaning, the rest of the verse shews. He
feels himself one with his converts
for life and for death.

4. *Great is my boldness...on your
behalf.* There is nothing to cause
reserve, or the loss of his old pride
in them. He can declare his pride
as boldly as ever, after the way in
which they have received Titus. Cf.
1 Thess. iii. 6–10.

5. For the history, cf. Introduction, p. lii. The Macedonian Christians were the best of all S. Paul's
converts, but not even to be with
them brought relief, till the success
of Titus' mission to Corinth was
known.

our flesh. A good example of the
wide meaning of "flesh" in the N.T.
It includes all that belongs to man

in his human weakness. "Fears," as
well as "fightings," assail the flesh,
the human "spirit" (ii. 13) being a
part of it.

6. Cf. ch. i. 3, 4, and Ps. cxxxviii. 6.
the lowly. Not in the moral sense
of "humble," but "cast down," or
"dejected."

the coming. Or "presence." The
word is that used for our Lord's
Second Coming. It combines the
thoughts of the "coming," and of the
"presence" which results from it.

7. *by the comfort...in you.* The
relief and exhilaration of Titus were
infectious, as he told his news.

your longing...zeal for me. All
three words refer to the new attitude
to S. Paul. The Corinthians were
longing to see him again, bewailing
the past, and zealous to have justice
done to him. Cf. *v.* 11.

rejoiced yet more. Better "rejoiced rather" than mourned over
the Corinthians.

8, 9. The meaning of these verses
is clear, but it is not clear how the
clauses should be arranged. The

with my epistle, I do not regret it, though I did regret;
[1]for I see that that epistle made you sorry, though but for
9 a season. Now I rejoice, not that ye were made sorry, but
that ye were made sorry unto repentance : for ye were
made sorry after a godly sort, that ye might suffer loss by
10 us in nothing. For godly sorrow worketh repentance [2]unto
salvation, *a repentance* which bringeth no regret : but the
11 sorrow of the world worketh death. For behold, this selfsame thing, that ye were made sorry after a godly sort,
what earnest care it wrought in you, yea, what clearing of

---

[1] Some ancient authorities omit *for.*　　　[2] Or, *unto a salvation which*
bringeth no regret

---

syntax is faulty, as so often when
the Apostle is deeply moved. The
following arrangement is perhaps
best: "For though I made you sorry
with my epistle, I do not regret it :
though I did regret it (I see that
that epistle made you sorry, though
but for a season), now I rejoice, not
that ye were made sorry, but that ye
were made sorry unto repentance."
Whatever arrangement is adopted,
the word "now" at the beginning of
v. 9 refers to time, and should have
emphasis placed upon it in reading;
it is not a conjunction of transition.

8. *though but for a season.* S. Paul
assumes that the pain is over for the
Corinthians, as well as for himself.

9. *after a godly sort.* The literal
translation "according to God" is
much better, as it is also in the next
two verses. The grief caused by the
severe epistle was in harmony with
God's character and will.

that ye might...in nothing. The
severity of the severe epistle, which
S. Paul now puts away, had robbed
the Corinthians of their satisfaction
with themselves, and tranquillity of
mind. If no good result had followed,
they would have suffered loss without any corresponding gain.

10. We should translate as R.V.
text, not margin. That salvation
brings no regret is too obvious to be
worth saying. In the Greek of this
verse the second word translated
"worketh" is a strengthened form of
the first, and probably marks the
completeness and finality of the
result "death." The examples of
S. Peter and of Judas in the Passion
story might well occur to S. Paul's
mind. The sorrow of the one was
"according to God"; the sorrow of
the other was not. We should observe that the grief brings the repentance; it is not identical with it.
Grief belongs to the emotions; repentance belongs to the will. The
practical character of repentance
becomes abundantly clear in the
next verse.

11. *this selfsame thing.* Better,
"this very thing."

what earnest care. This great verse
perhaps contains the best description
of repentance found in Scripture, and
repentance will be considered below.
But though the repentance which
S. Paul describes was "according to
God," what is chiefly in his mind is not
"repentance toward God" (Ac. xx.
21), but repentance toward himself.

yourselves, yea, what indignation, yea, what fear, yea, what longing, yea, what zeal, yea, what avenging! In everything 12 ye approved yourselves to be pure in the matter. So although I wrote unto you, *I wrote* not for his cause that did the wrong, nor for his cause that suffered the wrong, but that your earnest care for us might be made manifest 13 unto you in the sight of God. Therefore we have been comforted : and in our comfort we joyed the more exceedingly for the joy of Titus, because his spirit hath been 14 refreshed by you all. For if in anything I have gloried to him on your behalf, I was not put to shame; but as we spake all things to you in truth, so our glorying also, which 15 I made before Titus, was found to be truth. And his inward affection is more abundantly toward you, whilst he

The Corinthians awoke from their callousness ; they cleared themselves from complicity with the evil of the past ; they became indignant with S. Paul's enemies and with themselves ; they trembled to think what the result of their conduct to themselves might be ; they longed for S. Paul to come back ; they went to work in earnest to put things right ; they punished the chief offender ; and thus in every respect they cleared themselves of the evil of which they had been guilty. There was nothing further left for them to do.

12. *So.* This verse of course describes, not S. Paul's purpose in writing his severe letter, but the purpose which the letter had actually served, and which God had intended it to serve. It had led the Corinthians to recognize how great their regard for S. Paul really was. Cf. Introduction, pp. xxxviii, lii.

in the sight of God. This addition, apparently so unnecessary, is characteristic. God is the ever-present witness of the conduct of His people one to another, and of their changes

of feeling one to another. Who are respectively meant by the doer and sufferer of the wrong cannot certainly be known. Cf. Introduction, p. xxxvii.

13. *Therefore...comforted.* It is best to put a full stop after these words, and to connect them with the previous verses.

in our comfort. Better, "over and above this comfort of ours."

we joyed...Titus. The reason for this peculiar joy was apparently that Titus had not only fully shared S. Paul's anxiety, but had been far less hopeful as to the success of his mission to Corinth than S. Paul himself. He had not believed S. Paul's prediction that the Corinthians would come to a better mind.

14. *as we spake...found to be truth.* S. Paul had spoken the whole truth in his stern letter, sparing the Corinthians nothing that needed to be said ; but whether his assurances to Titus were as true as his words to the Corinthians it had been for the future to shew.

15. *his inward affection.* It was the more necessary to assure the

rembembereth the obedience of you all, how with fear and
16 trembling ye received him. I rejoice that in everything I
am of good courage concerning you.

Corinthians of the feeling of Titus,
because he had evidently been pessi-
mistic about them.

the obedience of you all. Titus had
been the bearer of an ultimatum ;

very definite demands had to be
satisfied. The word "all" is important, as in *v.* 13. The Church was
now obedient as a whole.

The foregoing passage affords a wonderful exhibition of the pastoral
spirit, and of S. Paul's sympathy and tact ; but its chief interest lies in its
teaching about repentance. S. Paul is not markedly a preacher of repentance,
as an examination of his sermons in the Acts of the Apostles, and of his
Epistles will shew. Apart from the passage before us, the word is only
found in his writings in Rom. ii. 4 and 2 Tim. ii. 25, and his authorship in
the last instance is uncertain. His method, like that of other great evangelists, was so to proclaim the Kingdom of God, and Jesus as the Christ, the
Bringer and Centre of the kingdom, that everyone understood that in
belief in Jesus as the Christ, and self-identification by baptism with Him
and with His people, renunciation of the old life, and the rising out of the
old life, were necessarily involved. We should however notice that, when
S. Paul had before him a Gentile audience, he seems to have said more about
repentance than when he spoke to Jews. Contrast Ac. xvii. 30, 31 with
Ac. xiii. 38, 39, though cf. also Ac. xx. 21. The Jews understood the moral
claims of God far better than the Gentiles.

Now this method of appeal ought not to cause us surprise. The real
teaching of the Bible from first to last is that God expects very little of the
heathen, since they can give very little (cf. Ac. xiv. 16 ; xvii. 30 ; Rom. iii.
25) ; and that what we call "original sin" calls out His pity rather than His
wrath. The great calls to repentance, which the O.T. and N.T. alike contain,
are always addressed to those who have been unfaithful to their covenant
relation to God as His people ; they are addressed to the members of the
Church, whether before or after the Lord's coming.

What then ought the repentance of Christians to be ? The seventeenth
verse of this chapter gives an admirable answer. Just as God is revealed to
men in Christ, so Christ is revealed to men through those who speak and
act for Him, and are in character and life identified with Him (cf. Mt. x.
40 ; xxv. 40 ; and in this Epistle ii. 10 ; xiii. 3) ; and, in seeing what was
involved in the repentance of the Corinthians for their conduct to the great
Apostle, whose children they were, and who had so wonderfully given himself for them and to them, we see what is involved in repentance toward
that heavenly Father, Whose authority over His children, and Whose love
and sacrifice, S. Paul in some measure incarnated and manifested.

How then is this repentance aroused, and what form does it take ? Its
beginning is in pain, but in pain that is "according to God." This pain may
be caused either by the stern appeal of the Christian teacher to the conscience,
as in the case before us ; or by the disasters which fall upon us, and which

the conscience interprets as divine judgments. This pain is not in itself repentance, nor does it necessarily lead to it; indeed it may be, as S. Paul says, a source of impoverishment, or even lead to our destruction. It is only according to God, if it arouses the right kind of emotion, and through this emotion the right kind of action; and it is in the action, which is thus brought about, that repentance chiefly consists. Repentance is not just a "change of mind," as the derivation of the Greek word for it so often leads Christian teachers to assert; it is a change in the whole thinking, feeling, and working personality, and so in that practical action from which personality is inseparable, and in which it not only manifests itself, but comes to be what it is. When S. Jerome translated the Greek word for "repent" in the Baptist's message by the Latin "Paenitentiam agite"—"Do penance"— he translated it admirably; though we must not suppose that the penance or repentance which has to be "done" consists only or chiefly in devotional exercises. It consists in an awakening from our general callousness to something like a true sense of God, and of His claims upon us; in a definite renunciation of our past sins; in indignation with ourselves, in fear of the consequences of our conduct, in longing for a renewed union with God,

> I hate the sins which made Thee mourn
> And drove Thee from my breast,

and above all in the two things in which alone repentance attains full reality, in earnest and anxious effort to put things right, and in punishing ourselves as we deserve. That is the "repentance unto salvation," which "brings no regret" because it invariably attains its object—the joy of God in us, the justification of His hope for us, our own joy in Him, and a new recognition of what He means to us. But there is no "approving ourselves to be pure," no real cleansing of ourselves from past evil on any easier terms. Repentance, like faith, is practical; it only finds itself in the action which it involves; and—again like faith—it is worth just what it costs.

Chs. VIII, IX. Reconciliation between S. Paul and the Corinthian Church as a whole is now complete. But restored good feeling is best strengthened and assured by common work; and S. Paul turns to that subject ever so dear to his heart, the support of the distressed Church of Jerusalem. On this cf. the note on 1 Cor. xvi. 1–4. The two following chapters are a conspicuous example of S. Paul's rudeness of speech, and neither the A.V. nor the R.V. clears away the resulting obscurity of much that he says. But they are none the less a wonderful example both of S. Paul's own mind and spirit, and of his exquisite tact, not even the Epistle to Philemon being superior to them. The words of a modern French writer are worth quoting:—

Quelle délicatesse de touche pour être insinuant sans devenir importun! Que de ménagements et d'adresse, pour stimuler la générosité tout en évitant de l'imposer! Quelles envolées de surnaturel pour corriger ce que le sujet a de fatalement banal! Le mot de quête n'est pas prononcé; celui d'aumône non plus : c'est un acte de bienfaisance et de miséricorde, un ministère sacré, un

VIII. 1 Moreover, brethren, we make known to you the grace of God which hath been given in the churches of 2 Macedonia; how that in much proof of affliction the abundance of their joy and their deep poverty abounded unto the 3 riches of their [1]liberality. For according to their power, I bear witness, yea and beyond their power, *they gave* of 4 their own accord, beseeching us with much intreaty in regard of this grace and the fellowship in the ministering 5 to the saints: and *this,* not as we had hoped, but first they

[1] Gr. *singleness.*

moyen de s'unir aux frères et de participer à leurs prières, c'est l'assistance destinée aux saints, c'est enfin une grâce, plus encore pour celui qui donne que pour celui qui reçoit.

Paul fait appel à trois motives qui manquent rarement leur but; l'émulation, l'amour-propre et l'intérêt. Ces sentiments sont tout-puissants pour le bien comme pour le mal. Il ne s'agit que de les diriger et de surnaturaliser : l'Apôtre s'y entend à merveille et il nous donne, en ces deux pages, un modèle exquis de ce genre de prédication. (Prat, *La Théologie de Saint Paul,* Tome I, p. 178.)

VIII. 1. *Moreover.* A bad translation, since this strong conjunction, though introducing a new point, links it with what has gone before. Better the simple "now," which is all that the Greek requires. S. Paul turns to a subject entirely new.

we make known to you. Again a bad translation, since the phrase is much too heavy, and suggests the revealing of a secret. The old English "do you to wit" of the A.V. is excellent; but, if this is too archaic, "let you know" is better than the R.V.

the grace of God ... Macedonia. S. Paul never forgets that all true Christian goodness has its source in the new life of grace. Such action as he proceeds to describe is "supernatural" in the true sense of that word ; it is beyond the normal range of unregenerate humanity. The Macedonian churches were the best of S. Paul's churches, and far superior

to that of Corinth, in spite of the latter's high intellectual gifts. Cf. 1 Thess. ii. 19, 20 ; Phil. iv. 1.

2. *in much proof of affliction.* An unintelligible translation. The A.V. "in a great trial of affliction" leaves little to be desired. The Revisers probably thought that the modern usage of the word "trial" put the stress too much on the suffering involved, and too little on its value as a test.

their deep poverty abounded. Not such a paradox as at first it seems. Not only is overflowing joy a great source of liberality, but great poverty often is also. Not only do the very poor alone understand what actual want means to others; but, having no power to provide for the future, they do not acquire the hoarding habit.

3–6. As so often with S. Paul, the general meaning is clear, but the exact meaning and the correct arrangement of the clauses uncertain.

gave their own selves to the Lord, and to us by the will of
6 God. Insomuch that we exhorted Titus, that as he had
made a beginning before, so he would also complete in you
7 this grace also. But as ye abound in everything, *in* faith,
and utterance, and knowledge, and *in* all earnestness, and
in ¹your love to us, *see* that ye abound in this grace also.

¹ Some ancient authorities read *our love to you.*

Neither the words inserted in italics
in the R.V., nor those similarly inserted in the A.V., have any justification in the Greek; and there
should be no full stop till the end of
v. 6. We should translate the words
without adding to them, and be
satisfied with that general impression
of S. Paul's meaning which they leave
upon our minds. "For according to
their power, I bear witness, and
beyond their power, of their own
accord (with much entreaty beseeching of us the grace and the common
sharing in the ministering to the
saints), and, not as we hoped, but
themselves they gave first to the
Lord and to us by the will of God,
so that we have asked Titus that, as
he made a beginning before, so also
he would complete unto you this
grace also." The chief points to observe are these: (*a*) S. Paul does not
say "they gave" (*v.* 3, R.V.), meaning
that they gave money, though the
passage implies it. Throughout these
chapters he avoids the mention of
money with remarkable skill. The
central statement is that the Macedonians "of their own accord gave"
not so much a contribution as "themselves to the Lord" and to the Apostle
who represented Him. S. Paul did
not have to appeal to them, though
he had hoped for their help. The
Macedonians asked as a favour that
they might be allowed to take part;
and, recognizing a call from the Lord

to minister to His members, threw
themselves into the work which
S. Paul had in hand. The ardent
interest was there from the first, the
money coming in as they were able
to collect it. (*b*) The "beginning"
which S. Paul here describes Titus
as making probably was in Macedonia, not at Corinth. S. Paul in
v. 6 says not "in you" (as A.V. and
R.V.), but "unto you." Titus was
treasurer of the fund; he had been
gathering contributions in Macedonia, and the Corinthian contribution would be the final one, to which
the earlier led up. He who had already been so useful to the Corinthians would be useful to them in
this matter also. Throughout *vv.* 3–6
the well-meant interpolations of our
translators obscure the meaning of
S. Paul's rapidly dictated words.

7. *in your love to us.* The reading
"our love to you" (R.V. margin) is
the better. Though it seems at first
sight less appropriate, and the scribes
would be likely to correct it, it is not
really so. The love of the Apostle
to the Corinthians, on which he has
already so often dwelt, was part of
their treasure; and the mention of
it here, like the reference in the
previous verse to what Titus had
done for the Corinthians, links these
verses with the previous chapter.
The Greek words here employed are
inadequately represented by the R.V.
translation. S. Paul speaks of "the

8 I speak not by way of commandment, but as proving
through the earnestness of others the sincerity also of
9 your love. For ye know the grace of our Lord Jesus Christ,
that, though he was rich, yet for your sakes he became

out of us in you love." The love of
the Apostle made light of the distance
between Macedonia and Corinth, and
dwelt among his children there, reproducing itself in them.

see that ye abound. The R.V. insertion "see" is a correct one. The
ellipse belongs to the colloquial Greek
of the time, and is found in the
papyri.

8. *proving.* i.e. testing.

the sincerity also of your love.
Better "how sterling is your love
also."

9. *For ye know.* The verse gives
the reason why S. Paul does not here
speak by way of commandment; the
example of the Lord should be enough
to constrain them, and they are well
aware what it was.

the grace of our Lord Jesus Christ.
The titles "Lord" and "Christ" (cf.
Ac. ii. 36) are advisedly used to bring
out the greatness of the Giver; and
His immeasurable grace and generosity are tacitly contrasted with the
little now asked of the Corinthians.
They cannot accept His gift, and
refuse the gift asked from them.

*though he was rich, yet for your
sakes he became poor.* Simple as the
words appear, they are, like the
parallel words of Phil. ii. 5-8, less
simple than they seem. (*a*) The words
"he became poor" do not refer to
the moment of the Incarnation, but
to the whole earthly experience of
the Lord, including the experience
of death. It is on this that the N.T.
writers dwell, and not upon the moment of the Incarnation; Jn. i. 14

affords no exception. (*b*) When
S. Paul says "though he was rich,"
does he mean that by the Incarnation
the Lord ceased to be rich, or that
He remained rich, in spite of living
the life of a poor man? It is clear
from Col. i. 16, 17 that S. Paul regarded the general relation of the
Son of God to the universe as in no
way affected by the Incarnation, and
in this sense our Lord always remained rich. But S. Paul also regarded the Lord, as Phil. ii. 5-8
shews, as having really emptied Himself of His divine glory by assuming
human form and living a human
life; and this thought of having
ceased to be rich within the sphere
of the Incarnate life is more appropriate here. (*c*) The words "for
your sakes" are very wide in their
meaning, and cover all forms of the
Lord's work for us. Cf. the words of
the Nicene Creed, "for us men, and
for our salvation."

We should observe that there is
never any question with S. Paul
about the pre-existence of the Lord.
Cf. Gal. iv. 4 (with Lightfoot's note);
1 Cor. x. 4; Rom. viii. 3, as well as
the later Phil. ii. 5-8 and Col. i. 16,
17. He refers to it as a matter of
which his converts have not the
slightest doubt, and to which he can
appeal in moral exhortation. But no
more than S. Peter does he refer to
it in the first preaching of the Gospel.
There is a right order in the communication of truth; and the redeeming power of Christ should be
known before the deeper questions

10 poor, that ye through his poverty might become rich. And herein I give *my* judgement: for this is expedient for you, who were the first to make a beginning a year ago, not

11 only to do, but also to will. But now complete the doing also; that as *there was* the readiness to will, so *there may*

12 *be* the completion also out of your ability. For if the readiness is there, *it is* acceptable according as *a man*

13 hath, not according as *he* hath not. For *I say* not *this*,

14 that others may be eased, *and* ye distressed: but by equality; your abundance *being a supply* at this present time for their want, that their abundance also may become *a supply*

are raised as to His Person. Before men are told that "Jesus is God," they should know a good deal about Jesus, and a good deal about God.

that ye through his poverty might become rich. These words shew conclusively that far more than the moment of the Incarnation is in S. Paul's mind. The Lord, like the Macedonians, gave Himself to God "and to us by the will of God," and through His sacrifice of Himself enriched us with the wealth which was eternally His own. Cf. Jn. xvii. 22, 24.

10. *herein I give my judgement.* Moffatt excellently "I will tell you what I think about it."

who were the first. Better "since you were the first."

a year ago. Probably "last year." So also in ix. 2. The Macedonian year, like the Hebrew, began in the autumn, and S. Paul may look back to the previous spring. Cf. 1 Cor. xvi. 1 ff.

not only to do, but also to will. The seemingly strange order of the two clauses is to be explained by S. Paul's words in *v.* 5. It was the goodwill of the Macedonians, upon which he had particularly dwelt, and he recognizes that not even in goodwill had the Macedonians been in advance of the Corinthians. The

Peshitto Syriac version transposes the two verbs, a good example of the supposed improvements made through misunderstanding of the true text.

11. *out of your ability.* Moffatt again excellently "so far as your means allow." The "for" of the next verse thus becomes intelligible.

12. *according as a man hath.* Better "may have." Cf. Tobit iv. 8.

13. *that others...distressed.* S. Paul knows well this familiar excuse for refusal to give.

but by equality. The literal translation "from equality" is preferable. The clause explains the principle out of which the call arises.

14. The R.V. insertions in italics are only harmful. The brief epigrammatic form makes what S. Paul says a watchword of Christian justice Cf. Rom. xv. 27. S. Paul hardly looks forward to a time when Jewish Christians may be better supplied with this world's goods than Gentile. The thought rather is of the spiritual blessings which may come from "the saints" at Jerusalem to the Gentile churches. As yet practically all the missionary work had been done by Jewish Christians; and all spiritual blessings had come through them.

15 for your want; that there may be equality: as it is written,
He that *gathered* much had nothing over; and he that
gathered little had no lack.

16 But thanks be to God, which putteth the same earnest
17 care for you into the heart of Titus. For indeed he accepted
our exhortation; but being himself very earnest, he went
18 forth unto you of his own accord. And we have sent together with him the brother whose praise in the gospel *is*
19 *spread* through all the churches; and not only so, but who
was also appointed by the churches to travel with us in
the matter of this grace, which is ministered by us to the

---

15. A most happy quotation from Ex. xvi. 18. The whole chapter should be read; it is full of spiritual teaching. The quails, at any rate in Numb. xi. 31–34 and Ps. lxxviii. 20–31, are given in anger; the manna is the Father's supply of daily bread. Cf. the longer note below.

16. *the same earnest care.* i.e. the same as my own.

17. *For indeed he accepted.* A misleading translation, English idiom demanding "he has accepted," and in the second part of the verse "he has gone forth." S. Paul is speaking of Titus as the bearer of the Epistle which he is writing, and not of his earlier mission.

18. *And we have sent together with him.* Here the R V., like the A.V., rightly follows the English idiom, though the tense in the Greek is the same as that twice used in the previous verse. Both bodies of translators apparently misunderstood the time to which *v.* 17 refers.

the brother whose praise in the gospel. Very probably S. Luke; Ac. xx. 4–6 suggests that he was the Philippian delegate. The point is that those sent with Titus to Corinth are not unknown people. But, though S. Luke may have been already

collecting materials for his Gospel, "the gospel" here means evangelistic activity. It must not be interpreted as it is naturally interpreted in the Collect for S. Luke's Day, since the use of the word to signify a written document did not arise till much later. It is, however, not unlikely that S. Luke's reputation already rested upon the knowledge he had acquired of the earthly life and teaching of the Lord. Cf. Luk. i. 3.

19. *appointed by the churches.* The fact that this appointment is not mentioned in the Acts suggests that it was S. Luke himself who received it. If he had already considerable knowledge of the beginnings of Christianity, his appointment to go to Jerusalem with S. Paul was the more natural.

to the glory of the Lord...our readiness. Quite apart from the need of the Christians at Jerusalem, S. Paul had two great objects in view. The first was the glory of Him, Who is Lord of Jewish and Gentile Christians alike (cf. Ac. x. 36). There was grave danger that over the question of the observance of the Mosaic law the Church would break asunder, to the dishonour of the Lord (cf. 1 Cor. i. 13) and the

20 glory of the Lord, and *to shew* our readiness : avoiding this, that any man should blame us in *the matter of* this
21 bounty which is ministered by us : for we take thought for things honourable, not only in the sight of the Lord,
22 but also in the sight of men. And we have sent with them our brother, whom we have many times proved earnest in

serious setback of God's purpose. The "collection for the saints" not only glorified the Lord by shewing the reality of His work among the Gentiles, but knit the hearts of Jewish and Gentile Christians together. Jewish Christians could not at once accept the self-sacrifice of the Macedonians, who were almost as poor as themselves, and deny their equal position in the Christian brotherhood. S. Paul's second object was a personal one. Charged as he was (cf. Ac. xxi. 20, 21, 28) with being the leader of a great apostasy from the religion of the people of God, it was essential for him to shew his zeal for his own nation in every legitimate way ; and there could be no better way than to turn that very activity among the Gentiles which the Jewish Christians misunderstood into a means of benefit to them. Cf. Gal. ii. 10. Thus the collection was not only to the glory of the Lord, but—in a way quite legitimate—to S. Paul's own glory ; and it is this which explains the omission of the verb in the last clause of this verse. "Glory" is the manifestation of inherent character, and in the last clause "to shew," or manifest, is supplied out of the meaning of the word "glory."

20. *avoiding this.* Strictly speaking, this clause should be constructed with "we have sent" at the beginning of *v.* 18, and refer to the mission of "the brother" to Corinth. But

S. Paul frequently loses his way in the long sentences that he dictates ; and probably what is here in his mind is the appointment by the churches of a commissioner to travel with him to Jerusalem. Beset by hostility and suspicion as S. Paul was, it was essential, not only at Corinth, but everywhere, to guard against the charge of appropriating to his own use the funds collected. He "ministered" the fund to the authorities of the Church of Jerusalem (cf. Ac. xi. 29, 30), but had no control over it.

bounty. i.e. munificence. Yet another substitute for the ill-sounding "money."

21. *thought for things honourable.* The Greek word defies translation, but "honourable" is needlessly misleading. S. Paul probably has in mind the LXX Version of Prov. iii. 4 ; and the A.V. and R.V. translation "favour and good understanding" suggests the right meaning here. S. Paul takes thought for what is not only good and beautiful in itself, but will be recognized as being so. Cf. Rom. xii. 17. In the Church all money matters require careful handling. Where the "mammon of unrighteousness" is concerned, suspicion almost always creeps in.

22. *our brother.* Possibly Timothy, an earnest worker, but one, as the N.T. seems to shew, a little disposed to be timid, and needing encouragement.

many things, but now much more earnest, by reason of
23 the great confidence which *he hath* in you. Whether *any
inquire* about Titus, *he is* my partner and *my* fellow-worker
to you-ward; or our brethren, *they are* the [1]messengers
24 of the churches, *they are* the glory of Christ. [2]Shew ye
therefore unto them in the face of the churches the proof
of your love, and of our glorying on your behalf.

IX. 1 For as touching the ministering to the saints, it is

[1] Gr. *apostles.*   [2] Or, *Shew ye therefore in the face…on your behalf unto
them*

much more earnest…hath in you.
Confidence is the parent of earnestness; discouragement of slackness.
Those who complain of the slackness
of the clergy should ask themselves
whether their own attitude is such
as to suggest that greater activity
would be followed by good results.

23. The insertions of the R.V. are
unnecessary, and the first—"any
inquire"—is absurd. Titus was already well known at Corinth, but it
was well to insist upon the complete
unity of purpose and work which existed between them.

messengers of the churches. Better
"representatives." The word used is
"apostles," and apostles are representatives, authorized to act in the
name of those who send them. By
the "apostles" in the N.T. is generally meant the Apostles of Christ;
but churches, as well as the Lord,
may appoint authorized representatives Cf. Phil. ii. 25, where, as here,
"messenger" is a mistranslation. In
both cases, the "apostles" of the
churches were authorized to carry
and bestow money; they had no
particular message to give.

the glory of Christ. The saints
are always the glory of Christ, manifesting the power of His grace, and
the beauty of His character, as it is
reproduced in them in their different

positions and callings. But S. Paul
(cf. *v.* 19) probably is thinking
especially of that manifestation of
the reality of Gentile Christianity
which the apostles of the churches
were to make to the Jewish Christians. As usual, his mind is absorbed
in the matter in hand.

24. *the proof of your love.* Better
"the demonstration." It is not a
question of any external proof of love,
but of love itself.

our glorying. Cf. ch. vii. 14.
S. Paul's confidence in the Corinthians had not been expressed to
Titus alone; the Corinthians had to
justify it before the Macedonian
churches. The words "in the face of
the churches" should come at the
end of the sentence, as in the Greek.
The apostles of the churches would
report the reception they had received; and the Corinthians have to
take account of the public opinion
of Christendom.

IX. 1. There is no break; but
S. Paul turns from the commissioners
back to the collection itself. The force
of the word "For" at the beginning
of this chapter is this. He has been
speaking about the commissioners,
"for" it is unnecessary to speak
about the collection. After the
trouble that had arisen at Corinth,
the good reception of the closest

2 superfluous for me to write to you: for I know your readiness, of which I glory on your behalf to them of Macedonia,
that Achaia hath been prepared for a year past; and [1]your
3 zeal hath stirred up [2]very many of them. But I have sent
the brethren, that our glorying on your behalf may not be
made void in this respect; that, even as I said, ye may
4 be prepared: lest by any means, if there come with me
any of Macedonia, and find you unprepared, we (that we
5 say not, ye) should be put to shame in this confidence. I
thought it necessary therefore to intreat the brethren, that
they would go before unto you, and make up beforehand
your aforepromised [3]bounty, that the same might be ready,
as a matter of bounty, and not of [4]extortion.
6   But this *I say*, He that soweth sparingly shall reap also

[1] Or, *emulation of you*   [2] Gr. *the more part.*   [3] Gr. *blessing.*
[4] Or, *covetousness*

associates of S. Paul was of supreme importance.

2. *readiness.* Better "keenness." "Readiness" is an ambiguous word, and may suggest that the work of collecting funds for Jerusalem was already accomplished at Corinth. The R.V. has probably two other mistranslations in this verse. S. Paul says, not "to them of Macedonia," but "to Macedonians"; it is chiefly the less zealous Macedonians who are in question. Perhaps there was a touch of legitimate provincial rivalry. After ch. viii. 1–5, this verse, as translated in the R.V., reads strangely. Again, "hath prepared itself" is probably right, and not "hath been prepared" (cf. 1 Cor. xiv. 8), which is hardly consistent with the verses which follow. Cf. note on viii. 10.

3. *in this respect.* Perhaps a delicate suggestion that S. Paul's praise of the Corinthians has not been confined to this one matter.

even as I said. Better "even as I have been saying, ye may have prepared yourselves."

4. *any of Macedonia.* Better "if Macedonians come with me." There is no suggestion that Macedonians are peculiarly likely to be absent.

5. *to intreat the brethren.* Better "to ask." There is no suggestion that they were unwilling to go.

as a matter...extortion. Moffatt excellently "as a generous gift, and not as money wrung out of you." But the mention of money is still avoided. It is very important to keep the spirit and motive right, both in collecting money and in giving it. The spirit of covetousness —of desiring to have more than can be fairly claimed—may enter into the collector who asks, as well as into those to whom his appeal is made. It is not unlikely that S. Paul was charged by some at Corinth with covetousness of this kind. Cf. vii. 2; xii. 18.

6. Cf. Prov. xi. 24–26; Mt. vi. 4; Luk. xiv. 14; 1 Tim. vi. 17–19. Are

sparingly; and he that soweth [1]bountifully shall reap also
7 [1]bountifully. *Let* each man *do* according as he hath purposed in his heart; not [2]grudgingly, or of necessity: for
8 God loveth a cheerful giver. And God is able to make
all grace abound unto you; that ye, having always all
sufficiency in everything, may abound unto every good
9 work: as it is written,

He hath scattered abroad, he hath given to the poor;
His righteousness abideth for ever.

[1] Gr. *with blessings.*   [2] Gr. *of sorrow.*

appeals of this kind, so clearly sanc-
tioned by the Lord, unworthy and
degrading? Not at all. There is a
right self-regard, as well as a wrong;
and Christian conduct is so difficult
to us all, that all legitimate appeals
should be employed. It is this which
the highbrow moral philosopher often
does not understand. But though
the servants of God, in their generosity to their fellow-servants, may
begin with childish conceptions of
the reward that they are to receive,
they do not end with them. God
gives more than they ask or think,
but not what at first they ask or
think, as S. Paul well explains in the
noble passage which follows.

bountifully. Translate literally, as
in the margin, "with blessings." Cf.
Jam. i. 5. Both S. Paul and S. James
think of such O.T. teaching as that
found in Ecclus. xviii. 17, 18; xx. 15.

7. *Let each man...in his heart.*
In giving, we should not yield to
pressure, but give only what we have
resolved to give. Otherwise we feel
ourselves robbed, and are embittered,
instead of growing in love.

God loveth a cheerful giver. That
is the witness of the O.T. teaching.
Cf. Deut. xv. 9, 10; Prov. xxii. 8,
9; Ecclus. xx. 14, 15; xxxv. 8, 9.
"Hilarem Dei similem," says Bengel.

8. *to make all grace abound unto
you.* All—the higher spiritual blessing as well as the lower temporal,
and the lower temporal as well as
the higher spiritual.

may abound unto every good work.
No one need fear that he will suffer
by generosity to the people of God.
At all times, under all circumstances,
every kind of need can by God be
fully supplied. But even so the gifts
of God are not for the immediate
recipient alone; they are equipment for further service. The reward
of giving what we have is not to
be "repaid a thousand-fold," and be
a thousand-fold selfish afterwards
without rebuke; it is that we may
serve a thousand-fold more effectively, and find our joy in doing so.

9. *as it is written.* In Ps. cxii. 9.
But the whole Psalm should be
studied, in order to understand
S. Paul's meaning. "Righteousness,"
as almost invariably with S. Paul, is
a religious rather than an ethical
conception. It is a gift rather than
an attainment—God's approval and
acceptance manifested by God's
practical action. Cf. Ps. cxii. 3, 6,
8–10. It has a forensic aspect—"He
shall maintain his cause in judgement" (*v.* 5). But the judgment of
God is declared by God's open and

10 And he that supplieth seed to the sower and bread for food,
  shall supply and multiply your seed for sowing, and increase
11 the fruits of your righteousness: ye being enriched in everything unto all ¹liberality, which worketh through us thanks-
12 giving to God. For the ministration of this service not
  only filleth up the measure of the wants of the saints, but
  aboundeth also through many thanksgivings unto God;

¹ Gr. *singleness.*

manifest action before the world, and it was this that the people of God ever desired. Cf. Is. lviii. 8. Thus the meaning of "his righteousness remaineth for ever" is that the practical manifestation of God's favour will never cease; and the statement is exactly parallel to the Apostle's statement in the preceding verse. For "He hath scattered"—"verbum generosum," as Bengel says—cf. Prov. xi. 24.

10. *he that supplieth...bread for food.* The word "scattered" at once suggests the thought of the sower, and supplies a beautiful illustration of the thought already expressed. God, Who will so richly reward His servants, is the same God Who in His harvest bounty gives not only bread for food, but seed for sowing for yet another harvest. Cf. Is. lv. 10, where, as here, the seed is mentioned before the food, as the more important.

supply and multiply your seed for sowing. The thought of bread for food passes away ; that the generous will not come to want is but a little thing. The great thing is the ever increasing surplus for service.

increase the fruits of your righteousness. Or "make the shoots of your righteousness to grow." The religious sense of righteousness is still maintained. It is the mani-fested approval that God rains down

(cf. Hos. x. 12), the blessing so fruit-ful for others as well as for those who immediately receive it. In Is. lv. 10, 11, which S. Paul has in mind, the parallel is between the rain, and the operative word of God which accomplishes the practical vindica-tion of His people.

11. *which worketh through us... to God.* It might seem that nothing more could be said about the blessed-ness of giving, but the highest reason of all is still to come. There is nothing egotistical about the words "through us." S. Paul knew himself to be God's chosen instrument, not only for the gathering of the Gentiles, but for the glory of God in the mutual love of all men within the Catholic Church.

12. *the ministration of this ser-vice.* The word for "service" sug-gests priestly service. The gift to the Christians of Jerusalem was part of the offering up of the Gentiles (cf. Rom. xv. 16, and 2 Cor. viii. 5).

filleth up...wants of the saints. Better "is filling up abundantly." The work is regarded as already begun. The Jewish Christians prob-ably knew of what was on foot, and were building upon it.

but aboundeth. Better "is abound-ing."

through...unto God. As in all sacrifice, God has His share. The thanksgivings offered are not only

13 seeing that through the proving *of you* by this ministration
they glorify God for the obedience of your confession unto
the gospel of Christ, and for the ¹liberality of *your* con-
14 tribution unto them and unto all; while they themselves
also, with supplication on your behalf, long after you by
15 reason of the exceeding grace of God in you. Thanks be
to God for his unspeakable gift.

¹ Gr. *singleness.*

those of the Jewish Christians, but those of all who, like S. Paul, have the unity of the Church passionately at heart.

13. *for the obedience of your confession unto the gospel of Christ.* An obscure phrase. The confession in view is the confession, or profession, of their faith by the Gentiles. Cf. Rom. x. 9; 1 Tim. vi. 12, 13; Heb. iii. 1; iv. 14; x. 23. "Unto the gospel" may be either (*a*) taken closely with "confession," the strong Greek phrase expressing that union with truth which open profession of it brings about, or (*b*) an additional clause referring to that advancement of the cause of the Gospel which the Gentile obedience to the Gospel brings about. But the great point is the "obedience." What the Christians of Jerusalem were inclined to doubt was the reality of Gentile Christianity. A faith in the Christ of Israel, which did not involve obedience to the divinely given law of Israel, seemed to many of them a valueless, because an inoperative, faith. The love shewn to them by the generous supply of their

needs was the very thing to remove their misunderstanding.

contribution unto them and unto all. The translation "contribution" gives too narrow a meaning to the word. Better "fellowship." The Gentile Christians had grasped the fact that they and their Jewish brothers were members of one body, with a common cause and common interests, and so helped their Jewish brothers to grasp it. The addition "unto all" brings out the Catholic outlook from which their generosity proceeded.

14. *long after you.* Cf. the "longing" of vii. 11. In both cases, the former alienation has been exchanged for a longing desire for closer union.

the exceeding grace of God in you. Better "resting upon you." It was a moral miracle that Macedonians and Corinthians should be exhibiting such self-sacrifice for Jews.

15. *his unspeakable gift.* The widest meaning should be given to this phrase. It refers to the gift of redemption in God's Son by His Spirit. The Gentile generosity was a striking example of what it effects.

These two chapters are, as has been said, the *locus classicus* for Christian charity; and there are few of which we are more in need. S. Paul does not speak "by way of commandment"; like S. Peter in Ac. v. 4, he fully recognizes the institution of private property. Each must decide for himself what he will give, and do "as he hath purposed in his heart." It is not a question of all or nothing; we can be mean, or rather mean, or fairly generous, or generous "according to" and even "beyond our power." But there, ever displayed before our astonished eyes, is God's "unspeakable gift." We "know the grace of our Lord Jesus Christ"; we know the sacrifice which our Lord and Master made for us, and the vast and abiding wealth, which (ever since He made it) is within our reach, and of which "the earnest" is already ours. Yes! and we know more than this. We know that there have been, and are, thousands of Christians far poorer than we, so moved by the divine love as to give on a scale, which not even one like S. Paul, who had himself sacrificed all, would feel that he could rightly ask of them. What, in view of all this, shall we ourselves give to help our brothers in their need? Our brothers in Christ—there lies the great appeal; the great sacrifices are not asked for those outside the Christian brotherhood. No doubt, like our heavenly Father (Mt. v. 45), we should do good to all, as opportunity is given to us; but the full claim is for those that are "of the household of the faith" (Gal. vi. 10). There—within the Church—God desires "equality." That does not mean that all good things should be equally distributed; but it does mean that no one should possess that of which he can make no rational use, and that no one should be without that which he requires for worthy Christian living. So we are taught in that chapter of the Book of Exodus to which S. Paul refers. The fleshpots of Egypt, the quails covering the camp, are no sign of the blessing of God; the hoarded manna "breeds worms"; what God gives in love is "a day's portion every day," and His eye watching us "whether we will walk in His law, or no." To gain or to keep what we do not want is covetousness, and the N.T., followed by all the great moral teachers of the Church, regards covetousness as a sin as serious as drunkenness or loose living (cf. Eph. v. 3). If we English Christians do not feel it to be so, and our teachers are afraid to tell us so, it only shews how far we have fallen from the principles of the Gospel.

But then, it will be said, this is to preach communism. No, it is not. Communism is an economic system of "the world"; not even the first Christians of Jerusalem practised that; in Ac. ii. 44, 45 the Greek tenses are imperfects, and what is described is the willing sacrifices that Christians were continually making. Communism can only be realized and maintained by the world's methods of violence; and those who "take the sword" to establish it will "perish by the sword." To attempt the enforcement of brotherhood—a contradiction in terms—upon a vast population not yet capable of brotherhood, is to put new wine into old bottles, and an incongruous pseudo-Christian patch upon an old garment, which will be rent the more by our misguided zeal. But the members of the Church are already brothers, children of God and members one of another; and to refuse to act as brothers is to refuse the immediate demand which membership makes of us. We cannot have what has been wittily described as "Christianity à la carte," selecting according to our taste what appeals to us; we must take it as it is, or not at all.

It is true that the Church has everywhere allowed itself to be not only mingled, but confused with the world. It has lost its discipline. It is hard to-day to distinguish those who are effectively members of the household of faith from those who are not; and thus the practical action which we ought to take is difficult to discover. But the immediate question is whether we accept the principle of equality as S. Paul lays it down, and are really seeking how best to apply it. The right thing to do with "abundance" is not to "lay it up for ourselves," but to "disperse" it by giving it to the poor in whatever way we judge to be the best and wisest; and our "righteousness," God's approval manifestly resting upon us, depends upon our doing so. "It is expedient for" us not just to intend to give, or to make a beginning only, but to "complete the doing also"; the abundance must pass to other hands than ours. Nothing else will do instead. We may, like the Corinthians, have a real faith, and be able to talk about it; we may be instructed Christians, really in earnest, and much attached to our teachers. But if the one thing lacking is the open hand, we must "see that we abound in this grace also," and shew in the face of the churches the proof of our love. "He that soweth sparingly shall reap also sparingly; and he that soweth" with words of sympathy "better than a gift" will find that God and man return to him a thousand-fold, to the vast increase of his power of service. For the harvest is not only bread to the eater, but seed to the sower; and the more generously in the morning we sow our seed, and in the evening withhold not our hand, the more year by year will be ours to sow. "God is able to make all grace abound unto us," not only the "very little" of this world which is but "another's," but "the true riches" which is "our own," since it enters into our personalities, and forms them for life eternal (cf. Luk. xvi. 9–12).

But not even this is all.

> The quality of mercy is not strain'd,

So Shakespeare tells us, reproducing x. 5 and 7.

> It droppeth as the gentle rain from heaven
> Upon the place beneath:

So he says again, almost reproducing x. 10; but

> it is twice blest;
> It blesses him that gives and him that takes,

and that in ways reaching further than at first we see. If it was hard to draw the Church together when S. Paul called the churches of Greece to help the Church of Jerusalem, the spirit of division has rent the Church far more terribly since his day. East against West, Catholic against Protestant, the poor of the flock against those who, as the poor think, "thrust with side and with shoulder," and feed "upon the good pasture, and tread down with their feet the residue of the pasture"—what shall make up the breaches of the house of Israel to-day? Will argument bring us all to one mind? Argument has its place; and S. Paul himself, as the chapters to come will shew us, can strike like a steam-hammer against those who rend the Church asunder by their ignorance and pride. But argument by itself may only make the breach wider. Alienation produces bad arguments, and bad arguments increase the alienation. Even the best arguments will not avail alone. S. Paul had used very good arguments before this against the Pharisaic Christians of Jerusalem; but they were Pharisees still, and had no

X. 1 Now I Paul myself intreat you by the meekness and gentleness of Christ, I who in your presence am lowly among you, but being absent am of good courage toward you : 2 yea, I beseech you, that I may not when present shew courage with the confidence wherewith I count to be bold against some, which count of us as if we walked according

faith in a Christianity without the law. But when the loving hand of Macedonia tamed their wild hearts, they ceased to ask whether Gentile Christianity meant anything, and glorified God for what it did mean. Instead of wondering whether it were lawful for them to join in love-feast and Eucharist with these "sinners of the Gentiles," they "longed after them for the exceeding grace of God in them." So it is with our divisions to-day. The first thing is not to argue, but to create the atmosphere of mutual love and confidence, in which the voice of reason can be heard. What creates it is acts of love, and words that are equivalent to acts of love. But it is acts that are best understood, and remembered longest; and thus the sorrows of our brothers in churches far off, and long severed from our own, as well as of our poor brothers here, may win blessing for us and for them, if they afford us the opportunity of service.

X. 1. *Now I Paul myself.* The question with which he must now deal is intensely personal; he is not, as so often in the earlier chapters, speaking for the apostolic body, or for his companions as well as for himself. The very Paul, who is charged with being bold only at a distance, is going to fight his battle. Cf. Gal. v. 2.

by the meekness and gentleness of Christ. Matthew Arnold's paraphrase for gentleness—"sweet reasonableness"—is very good. "Of the Christ" is here better than "of Christ." It is the place of the Lord in the divine purpose which makes His gentleness so moving. Both the characteristics which the Lord claims for Himself in Mt. xi. 29 are claimed for Him here; and the words recorded in Mt. xi. 28–30 may be actually in S. Paul's mind (cf. Zech. ix. 9). But, as in viii. 9, he probably thinks chiefly of the Passion story (cf. Wisd. ii. 19), since it is the Passion of the Lord

that he regards himself as sharing (ii. 15, 16; iv. 10, 11). Cf. xiii. 3, 4.

in your presence...toward you. This was, of course, the taunt of S. Paul's enemies. His reply is that he is but following his Master. The Lord too was gentle, when face to face with His enemies; but He warned them, as S. Paul is doing, of impending judgment, if they did not repent.

2. *I count to be bold.* i.e. I reckon upon being bold.

some, which count of us...the flesh. To whom does S. Paul refer ? Two things should be noticed: (*a*) The indefinite "some" (better "certain people") suggests that he is not referring to the Corinthians. (*b*) On the other hand, the appeal of the verse presupposes that it depends upon the action of the Corinthians whether S. Paul has to act sternly or not. It is probably this consideration which leads so many to

3 to the flesh. For though we walk in the flesh, we do not
4 war according to the flesh (for the weapons of our warfare
are not of the flesh, but mighty before God to the casting
5 down of strong holds); casting down [1]imaginations, and
every high thing that is exalted against the knowledge of
God, and bringing every thought into captivity to the
6 obedience of Christ; and being in readiness to avenge all

[1] Or, *reasonings*

suppose that the Corinthians are intended, and so to find the last four chapters of the Epistle inconsistent with the restored good relations presupposed in the earlier chapters. But there is no real difficulty. S. Paul's opponents, the Pharisaic mission from Jerusalem, are either present at Corinth, or likely to return to it. They are not S. Paul's spiritual children; and, as long as they do not interfere with those who are, they are outside his jurisdiction (cf. Gal. ii. 9). But, if they pervert a Church under his authority, or in any way interfere with his apostolic mission, the situation is changed. He must act both against them, and against any who may support them. They maintain that he walks "after the flesh," i.e. that he has no apostolic position, or apostolic powers, but is simply following his own sweet will: he will shew them the contrary. Thus our first impression that the "certain people" are not Corinthians is correct, and quite consistent with the appeal which the verse contains. Whether or not S. Paul will have to act against the Pharisaic mission depends upon the attitude adopted towards it by the Corinthians themselves.

3. *For though we walk in the flesh*. S. Paul has recognized this in the fullest way (iv. 7 ff.), and will recognize it again (xii. 5-10). But

human weakness in no way implies lack of apostolic power.

4. *mighty before God.* Better, either "mighty for God," or (as Moffatt) "divinely strong." The latter suits the context best.

to the casting down of strong holds. The strong fortresses of the enemy are not avoided, or masked, but destroyed. See the fuller note below.

5. *imaginations.* Better, as R.V. margin, "reasonings." The Pharisees were not dreamers; they had arguments of much force to urge.

high thing, "towering structure." The Jewish nationalist claims may be in view.

against the knowledge of God. The conflict was one of specious argument versus spiritual experience—a conflict which frequently arises.

every thought into captivity...of Christ. The fullest victory lies not in silencing, but in convincing. The best way to "stop the mouths" of "those of the circumcision" (Tit. i. 11) was so to bring their minds and wills beneath the yoke of Christ, that they would no longer wish to open their mouths against the truth.

6. *in readiness...disobedience.* Better "being equipped for the punishment of all disobedience." S. Paul speaks, not of his own resolution, but of the apostolic powers of the Spirit present in him to carry it out.

disobedience, when your obedience shall be fulfilled.

when your obedience shall be ful-filled. Cf. ii. 9. The earlier chapters, as well as the last four, presuppose that the Corinthian obedience is not yet perfect, though S. Paul can be "in everything of good courage" (vii. 16). Cf. Introduction, pp. xxxix ff.

The apparent contradiction of the first clause of this verse by the second is to be explained by an important principle. The right exercise of spiritual discipline is only possible in a church, which as a whole wel-comes it, and is ready to support it. Cf. 1 Cor. v. 2–5. Modern demands for the exercise of discipline in the Church of England often ignore this.

Of what character were the weapons of S. Paul's warfare to which he here refers? That they were "supernatural" powers, divinely bestowed upon S. Paul as an Apostle for the carrying out of his apostolic work, is obvious from his words ; and it was, of course, "the Spirit" Who bestowed them. But were they purely "spiritual," in the sense which we give to that word to-day, or did they include such powers as are illustrated by Ac. v. 1–11 ; xiii. 8–11 ; and above all by 1 Cor. v. 3–5 ? Almost certainly S. Paul thinks of them as including the latter (cf. 1 Cor. iv. 21 and xiii. 2–4 of this Epistle). Modern psychology may suggest to us an explanation of these powers different from that which S. Paul himself would have given ; but that the Apostles possessed them can hardly be doubted. Face to face at Corinth with the leader of the Pharisaic mission, S. Paul would probably have acted much as he did at Paphos. But that, as *v.* 6 suggests, would only have been in the last resort. S. Paul began by dealing with the "reasonings" of the Pharisees. He met their case point by point, as he meets it in the Epistles to the Romans and the Galatians, and in this Epistle. He proved the reality of his own apostleship ; he shewed that the O.T., rightly interpreted, was on his side ; and he appealed to "the know-ledge of God," the spiritual experience of the Gentile Christians, as con-clusively demonstrating that non-observance of the law was compatible with the very highest Christian character and power (cf. e.g. Ac. xv. 7–11 ; Gal. iii. 1–6). In a word, he turned his batteries upon every one of the "forts" in which the Pharisees placed their confidence, and laid them in ruins. "In demonstration of the Spirit and of power" (1 Cor. ii. 4) he did every-thing possible to bring the minds and consciences of all who would listen to him into obedience to the mind of the great Christ, Who came to save His people from their sins by the gift of the same Spirit as that by which S. Paul himself spoke. But, if all this failed—if the Pharisees, like their forefathers (Ac. vii. 51), obstinately "resisted the Holy Ghost" for no better reasons than national pride and fear of persecution at the hands of their unbelieving fellow-countrymen (Gal. vi. 12)—S. Paul would have shewn them very plainly that he had other powers in reserve than those of argu-ment, and would, in the last resort, have defended the faith of his converts by strong punitive action just as "spiritual" in the true sense of the word as his speech. S. Paul was no rose-water Apostle ; and he would have known, not the word of the puffed up, but the power (1 Cor. iv. 19) of discipline which the Spirit gave to him.

7 [1]Ye look at the things that are before your face. If any
mantrusteth in himself that he is Christ's, let him consider
this again with himself, that, even as he is Christ's, so also
8 are we. For though I should glory somewhat abundantly
concerning our authority (which the Lord gave for building
you up, and not for casting you down), I shall not be put
9 to shame: that I may not seem as if I would terrify you
10 by my letters. For, His letters, they say, are weighty and
strong; but his bodily presence is weak, and his speech of

[1] Or, *Do ye look...face?*

7. *the things that are before your
face.* i.e. the outward appearances of
things, such as S. Paul's own apparent weakness. But Moffatt's
translation "Look at this obvious
fact" may be right.

trusteth in himself. Cf. 1 Cor. i.
12, which suggests that the Pharisaic
party claimed to be the party "of
Christ," and their leaders Christ's
representatives.

consider this again with himself.
Second thoughts are best. The Pharisees denied the apostolic position
of S. Paul and the equality of his
Gentile converts with Jewish Christians.

8. *though I should glory.* Better
"though I may glory." S. Paul speaks
of what he intends to do, and indeed
has already begun to do.

which the Lord gave. When i.e. he
called me to be His Apostle. The
purpose is a purpose of blessing;
and, even when for the time the
authority is used for stern discipline,
the purpose of blessing remains the
ultimate purpose. Cf. once more
1 Cor. v. 5, and in the same Epistle
xi. 30–32.

I shall not be put to shame. i.e.
by lack of spiritual power to make
good my words.

9. *terrify you by my letters.* The

charge was that the letters were only
an effort to scare those who opposed
him.

10. *they say.* The better reading
is "he says," the reference being to
the leader of the mission of the
Pharisees. The same person is
referred to as "such a one" in
v. 11, but we do not know who he
was.

*his bodily presence...speech of no
account.* For the meaning of "presence," cf. note on vii. 6. It is now
clear why S. Paul has laid so much
stress upon his bodily weakness, and
the divine purpose which it served.
It was urged that his infirmities
shewed that he was no divinely
blessed Apostle. The charge that
his "speech was of no account" probably meant that when he came to
Corinth he failed to make good his
bold words. They were "proved to
be of no account," and the Corinthians were "not to be afraid of
him" (cf. Deut. xviii. 21, 22). A reference to S. Paul's "rudeness of
speech" is less appropriate here.
The charge of "bluff," if we may use
the word in this connexion, was the
more plausible, because S. Paul had
not vindicated his authority at the
time of his painful visit. Cf. Introduction, pp. xxxv f. The reason why he

11 no account. Let such a one reckon this, that, what we are
in word by letters when we are absent, such *are we* also in
12 deed when we are present. For we are not bold [1] to number
or compare ourselves with certain of them that commend
themselves: but they themselves, measuring themselves by
themselves, and comparing themselves with themselves,
13 are without understanding. But we will not glory beyond

[1] Gr. *to judge ourselves among,* or *to judge ourselves with.*

had not done so is shewn in the note
on *v.* 6.

11. *such are we.* Better "such
we shall be." Reckoning has to do
with the future.

12. *For we are not bold...compare
ourselves.* Better "we have not the
face to class or compare ourselves."
There is a slight play upon words
here, but it is scarcely worth while
to attempt to reproduce it in English.
Waite and Plummer suggest "pair
or compare," but there is no actual
pun in the Greek.

*measuring themselves...are with-
out understanding.* There is more
than sarcasm in this verse; there is
an ethical principle of the greatest
importance. The Pharisees took for
granted exactly the point at issue.
They assumed that the divine standard of righteousness was the Mosaic
law, as they had come to interpret
it. Their spiritual pride was due to
the fact that they judged themselves
simply by this standard, no Pharisee
comparing himself with anybody
except other Pharisees. Cf. our
Lord's criticism in Mt. xxiii. 23, 24.
S. Paul could in fact claim for himself all that they claimed (cf. xi. 22,
23; Phil. iii. 5, 6); but the law itself led him to die to the law (Gal.
ii. 19). Facing, as the Pharisees did
not, the real divine standard, he
found that it led him, not to self-

congratulation, but to self-despair;
and so was ready for the gospel of
redemption by the Cross. Cf. Rom.
vii. 7 ff. and ch. iii of this Epistle.
Again and again, self-satisfaction is
due to just such a blunder as that of
the Pharisees. The Roman Church,
to take one example, claims that
"authority" is only found in its fold.
Nowhere else can we all be told
exactly what we are to believe, and
exactly what we are to do. Quite so.
But the prior question which arises is
this: Is it in the least desirable for
our intellectual, spiritual, and moral
growth that we should submit to an
authority of this kind? If it is, the
Roman Church is undoubtedly the
place in which to find it. But is it?
It is noticeable that the MS. D, and
some early Latin versions, shorten
the text, and so greatly alter the
meaning. In the shorter text it is
S. Paul who measures himself by
himself, and judges himself by his
own standard. But this makes
S. Paul himself a Pharisee, and is
quite inconsistent with his real spirit
(cf. 1 Cor. iv. 1–5).

13–16. As so often in this Epistle,
S. Paul's drift is quite clear, but the
language most confused. He dictates
rapidly without thought of literary
exactness. The point is this: S. Paul
is the Apostle of the Gentiles, and
has been recognized as being so. Cf.

our measure, but according to the measure of the [1]province
which God apportioned to us as a measure, to reach even
14 unto you. For we stretch not ourselves overmuch, as
though we reached not unto you: for we [2]came even as
15 far as unto you in the gospel of Christ: not glorying beyond
our measure, *that is*, in other men's labours; but having
hope that, as your faith groweth, we shall be magnified in
you according to our [1]province unto *further* abundance,

[1] Or, *limit* Gr. *measuring-rod.*　　　　[2] Or, *were the first to come*

Gal. ii. 9, 10. The churches who
owe their Christianity under God to
him are under his jurisdiction. The
Pharisaic mission from Jerusalem is
a totally unjustified interference;
and the Pharisaic Christians would
be better employed in breaking new
ground for themselves.

13. *will not glory beyond our
measure.* Better perhaps "we"—
the word is emphatic—"will not
carry our glorying into regions beyond our allotted sphere."

*according to the measure...even
unto you.* It is for God to measure
out to each his appointed sphere of
labour; it is for the servant to keep
to the sphere appointed to him. The
Corinthians are within S. Paul's
sphere of apostolic activity, and
Corinth is the furthest point which
as yet he has reached. It is one
thing for a man to insist upon his
claims in dealing with those under
his jurisdiction; it is quite another
for him to carry his claims into
regions outside it.

14. *stretch not ourselves overmuch.* i.e. extend our claims too
far.

came even as far as unto you.
The translation of R.V. margin suits
the context, and is in accordance
with the use of the verb in classical
Greek: but that of the text is most
in accordance with later usage.

15. *not glorying beyond our
measure.* Translate as in *v.* 13.

that is, in other men's labours.
The insertion of our translators
"that is" is not only unnecessary,
but misleading. The phrase adds a
new point. The Pharisees are in-
truding, where another has done the
hard work.

magnified in you...abundance.
Again, the insertion of our R.V.
translators is pointless; and "overflow" is perhaps better than "abundance." The Gospel to the Gentiles
has been entrusted to S. Paul, and it
is creeping on westward like an in-
coming tide. But so closely is it
bound up with S. Paul himself, that
he uses metaphors of himself, which
seem more appropriate to the Gospel
which he is preaching. To understand the words "according to our
province," we must remember that
S. Paul's province was not geographical, but racial, and included Gentiles
at Rome as well as at Corinth. He
would only have gone beyond his
province, if he had betaken himself
to Jerusalem, and begun a campaign
there against the observance of the
law. Contrast his real action in Ac.
xxi. 17–26. Apparently he went so
far as to pay for sacrifices in the
Temple. How great a contrast with
the action of the Pharisees at Corinth
and elsewhere!

16 so as to preach the gospel even unto the parts beyond you,
   and not to glory in another's ¹province in regard of things
17 ready to our hand. But he that glorieth, let him glory in
18 the Lord. For not he that commendeth himself is approved,
   but whom the Lord commendeth.

¹ Or, *limit* Gr. *measuring-rod.*

16. Cf. Rom. xv. 24, 28. Rome is already in view, and Spain beyond.

things ready to our hand. The point is once more that the Pharisees are interfering with the work of another, instead of evangelizing on their own account.

17. A favourite text with S. Paul. Cf. 1 Cor. i. 31. The two verses Jer. ix. 23, 24 should be carefully read, if we would understand rightly that "glorying" of S. Paul, which might otherwise offend us. His glorying is always in God—in the personal and sanctifying knowledge gained of Him through Christ, and being extended to the world (cf. *v.* 5)— in the manifestation of His "loving-kindness, judgement, and righteousness in the earth" by His vindication of His Son by the Resurrection, and of His people by the gift of the Holy Ghost.

18. Again, we must remember that God's commendation or justification is practical. The words are not an appeal against the Pharisees to the unseen bar of God; but, as the coming chapters will shew, an appeal to facts.

approved. Better "accepted."

S. Paul's attack upon the mission from the Pharisees as an unwarrantable intrusion into his own sphere of labour, and his suggestion that they would be much better employed in doing missionary work themselves, were no doubt justified. But we must none the less remember that the Concordat of Gal. iii. 9, 10 was most difficult to work, just because "the circumcision" was so widely distributed in the Gentile world. S. Paul found Jews in almost every city that he visited, and he could only reach the Gentiles by beginning with the Jews, and going on to the Gentiles most closely associated with them. Moreover, Jewish Christians, who had derived their Christianity from the original Apostles, or even from other Jewish Christians of a more Pharisaic type, would frequently find themselves visiting "on their lawful occasions" churches founded by S. Paul. The Christians at Corinth who said "I of Cephas" (1 Cor. i. 12) are perhaps to be thus explained. On the other hand, Cornelius and his friends (Ac. x. 1–xi. 18) were not the only Gentiles in Palestine ready to receive the message of the Gospel. Thus, quite apart from the complications introduced by such casual evangelization as that described in Ac. xi. 19–21, the division of spheres arranged in the Concordat could only be treated as a rough geographical division rather than a racial one. But then this inevitably meant that, though the charge brought against S. Paul (Ac. xxi. 20, 21) was not true, it had a great deal of practical justification. S. Paul would have said that he never taught the Jews that were among the Gentiles to forsake

XI. 1 Would that ye could bear with me in a little foolish-
2 ness: ¹nay indeed bear with me. For I am jealous over

> ¹ Or, *but indeed ye do bear with me*

Moses (cf. Ac. xvi. 1–3); and that he not only regarded the observance of
the law by them as harmless, and perhaps even desirable, as long as they
did not regard it as the means of salvation (cf. Ac. xv. 11; Gal. ii. 15, 16),
but was quite willing himself to practise its observances (cf. Ac. xviii. 18 ;
xxi. 17–26 ; 1 Cor. ix. 20). But the fact remained that he regarded Moses
and the law in a way very different from that in which the Pharisaic Christians regarded them—what would they have thought of ch. iii of this
Epistle?—and that to teach that the fullest Christian status and blessing
were compatible with the non-observance of the law was in effect to
encourage Jews as well as Gentiles not to observe it. There was probably
among the Jews of the Dispersion a good deal of "Liberal" Judaism of
various types. Quite apart from S. Paul many of them were disposed to
sit loosely to the law; and very many of those who became Christians would
almost certainly cease to trouble themselves about it. The truth is that
though Concordats may help to tide over times of difficulty, questions of
principle must always sooner or later be fought to a finish. To take a modern
example, the acceptance of the Papal claims either is necessary to membership in the Catholic Church, or it is not. We cannot say "You must accept
them, if you live in France; and you are heretical, or schismatic, if you do
not. But if you live in England or Russia, you must acquiesce in their
rejection, and you are a schismatic if you do not":

> Caelum, non animum, mutant qui trans mare currunt.

And what about the new world, or the mission field ? Is the position of one
body of Christians permanently Catholic, and that of another permanently
schismatic, because one ship sailed a little faster than another, and reached
a particular country a few days in advance. The "comity of missions" is a
very good thing; and, with the wide world before us, we should interfere
one with another as little as may be; but in the long run, in all matters of
real importance, there is no way out of our difficulties except by being
through the Spirit of God "perfected together in the same mind and in the
same judgement" (1 Cor. i. 10).

XI. 1. *a little foolishness.* This
word, and the corresponding adjective, will appear again and again (xi.
16, 17, 19, 21 ; xii. 6, 11). It is possible,
as has been suggested, that S. Paul's
enemies had spoken of his "foolishness"—perhaps in relation to his self-
commendation—and that the word
had stung him. But, in view of xi. 17,
23, and xii. 11, it is more probable

that he is not thinking of any special
taunt, but speaking as he feels. He
is about to say a good deal not apparently consistent with the great
maxim of x. 17.

nay indeed bear with me. This
translation is certainly to be preferred to that of R.V. margin, which
is hardly consistent with the first
clause of the verse.

you with [1]a godly jealousy : for I espoused you to one husband, that I might present you *as* a pure virgin to
3 Christ. But I fear, lest by any means, as the serpent beguiled Eve in his craftiness, your [2]minds should be corrupted from the simplicity and the purity that is toward
4 Christ. For if he that cometh preacheth another Jesus, whom we did not preach, or *if* ye receive a different spirit, which ye did not receive, or a different gospel, which ye

---

[1] Gr. *a jealousy of God.* [2] Gr. *thoughts.*

---

2. *a godly jealousy.* A feeble and inaccurate translation. S. Paul says "with God's jealousy." All love involves jealousy, if its exclusive claim is set aside. Jealousy is right or wrong, according as the exclusive claim is right or wrong. The divine jealousy is a thing wholly right, since our Creator and Redeemer has a claim over us peculiarly His own. It is this jealousy which S. Paul shares. A Church which looks partly to Christ, and partly to the law, can be no true bride for Christ. "Hoc versu et seq. exprimitur causa insipientiae," says Bengel; "amantes enim videntur amentes."

espoused you to one husband. Better "betrothed you."

that I might present you as... Christ. The words "you as" are not in the Greek and are quite unnecessary. According to the Rabbis, Moses was the paranymph who presented Israel to God as His bride. Cf. Jn. iii. 29. Those who arranged the marriage of a girl were responsible for her conduct from the betrothal to the wedding day. S. Paul uses the symbol of marriage freely of the relation of Christ to the Church, as the O.T. uses it of the relation of Yahweh to Israel; and, just because the union begins now, but awaits consummation at the Second Coming,

the Church here and now can be regarded either as the wife of Christ (Rom. vii. 4; Eph. vi. 23, 24), or as His betrothed. It is noticeable that in Rom. vii. 1–4 the thought of a certain rivalry between Christ and the law appears, and a similar thought may here be in the background. The main thought of this verse has already appeared in ch. ii. 14.

3. *beguiled Eve in his craftiness.* Eve was beguiled; Adam sinned with a high hand. Cf. 1 Tim. ii. 14. This identification of Satan with the serpent, which is probably found also in Rom. xvi. 20, first appears in Wisd. ii. 24. S. Paul is not blaming the Corinthians, but warning them of a danger in which they stand. There must be no divided allegiance. The Church's trust and devotion belong to Christ alone; not in part to Him, and in part to the law.

4. A difficult verse. (*a*) Who is meant by "he that cometh"? Is it the leader of the Pharisaic mission, or is it a generic term? The Corinthians were only too disposed to listen to any teacher who came to them. (*b*) Does S. Paul imply that the newcomer does preach another Jesus, and bring a different Spirit and a different Gospel, or that the newcomer has in fact nothing to offer but what S. Paul himself has already

5 did not accept, ye do well to bear with *him*. For I reckon
that I am not a whit behind [1]the very chiefest apostles.

[1] Or, *those pre-eminent apostles*

brought? (*c*) Is the last clause of the
verse a simple and direct statement,
or is it sarcastic? (*d*) Is the object
to be supplied to the verb "him" or
"me"? The following solutions seem
to be the best: (*a*) "He that cometh"
is the leader of the Pharisaic mission,
the rather magniloquent phrase being
quoted by S. Paul from his opponents,
or used by him with a touch of sarcasm. The issue has been too directly
joined for generalities to be in place.
(*b*) S. Paul regards his chief opponent
as really offering a different religion.
It is true that, historically speaking,
both preached the same Jesus, and
that both presumably offered the
same Spirit, and the same Gospel of
the Kingdom. Had the new teachers
taught a different doctrine of the
Lord's Person, S. Paul would have
dealt with it. But to S. Paul the
issues raised by the Judaizers were
so vital, that he felt the whole truth
of the Gospel to be at stake. No one
familiar with the Epistle to the
Galatians will think it likely that he
would have been content to urge that
his opponents had nothing fresh to
offer. Cf. Gal. i. 6–9; v. 2–4. (*c*) The
last clause has a touch of sarcasm,
and anticipates *v.* 20. Translate "ye
bear with him well enough," or "ye
put up with it well enough." This
is the only charge which S. Paul
makes against the Corinthians. He
feels, as will soon appear, that they
are not as ardently on his side as
they ought to be. The Corinthians,
he would say, bear well enough with
what is really destructive of the
Gospel; it is not much to ask that

they should bear with him in a little
"folly." (*d*) We thus follow the R.V.
in supplying "him." The real extent
of the difference between S. Paul's
Gospel and that of the Pharisaic
Christians will be discussed below.

Two slight points may be observed
in this verse: (*a*) The R.V. rightly
distinguishes between the Greek
words for "another" and "a different." In speaking of the historic
Jesus there would be far less difference between S. Paul and the
Pharisaic Christians than in speaking
of the Spirit and of the Gospel.
(*b*) The Spirit is "received"; the
Gospel is "accepted." The heart and
will of man must cooperate with
God in receiving the Gospel and
acting upon it, but not in receiving
the Spirit. That is simply a divine
gift, though we must respond to it
after its reception.

5. *For I reckon.* If the previous
verse has been rightly understood,
the verse gives a reason for the Corinthians being as patient with S. Paul's
"folly" as with his opponents' false
teaching.

the very chiefest apostles. R.V.
margin is probably right—"those
only too apostolic persons." Cf. *vv.* 13,
20. S. Paul certainly claimed an
apostleship as authoritative as that
of the Twelve; but it is not likely
that he refers to them here. It is
true that he speaks of them somewhat cavalierly in Gal. ii. 6; but
S. Peter's inconsistency at Antioch
was then fresh in his recollection
(cf. Gal. ii. 11 ff.). Here we should
rather expect him, if he referred to

6 But though *I be* rude in speech, yet *am I* not in know-
　ledge; nay, in everything we have made *it* manifest among
7 all men to you-ward. Or did I commit a sin in abasing
　myself that ye might be exalted, because I preached to
8 you the gospel of God for nought? I robbed other churches,
9 taking wages *of them* that I might minister unto you; and
　when I was present with you and was in want, I was not
　a burden on any man; for the brethren, when they came

them at all, to lay stress upon his
union with them, and the clear recognition, which they had afforded to
him. Not only S. Peter and S. John,
but even S. James of Jerusalem had
accepted fully S. Paul's Gospel and
his mission to the Gentiles. Cf. Gal.
ii. 6–10, and Ac. xv. 7–11; 14–29.

6. *rude in speech...knowledge.*
The point is that though he has no
special qualifications as a speaker, he
has the very highest as a teacher;
and has fully proved it in the face of
the world by his work among the
Corinthians. Cf. ch. iii. 2, 3. The
best commentary on this verse is
found in 1 Cor. ii, and in our own
experience as students of S. Paul,
perhaps especially in this Epistle.
The depth and power of S. Paul's
teaching is most wonderful; and
there are places where the beauty of
the thought seems to force the expression into conformity with it (cf.
e.g. 1 Cor. xiii). But it is not so as
a rule. S. Paul lacks both the power
of logical arrangement, and that of
lucid expression. His sentences are
often far too long, and he loses his
way in them. As a writer, he is not
to be compared with the author of
the Epistle to the Hebrews, or even
with S. Luke, S. Peter, or S. James.
But what he says of the weakness of
his body is equally true of the rough-
ness of his style. The treasure is in

an earthen vessel, that the exceeding
greatness of the power may be of
God, and not from him. S. Paul
was the greatest Evangelist and
teacher of the Church, while the
Greek rhetoricians merely pleased
the ear, and effected nothing. Cf. Ac.
iv. 13. But the point there probably
is that the Apostles lacked the proper equipment of a Rabbi; and this
S. Paul possessed. His learning
could not be denied. Cf. Ac. xxvi.
24.

7. The whole of this passage
should be read with the words of
v. 12 in our minds. S. Paul is not
primarily answering the attacks of
the Corinthians upon him, but the
attacks of the Pharisees, and shewing
the Corinthians how to deal with
them. It is the failure to observe
this which leads so many to suppose
that the last chapters belong to an
earlier Epistle. The charge which
S. Paul is here answering probably
is that he has set aside the Lord's
command, which the Twelve followed.
Cf. Mt. x. 10; Luk. x. 7; 1 Cor. ix.
4, 5, 12.

8. *I robbed other churches.* Cf.
Phil. iv. 10, 13. The robbery con-
sisted in taking wages from other
churches for ministering to the
Corinthians.

9. *and was in want.* "Ran short,"
as we should say.

from Macedonia, supplied the measure of my want; and in
everything I kept myself from being burdensome unto you,
10 and *so* will I keep *myself*. As the truth of Christ is in me,
no man shall stop me of this glorying in the regions of
11 Achaia. Wherefore? because I love you not? God knoweth.
12 But what I do, that I will do, that I may cut off ¹occasion
from them which desire an occasion; that wherein they
13 glory, they may be found even as we. For such men are
false apostles, deceitful workers, fashioning themselves
14 into apostles of Christ. And no marvel; for even Satan
15 fashioneth himself into an angel of light. It is no great
thing therefore if his ministers also fashion themselves as

¹ Gr. *the occasion of them.*

supplied the measure of my want.
A very obscure translation. Better
"did more, and made up my de-
ficiency." The Greek word seems to
speak of an additional gift. S. Paul
came to Corinth, with supplies provided by the Macedonians for a short
visit. Silas and Timothy brought
him a further supply from the same
source (Ac. xviii. 5). We have here
a good example of those "undesigned
coincidences" between the Acts and
the Epistles, which Paley brought
out in his *Horae Paulinae*.

10. *no man shall stop me.* The
R.V. paraphrase misses the point;
no one was attempting to stop him.
S. Paul merely expresses his intention
to continue in his chosen course.
"This glorying shall not be barred
to me."

11. "Saepe laeditur amor," says
Bengel, "etiam recusando." The
true answer to the question here
asked will be discussed below.

12. This verse was probably less
obscure to the Corinthians than to
us. It is best translated, with
Plummer, "that I may cut off occasion from those who wish for an
occasion of being found, in the

matter wherein they glory, on a level
with us." The Pharisaic teachers
accepted maintenance from the
Corinthians (*v.* 20) as apostolic
teachers, and would have liked
S. Paul to do the same.

13. The Jewish teachers evidently
claimed in some sense the title of
Apostles. Cf. *v.* 5. Probably they
had the same kind of commission
from some Jewish-Christian com-
munity as S. Paul and S. Barnabas
had from the Church of Antioch
(Ac. xiii. 1–3). Cf. iii. 1. They may
even, like the Twelve and S. Paul,
have seen the Risen Lord (1 Cor.
xv. 6).

14. *fashioneth himself into an
angel of light.* Cornelius a Lapide
has a collection of stories of Satan's
doing this; and evidently the Jews
had them also. It is as an angel that
Satan appears to Eve in the Apocalypse of Moses xvii, and S. Paul
both here and in *v.* 3 may have this
story in view. The story of our
Lord's Temptation may even have
been interpreted in this way. It is
possible, but not likely, that S. Paul
is simply employing a metaphor.

15. *his ministers.* They are doing

ministers of righteousness; whose end shall be according
to their works.

the work of the Accuser, and of the
Tempter; the one to S. Paul, the
other to the Corinthians.
ministers of righteousness. This

they no doubt claimed to be as
ministers of the law. S. Paul has
dealt with this claim in advance in
ch. iii.

The attitude of S. Paul to the Pharisaic mission, and the violence of his
denunciation, will be considered at a later stage. But two points have come
up in this last section whose connexion with the Pharisaic mission is
obscure; and it may be well to say something about them here. The first
is S. Paul's rudeness of speech; the second is his refusal to accept support
from the Corinthians. We find much reference to both in the First Epistle
also. For the rudeness of speech cf. 1 Cor. ii. 1–5, and for the refusal 1 Cor.
ix. 3–18. It is possible, as we shall see, that there was a connexion between
them.

We notice, first, that, in refusing to accept support from the Corinthians
in the earliest stage of his work among them, S. Paul was only doing what
it was natural that he should do. When the Lord first sent out the Apostles
into the towns and villages of Galilee, he was sending them to members of
the Church of God (cf. Mt. x. 5, 6). The people of God were expecting the
coming of the Kingdom, and the signs and wonders were to be interpreted
as the first drops of the coming torrent of blessing (Mt. x. 7, 8). It was
only to be expected of the people of God that they should welcome the
messengers of the Kingdom, and feel it an honour to entertain them (Mt. x.
9–13); unbelief and rejection would bring destruction in the coming judgment, by which the Kingdom would be ushered in (Mt. x. 14, 15). In this case
to say that the labourer was worthy of his food (Mt. x. 10; cf. Luk. x. 7) was
to say what was obviously true, and the Lord told His messengers to ask for
support at the hands of those to whom He sent them. But when S. Paul
went to the heathen world, the situation was altogether different. The
Jews of the Dispersion themselves probably had not their minds as much
fixed upon "the kingdom" as the Jews of Palestine, and the Gentile world
was not expecting it at all. Why should Gentiles support the preacher of
a new and unwelcome religion? We do not expect the heathen to support
our missionaries to-day. Thus there was nothing remarkable in the fact
that when S. Paul first preached the Gospel at Corinth, he in part supported
himself by his own labour, and in part was supported by his Macedonian
converts. He had acted in the same way at Thessalonica, and presumably
everywhere else. Cf. 1 Th. ii. 9; iii. 8. When however the Gospel had been
accepted, and a Christian Church had come into being, it was only right
that S. Paul should receive help from his converts; and, though it is only
in the case of Philippi that we have detailed information about the help
given to him (Phil. iv. 10–18), *v.* 8 of the chapter before us shews that the
case of Philippi was not exceptional. S. Paul was fully aware of our Lord's
teaching (1 Cor. ix. 14), of the practice of the older preachers of the Gospel

(1 Cor. ix. 5), and of the obvious justifications for that practice (1 Cor. ix. 7–14). Why then was it that at Corinth, where his stay was a long one, and where he continued to live after the church of Corinth had come into existence, he steadily refused to accept the maintenance to which he declared his right? Why did he, as he puts it, rob other churches poorer than the Corinthian, in order to avoid taking money from it? He gives two reasons: one, which he explains in 1 Cor. ix. 16–18 (see notes there), and another, which had to do with the success of the work itself. "We bear all things," he says, "that we may cause no hindrance to the gospel of Christ" (1 Cor. ix. 12). "What I do, that I will do, that I may cut off occasion from them which desire an occasion" (2 Cor. xi. 12). Now it is here that we find the difficulty. Why did S. Paul think that to take money from Corinthian Christians would be a hindrance to the Gospel? It was surely in itself a great waste of his time to spend it in making tents with Aquila and Priscilla; his action was, as he recognizes, straining the resources of his beloved Macedonians; and it is not as a rule at all desirable that Christians should be relieved from the duty of supporting their pastors. In the English Church, where partly owing to ancient endowments, and partly owing to the number of clergy who possess "private means," this freedom on the part of the laity is common, it works evil rather than good. It tends to make the clergy too autocratic, and the laity slack and uninterested in what is going on. Even at Corinth, the very way in which S. Paul speaks of his practice shews that it was criticized, and led to some amount of misunderstanding. Why then, we ask again, did he persist in this "work of supererogation," as he himself in 1 Cor. ix. 16–18 describes it as being?

May it not be possible that we find a clue in the transition, apparently so abrupt, from *v.* 6 in this chapter to *v.* 7? It is only in the Epistles to the Corinthians that S. Paul dwells upon his own rudeness of speech, and only there that he dwells at any length upon his financial arrangements. Corinth was a home of rhetoric; professional sophists and rhetoricians abounded there. Was it perhaps necessary for S. Paul, not only to dwell upon the difference between his manner of speech and theirs (cf. 1 Thess. ii. 5 ff.), but to mark his difference from them by steadily refusing the remuneration which they demanded and received? This suggestion is probably incapable of proof, but it fits well enough the data of this chapter. In attacking S. Paul's apostolic position, the Pharisees evidently made capital both out of S. Paul's deficiencies as a speaker, which, they maintained, threw doubt upon his commission; and out of his refusal to be supported by the Corinthians, which, they maintained, threw doubt upon his own belief in it. The two points were only two out of many, and yet the mention of the one seems at once to lead S. Paul to think of the other, and to pour out his heart about it. Again, this suggestion explains *v.* 12. Obviously, the emissaries of the Pharisees, coming as they did to interfere with S. Paul's churches, occupied an invidious position. They themselves (*v.* 20) evidently did ask for support. If S. Paul had been receiving regular support from the Corinthians, he would have been on a level with them. As we have seen, S. Paul's action laid him open to their criticism, but that criticism was at

16 I say again, Let no man think me foolish; but if *ye do*,
    yet as foolish receive me, that I also may glory a little.
17 That which I speak, I speak not after the Lord, but as in
18 foolishness, in this confidence of glorying. Seeing that
19 many glory after the flesh, I will glory also. For ye bear
20 with the foolish gladly, being wise *yourselves*. For ye bear
    with a man, if he bringeth you into bondage, if he devoureth
    you, if he taketh you *captive*, if he exalteth himself, if he

best a *pis aller*. They would immeasurably have preferred to charge him
with working for what he could get.

XI. 16–33. S. Paul's purpose in this section of the Epistle is twofold.
First, he desires to emphasize the contrast between his own sufferings and
the lack of suffering in the lives of his opponents as constituting a great
appeal to the heart of the Corinthians. He has all that his opponents can
claim, and the glory of the Cross beside. Secondly, he desires to urge that
his sufferings are the signs of the reality of his apostleship. No one can in
the deepest sense represent the Lord but he who has been by suffering
conformed to the Lord. This thought has already been anticipated in
ii. 14–16; iv. 7–10; vi. 4–10.

16. Cf. note on *v.* 1. Even a fool
may ask for a hearing.

17. *not after the Lord.* i.e. not
according to His example and teaching, e.g. in Luk. xviii. 14.

in this confidence of glorying.
Better, perhaps, "in this basis of
glorying." If S. Paul is at all un-
wise, it is not in being confident in
the strength of his position, but in
basing his claim in part upon facts
that possess no spiritual significance.

18. *many...flesh.* To glory after
the flesh is to take advantages of
this world as the foundation for our
satisfaction with ourselves. The reference in the word "many" is
primarily, but not exclusively, to the
Pharisaic teachers. Cf. Gal. vi. 14,
which expresses a great principle
recognized in this chapter from *v.* 23
onward, but not in *v.* 22.

19. The word for "gladly" comes
first in the Greek, and is emphatic.
For the irony, cf. 1 Cor. iv. 10;

viii. 1. There is such a thing as a
"patient" listener, whose patience is
more insulting than any violence of
opposition. His "patience" means
—and at its worst is intended to
mean—that his wisdom and knowledge are so obviously far above
those of the man who is speaking to
him, that he cannot be affected by
anything which the latter may say.
When, as in the case of the Corinthians, there is a good deal of knowledge, but little development of insight or of character, this kind of
patience is apt to flourish. Anger,
on the other hand, implies some
measure of respect.

20. A characteristic example of
the way in which S. Paul "goes off
at a tangent." This verse is not a
logical development of the previous
one, the new example of undesirable
patience being wholly unlike the old.
A little more self-respect on the
part of the Corinthians in dealing

21 smiteth you on the face. I speak by way of disparagement, as though we had been weak. Yet whereinsoever any is 22 bold (I speak in foolishness), I am bold also. Are they Hebrews? so am I. Are they Israelites? so am I. Are 23 they the seed of Abraham? so am I. Are they ministers of Christ? (I speak as one beside himself) I more; in labours more abundantly, in prisons more abundantly, in stripes 24 above measure, in deaths oft. Of the Jews five times received

with the new teachers was much to be desired. They allowed themselves to be brought into abject slavery (Gal. ii. 4), to be eaten out of house and home (Luk. xx. 47), to be caught like birds in a snare (xii. 16); they put up with the airs of their new teachers, and even with personal violence. Cf. 1 Kgs. xxii. 24; Mt. xxiii. 15; Ac. xxiii. 2. Here, again, the anger of S. Paul is much less with the Corinthians than with those who were injuring them.

21. *I speak...been weak.* Moffatt's paraphrase probably gives the true sense: "I am quite ashamed to say I was not equal to that sort of thing." Cf. x. 10, 12.

22. There is not much distinction to be drawn between "Hebrews," "Israelites," and "seed of Abraham." The new teachers rang the changes upon all the titles of the people of God. But the word "Hebrews" may mean that the Apostle, like his opponents, was a Jew, whose ordinary language was Aramaic, and not a Hellenist (cf. Phil. iii. 5; Ac. xxi. 40; xxii. 2). "Israelites" is the word for the Jews regarded as a sacred people (Rom. ix. 3, 4), while "seed of Abraham" introduces the thought of the promises made to him. S. Paul in this verse uses words in the sense which his opponents attached to them; we should not here take account of his doctrine

of the Church as the true Israel (Gal. vi. 16). As a man of Tarsus he may have been represented as a half-Gentile, just as the Lord was charged with being a Samaritan (Jn. viii. 48), and for the same reason, his criticism of his fellow-countrymen.

23. *I more.* i.e. I am more a minister of Christ than they, not I am more than a minister of Christ. "Quo quisque plus patitur," says Bengel, "eo magis ministrat." The Acts tells us of five imprisonments of S. Paul; Clement of Rome tells us of seven (1 Ep. Cor. v).

24. These flagellations by the Jews are not mentioned elsewhere; but we must remember them, if we are rightly to understand S. Paul's relations with his fellow-countrymen. Cf. Deut. xxv. 1–3; Mt. x. 17; Jn. xvi. 2. S. Paul was probably ex-communicated—a punishment which sometimes led, not only to exclusion from social intercourse, but to beating, and the confiscation of property (cf. Phil. iii. 8). Had he been willing to appeal to the Romans against his own countrymen, he would almost certainly, as a Roman citizen, have escaped this suffering; but he was too loyal a Jew for this. Cf. his apology for appealing to Caesar in Ac. xxviii. 19. The beautiful reason given for the limitation of punish-ment in Deut xxv. 3 is most notice-

25 I forty *stripes* save one. Thrice was I beaten with rods,
once was I stoned, thrice I suffered shipwreck, a night and
26 a day have I been in the deep; *in* journeyings often, *in*
perils of rivers, *in* perils of robbers, *in* perils from *my*
[1]countrymen, *in* perils from the Gentiles, *in* perils in the
city, *in* perils in the wilderness, *in* perils in the sea, *in* perils
27 among false brethren; *in* labour and travail, in watchings
often, in hunger and thirst, in fastings often, in cold and

[1] Gr. *race.*

able. We may punish, but never
contemn (1 Pet. ii. 17); an erring
brother is still a brother. Unjust
and excessive punishment is a con-
temptuous denial of brotherhood,
and increases the contempt from
which it proceeds. The forty stripes
permitted were reduced to thirty-
nine from fear that they might be
miscounted.

25. To beat with rods was a
Roman method of punishment; and
we might expect to find it only at
Roman colonies such as Antioch in
Pisidia, Lystra, and Philippi, or at
the great seats of Roman jurisdiction
such as Ephesus, Thessalonica, and
Corinth itself. S. Luke, who writes
for the Roman world, and perhaps
makes the best of the Roman magis-
trates, has only recorded the beating
at Philippi (Ac. xvi. 22, 23, 37),
where S. Paul came triumphantly
out of his ordeal. But he worked
after his conversion in Syria and
Cilicia (Ac. xi. 25; Gal. i. 21); and
the subject princes, Antiochus of
Commagene and Polemon of Cilicia,
are not unlikely to have used Roman
methods.

once was I stoned. At Lystra. Cf.
Ac. xiv. 19.

thrice...in the deep. Of these
shipwrecks we know nothing, that of
Ac. xxvii being of course later.
When S. Paul gave his advice in Ac.

xxvii. 10, 11, he did not speak without experience. The tense employed
in the last clause of this verse may
suggest that the occurrence was
recent. It may have taken place
when S. Paul was either going to or
returning from Corinth. Cf. Introd.
pp. xxxv, xxxvi.

26. Orientals have seldom our love
of adventure. S. Paul, unlike many
of ourselves, would have far preferred
to avoid all these dangers. Both
robbers and rivers in flood were
common in many districts where he
travelled. Though his period was
the best period of Roman rule in
Asia Minor, yet even then the roads
were not safe in mountainous districts, while the road from Derbe to
Tarsus passed through non-Roman
territory.

false brethren. Either Christians
unworthy of the name, or Jews
treacherously pretending to be
Christians. Cf. Gal. ii. 4.

27. Moffatt well paraphrases this
verse: "Through labour and hard-
ship, through many a sleepless night,
through hunger and thirst, starving
many a time, cold and ill-clad." But
A.V. and R.V. "fastings" is probably right, as something different
from natural hunger and thirst is
probably intended. Like the saints
of the O.T. and of after days, S. Paul
would fast to add power to his

28 nakedness. [1]Beside those things that are without, there
is that which presseth upon me daily, anxiety for all the
29 churches. Who is weak, and I am not weak? who is made
30 to stumble, and I burn not? If I must needs glory, I will
31 glory of the things that concern my weakness. The God
and Father of the Lord Jesus, he who is blessed [2]for ever-
32 more, knoweth that I lie not. In Damascus the governor
under Aretas the king guarded the city of the Damascenes,
33 in order to take me: and through a window was I let down
in a basket by the wall, and escaped his hands.

---

[1] Or, *Beside the things which I omit*   Or, *Beside the things that come out of*
course   [2] Gr. *unto the ages.*

prayers for his converts and for the whole Church. Cf. Ezr. viii. 21; Neh. i. 4; Est. iv. 16; Dan. ix. 3. Indeed his departure into Arabia after his conversion may well have been for a time of fasting and prayer, in imitation of Moses (Ex. xxiv. 18), Elijah (1 Kgs. xix. 8), and the Lord Himself. In the Bible the expression of sorrow, and the strengthening of prayer, are the purposes of fasting, rather than the discipline of the body. Cf. note on 1 Cor. ix. 27.

28. *things that are without.* The second marginal translation of R.V. makes the best sense. The exceptional troubles are contrasted with the daily burden of anxiety.

29. *and I burn not.* The "I" is emphatic in the Greek. The burning is probably with indignation. "Non solum ecclesias," says Bengel, "sed singulas animas curat." Cf. Gal. v. 12, where the Jewish mission is in view. S. Paul is so one with his converts that he bears the burden of their sorrows and sins. Cf. Myers, *S. Paul*:

Desperate tides of the whole great
     world's anguish
Forced through the channels of a
     single heart.

The fire that burns in these chapters is the fire of love, and not of any unworthy jealousy.

32, 33. These verses may be a gloss which has crept into the text. S. Paul is no master of rhetoric; but the bathos here is almost intolerable, the two previous verses having brought the recital of his sufferings to a natural close. If the words are his, they must have been added as an afterthought, the Apostle perhaps thinking of himself as reproducing the experience of the spies of Israel (Josh. ii. 15). The Arabian king Aretas and his successors are shewn by numismatic evidence to have probably been in possession of Damascus from A.D. 34 to A.D. 62. The ethnarch is evidently the resident governor. Aretas probably desired to stand well with the Jews. Thus S. Paul before his conversion could persecute the Christians at Damascus (Ac. ix. 2), while after it he was himself persecuted there. Cf. Ac. ix. 23-25. Such facts as these strikingly exhibit the truth of the N.T. story.

The contrast between the Spirit and the letter has already been considered. But the language of xi. 3 and 13 brings up once more the contrast between S. Paul's Gospel and that of his opponents at Corinth, and it is necessary more fully to consider it. There is a tendency to-day to reopen the old controversy, to regard the Pharisaic view as tenable, and S. Paul's theology as peculiarly his own. Judaizing Christianity is by no means dead; there is something very like it widely held among ourselves. Of late years, many of our best scholars have been chiefly occupied with the study of the Synoptic Gospels, and with the Lord as He is there revealed. Did S. Paul, it may be asked, who probably never saw or heard the Lord, rightly understand Him, or was He "another Jesus," nearer perhaps to the Judaizers than to S. Paul? What e.g. was our Lord's own teaching, as we find it in the Synoptic Gospels, about the law, about justification, and about the national claims of Israel?

We observe first that our Lord Himself undoubtedly observed the law. He believed it to come from God, and contrasted it with the tradition of men (Mk. vii. 8); and, though (like the best Jewish teachers) He recognized that some things which it contained were more important than others, He taught that the lesser commandments were to be kept as well as the greater (Mt. xxiii. 23, 24). Indeed in the Jewish Gospel of S. Matthew we find words which may easily be regarded as diametrically opposed to S. Paul's teaching (Mt. v. 17–20; xxiii. 2, 3; cf. Luk. xvi. 17, 18). S. Paul of course fully recognized that our Lord was "born under the law," and saw a providential purpose in the fact; here, as elsewhere, it was only by sharing our burden that the Lord was able to remove it from our shoulders (Gal. iv. 4, 5). But he certainly could not have admitted that the Lord had intended the law to be permanently binding upon His followers. But the truth seems to be that the Synoptic witness is misunderstood, when it is supposed to teach the permanent obligation of the law. Our Lord proclaimed the immediate coming of the Kingdom of God; and it was only until it came that He declared the law to be binding. The key to His meaning is found in the last words of Mt. v. 18—"till all things be accomplished" (cf. Luk. xvi. 16). The Kingdom will bring this accomplishment; and, when it comes, the old law and prophecy, like Moses and Elijah on the Mount of Transfiguration, will pass away, and leave "Jesus only" (Mk. ix. 8). The claims of the moral law will all be gathered up and perfected in the one great commandment of love, and the gift of the Holy Spirit will enable us to obey it (cf. Gal. v. 14; Rom. viii. 1–4); even the lesser ordinances, as yet "a shadow of the things to come" (Col. ii. 17), will find in Christian realities what they could only dimly suggest. But till the Kingdom comes, the old law stands; and must be obeyed with a deeper obedience than even the Scribes and Pharisees had given; there will be no entering the Kingdom otherwise (Mt. xix. 17). That, and no more, seems to be the Lord's teaching about the law in the Synoptic record. No doubt, He does not clearly distinguish between the first coming of the Kingdom in the gift of the Holy Ghost and its final coming at His return. But in relation to obedience to the law, that gift of the Holy Spirit, which is the earnest of the final Kingdom, is the one important matter; we find in the Spirit's teaching a better guide than the law could ever be; and thus, in relation to the claims of the law, God has already "translated us into the kingdom of the Son of his love" (Col. i. 13). S. Paul's attitude to the law is entirely faithful to his Master's. He had no objection to its observance by the Jews ; he was even willing to conform to its observance himself (Ac. xxi. 17-26 ; 1 Cor. ix. 20), if there were good reason ; but he could not admit that Christians were still under its dominion.

Secondly, we have to consider the question of justification. It is almost always in this connexion that S. Paul deals with the law. The question e.g. whether for Christians the law is of value as a spiritual discipline, and as a guide to the true claims of love, hardly seems to have occurred to him. Nor do his opponents appear to have urged its claims upon any such grounds. When they spoke of Christians as being "perfected" by it (Gal. iii. 3), they had in view the Pharisaic ideal, and not growth in Christian living. How then did our Lord teach that we were to be "justified"? The word seldom occurs in His teaching—only twice indeed in relation to our standing with God (Mt. xii. 37 ; Luk. xviii. 14). But that great vindication or justification of the people of God, which will come in the coming of the Kingdom, and in the divine judgment which will overthrow all hostile forces which stand in its way, is ever in His mind ; and He never thinks of this justification as attained by obedience to the law, but always by faith in, and attachment to Himself. The immediate duty is to answer to His call, and follow Him ; and every one who confesses Him before men He will confess before His Father in heaven (Mt. x. 32). It is in the Jewish Gospel itself that we find Him saying "that many shall come from the east and the west, and shall sit down with Abraham, and Isaac, and Jacob, in the kingdom of heaven," and it is the faith of the Gentile centurion, and not obedience to law, which is the occasion of this saying (Mt. viii. 10, 11). Thus S. Paul's teaching that it is faith, and nothing else, that God primarily requires of us is stamped upon the whole Synoptic story from first to last. Neither the Kingdom itself, nor those blessings of bodily and mental healing which shew its powers already at work, does the Lord ever regard as earned, or to be earned, by obedience to the Mosaic law. They are the free gifts of God— "not of works, that no man should glory" (Eph. ii. 9)—to be made our own through faith. Here again there is not the slightest difference between S. Paul's teaching and that of the Lord before him ; the language differs, but the meaning is the same.

Once more, as to those national claims of Israel, which were the great source of the Jewish hatred to S. Paul. Our Lord no more recognized them than S. Paul did. It is true that He recognized fully the great place of Israel in the divine purpose. The Jews are "the sons of the kingdom" (Mt. viii. 12), and Jerusalem is "the city of the great king" (Mt. v. 35). He Himself, we read in the Jewish Gospel, is "not sent" during His life of ministry "but unto the lost sheep of the house of Israel" (Mt. xv. 24), and His great effort is to gather them to Himself (Mt. xii. 30; xxiii. 37). But the Jewish Gospel itself is as clear as any other that, as S. Paul expresses it, "they are not all Israel, which are of Israel" (Rom. ix. 6). "The kingdom of God," the Lord says, "shall be taken away from you, and shall be given to a nation bringing forth the fruits thereof" (Mt. xxi. 43); and the foundation upon which the new and reconstituted Church will rest is the faithful remnant who believe in Him as the Christ (Mt. xvi. 18). Indeed the rejection of the nation as a nation and the coming destruction of the city of the Great King are taught again and again by the Lord, both directly and by parable. Moreover, it was apparently the Lord's rejection of Jewish nationalism that was the first thing which incensed the Jews against Him (cf. Luk. iv. 25–29); and, as far as the people as a whole were concerned, the chief cause which led to His death. If there is any contrast here between S. Paul and the Lord, it lies in the fact that S. Paul insists more, not less, than the Lord upon the privileges of Israel after the flesh (Rom. ix. 1–5).

We see then that when S. Paul speaks of his opponents as preaching another Jesus, and offering a different Spirit, and a different Gospel, and styles them "false apostles, deceitful workers, fashioning themselves into apostles of Christ," he says not a word too much. No doubt they taught that Jesus was the Christ, and accepted His moral teaching. But what sort of Christ did they hold Him to be ? A Christ Who would return in glory to vindicate none but Jews, and those who had been by circumcision incorporated into their nation ; a Christ Who would judge men by their obedience to the Mosaic law, and so had died for nothing (Gal. ii. 21). That was "another Jesus" indeed—S. Paul will not say "another Christ," for such a Jesus would have been unworthy of the title—and the Gospel which proclaimed Him a different Gospel. So with the Spirit also. What the Judaizers taught about the Spirit we do not know; but so dependent is the doctrine of the Spirit upon the doctrine of the Christ from Whom He comes, that to lower the position and work of the One is always to lower the position and work of the Other. Probably their doctrine here went little further than a recognition of the Spirit's miraculous gifts. In a word these Jewish teachers were not really Jewish Christians, like the Twelve and S. James of Jerusalem, but little better than ordinary Jews. If their Christology made of the Lord more than a glorified man, it did so in word more than in fact. The essential thing in our Christology is not the titles that we give to the Lord, but the confidence that we repose in Him, and the character of the salvation that we expect from Him ; and those who look for salvation to the law can have no right conception of the Lord's place, whatever language they may employ. In a word, the doctrine of the Lord's Person and the doctrine of His work always go together ; and if the one is lowered, the other will be lowered with it. So apparently it was with this Jewish Christianity, which clung to the law. If it was not heretical about the Lord's Person in S. Paul's day, it very soon became so.

A few words must be added as to the importance of these considerations to-day. The past never exactly repeats itself; but there is to-day a great deal of so-called Christianity which seems closely to resemble that of S. Paul's opponents. It does not explicitly reject the doctrine of the Lord's Divinity, for "divinity" may be ascribed to the Lord in many different senses, and on many different grounds. But the place, which it gives to the Lord in relation to our salvation, is a place so humble that it does not differ very much from the place which a devout Jew might be willing to give to Him. Many Jews to-day have a profound reverence for Jesus

G.

XII. 1 [1]I must needs glory, though it is not expedient;
2 but I will come to visions and revelations of the Lord. I

[1] Some ancient authorities read *Now to glory is not expedient, but I will
come &c.*

of Nazareth ; some may even regard Him, not only as a great moral teacher,
but as the best interpreter of the deepest meaning of their law. Nor will
they necessarily refuse to regard Him as by the nobility of His human
character the highest revelation of the God Whom with us they worship.
It is very natural that we should feel drawn towards such Jews as these.
Always we have venerated with them the saints and heroes of the O.T. ;
and in recent years we have learned much from Jewish interpreters which
has helped us in the understanding of the N.T. itself[1]. But we must not
forget that there still remains the great gulf upon which S. Paul insists.
Judaism is a religion of law, while Christianity is the religion of grace and
of the Spirit. To Catholic Christians, as to S. Paul, the Lord is not primarily
either a moral teacher, or an interpreter of the teaching of the O.T. ; He is
the Glorified Lord, the Head of His Body the Church, and its Saviour by
His Death and Resurrection and the gift of the Spirit. Just in so far as
Christians come to sit lightly to the truths which the Jews reject, they
themselves cease to be Christians. In the twentieth century, as in the first,
it is not enough to say that Jesus is the Christ, if that only means that He
is the great preacher of the Kingdom of God ; He must be to us its Head
and Centre, through Whom alone we can become its members, in Whom
alone we can continue such, and from Whom alone can come to us the Spirit
of life, through Whom we are justified. To regard Him as but the highest
of moral teachers and revealers of God, and to place our hopes upon our
efforts to obey Him, is to refuse the faith which He asks. Now, as then,
there may well be a Jewish Christianity as there may be an English
Christianity ; strange indeed it is that the Jews should be the one nation
asked to forget their own people, and their fathers' house, when they
enter the Church. But it must be the Jewish Christianity of S. Peter and
S. James, not that of those who still put their trust in obedience to the
law, and dogged the footsteps of the Apostle to the Gentiles to overthrow
his work.

XII. 1–13. The subject of S. Paul's credentials is continued. He first
speaks of his strange spiritual experiences and then returns to his sufferings
and their purpose. He has been, he would say, no less privileged than the
seers of the O.T. (cf. e.g. Ez. viii. 3 ; Dan. x. 1) and S. Peter himself (Ac. x.
10 ff.). Probably the words of *v.* 9 were spoken in the course of a vision.

1. *visions...of the Lord.* i.e. probably visions and revelations sent by
Him. In some cases the Lord Himself was seen, and in some cases not.

[1] Cf. the valuable Essay of Mr Abrahams on Jewish Interpretation of the
O.T. in *The People and the Book.*

know a man in Christ, fourteen years ago (whether in the
body, I know not; or whether out of the body, I know not;
God knoweth), such a one caught up even to the third
3 heaven. And I know such a man (whether in the body, or
4 apart from the body, I know not; God knoweth), how
that he was caught up into Paradise, and heard unspeakable words, which it is not lawful for a man to utter.

2. *in Christ.* The words should
probably be taken, not with "a man,"
but with "caught up." All Christian
experience takes place "in Christ,"
and union with Him means perfect
safety. Cf. the long note below.

fourteen years ago. Shortly before
the beginning of his work among the
Gentiles. He remembers the time as
a definite point in his Christian experience. Cf. Ez. i. 1; viii. 1.

the third heaven. Cf. Eph. iv. 10;
Heb. iv. 14; vii. 26. "Primum coelum
nubium," says Bengel, "secundum
stellarum; tertium spirituale"; and
so substantially the Christian Fathers.
But some of the Jews reckoned seven
heavens. In 2 Enoch viii. 1-3, and
in the Apocalypse of Moses xl,
Paradise is in the third heaven.

4. *caught up into Paradise.*

S. Paul probably does not speak of a
second ecstasy, but further describes
the one already mentioned: for
(*a*) he probably thought of Paradise
as in the third heaven, and (*b*) if he
were speaking of a second ecstasy,
we should expect him to date it as
he does the first. The word "Paradise" is an old Persian word for
"garden" or "pleasaunce." It is
applied to the garden of Eden in
Gen. ii and iii, xiii. 10, and Is. li. 3;
but in Ez. xxviii. 13 and xxxi. 8 it
seems to refer to a heavenly region,
and our Lord uses it of the abode of
the blessed dead (Luk. xxiii. 43). Cf.
also Rev. ii. 7. Both the heavenly and
the earthly Paradise are mentioned
in 2 Enoch viii. 1-6.

which...utter. Cf. 1 Cor. ii. 9, 10;
Rev. x. 4.

How are we to regard such experiences as those to which S. Paul here
refers? The Jews knew nothing either of Copernican astronomy or of
modern psychology; and S. Paul probably thought of his visions and ecstasy
very simply, regarding them as plain matters of fact. He had read in the
O.T. of experiences similar to his own, and heard of them from his fellow-
Christians (cf. Ac. vii. 55, 56; x. 9-16). He had read that Enoch and Elijah
had ascended to heaven in their bodies, and may have heard the stories that
some of the Rabbis had done the same. But our attitude cannot be quite
the same as his. Certainly we shall not dismiss his experiences as mere
hallucinations; modern knowledge has rendered such an attitude as that
out of date. Such experiences are widespread, and in no way a mark of
mental or bodily disorder; indeed some of those who have had them,
Isaiah, S. Paul and S. Teresa—in view of Mt. iii. 16, 17; iv. 1-11 (cf. Jn. iii.
11-13; viii. 38), we may surely add our Lord Himself—have been among
the sanest and most practical of mankind. But we shall not regard what
is seen and heard in such visions and auditions as seen and heard just as

are the sights and sounds of our workaday world. "Objective" they may be, for all perception has both an objective and a subjective element; but they are not a part of that world which physical science investigates, nor are they perceived in the same way.

Let us consider the experience of S. Paul himself. He was not what we usually understand by a mystic. A man is often called a mystic for no better reason than that he takes seriously the N.T. teaching, and thinks of the Lord as the soul of his soul, and not as one removed from him to a distant heaven. But by a mystic we usually understand one who, whether a Christian or not, habitually seeks for union with the divine by strange methods of fasting and contemplation and prayer; and S. Paul was far too pressed by anxiety for all the churches, and the demands of his missionary life, to have leisure for that. In the life of simple faith and obedience he found through union with Christ all the union with God for which he looked in this life (cf. Gal. ii. 20; 2 Cor. v. 6-8). But, though not a mystic like Plotinus or S. John of the Cross, he was what we should now call "psychic," and it is of interest to notice the forms which his experience took.

Of the gifts of prophecy and speaking with tongues, something has been said in the Commentary on the First Epistle to the Corinthians (cf. pp. 134-137). Both appear to have been wholly or in part activities of what we term the subconscious mind, like automatic writing; and S. Paul seems to have exercised both (1 Cor. xiv. 1-19). The Spirit of God may be active in what goes on, to use spatial language, below the level of conscious life, as well as in what goes on upon it; and in the speech, which rises out of these strange depths, the sign of His presence is not the strangeness of the manner in which we speak, but the value and fruitfulness of what we say.

But let us "come to visions and revelations of the Lord." Of what character, we first inquire, was the revelation of the Lord upon the Damascus road? A "vision" it undoubtedly was; but S. Paul leaves us in doubt as to its character. He seems to class it, not with subsequent visions like that of Ac. xviii. 9, 10, but with the appearances of the Lord during the great Forty Days (1 Cor. xv. 5-8; cf. ix. 1). Now these appearances in several cases, if not in all, seem to defy explanation on ordinary psychological lines. The great numbers who together "saw" the Lord according to our very earliest information (1 Cor. xv. 5-7) are a grave difficulty in the way of this; and still more is such a narrative as that of the walk to Emmaus (Luk. xxiv. 13-31; cf. v. 50). Though we need not suppose that the Lord would have been seen and heard by casual passers by, He was with the disciples as they walked, and seen against an ever-changing background. It may be, as Jn. xx. 17 suggests, that the conditions of the Lord's glorified life differed before and after the Ascension, and that His modes of self-manifestation differed with them; in this case His self-revelation to S. Paul would be different in character to those previously granted to the eleven, without necessarily being a vision of the ordinary kind. There are facts which suggest a difference. In ordinary visions both the picturing and the audition are as a rule largely explicable by the previous furniture of the recipient's mind. The angel's message to Mary, to take one example, though containing a real revelation of truth, was expressed in the language of O.T. prophecy, and described the Messiah whom Mary was expecting rather than the Messiah that the Lord actually proved to be (Luk. i. 31–33). But it seems to have been otherwise in the vision on the Damascus road. Is it likely that S. Paul at this time knew of our Lord's characteristic way of repeating the name of those with whom He expostulates (cf. Luk. x. 41 ; xxii. 31); or of His way of expostulating by asking quietly the reason for what is done (Mt. xiv. 31; xxvi. 50; Mk. v. 39; Jn. xviii. 23); or once more that he was familiar with that doctrine of the union of the Lord with His people which the Lord's words presuppose ? The facts, when we examine them with care, make it almost as difficult to regard the Lord's appearance as an ordinary vision as to accept Jung's explanation of it on psycho-analytic lines.

With those later visions of S. Paul which S. Luke records the case is otherwise. In two cases (Ac. xviii. 9, 10 ; xxiii. 11) they are visions of the Lord ; in one of a man of Macedonia (Ac. xvi. 9); and in one of an angel (Ac. xxvii. 23). But not one presents any difficulty. Such revelation of the future as they contain finds abundant parallels in the facts collected by modern psychical research. The visions are all expressly said to have taken place by night, and are hardly to be distinguished from veridical dreams (cf. Numb. xii. 6 ; Job iv. 12 ff.; Joel ii. 28). The same may be said of S. Peter's symbolic vision (Ac. x. 9–16). Important as it was, the data for reaching the conclusion to which he was led were already present in his mind (cf. supra, pp. 111 f.); and it is not uncommon for problems, both intellectual and aesthetic, which have puzzled the conscious mind, to be solved by the unconscious. In all these cases even a psychologist who is not a Christian will find little difficulty in the Bible story.

We pass now to the experience mentioned, though not described in detail, in xii. 2–4. That this stood by itself S. Paul implies in two ways. He will not reveal the words which he heard, though the record of the Acts shews that normally he spoke without reserve of what he heard in his visions ; and he suspects, though he is not certain, that he was out of the body, when the experience took place. To this experience also there is no lack of parallels either in Scripture (e.g. Ez. iii. 12–14 ; viii. 3 ; xi. 24 ; Mt. iv. 5–10) or in wider fields of research. Indeed it has been said that "the evidence for ecstasy is stronger than the evidence for any other religious belief." But what precisely it is which takes place in such experiences it is as yet impossible to say. Almost certainly the earthly bodies of Ezekiel, of S. Paul, of our Lord, and of others who have had this experience, would have been seen wrapped in complete unconsciousness ; but what of their souls or spirits ? If the connexion with their bodies was unbroken it was not through the physical body, as far as we can judge, that their experience took place ; and there is much evidence to shew that the living, under such abnormal conditions, are seen and recognized in places far removed from those where their bodies lie in apparent slumber. But even here it would seem that the previous furniture of the mind is not without its influence. S. Paul, we may be sure, did not derive his map of the heavens from his experience in ecstasy; rather his experience took the form that it did because he already believed that there were more heavens than one.

Now these questions have a very practical bearing upon Christian duty. There is to-day a great revival of interest in supranormal experience, and Christians should welcome it. The more wonderful that we find the soul of man to be—the clearer it becomes that we have powers within us that cannot possibly find their full exercise in our threescore years and ten—the greater will be our assurance that we are destined for another life than this. But caution is necessary; for the greater our powers, the greater the peril of misusing them. What is the teaching of the Bible and the Church?

First, it assures us that all our natural powers, from the humblest to the most exalted, are from God, and to be used for His glory; and that the Spirit is given to raise and consecrate them to the service of God, and the edification of the Church (cf. 1 Cor. xii. 4–11). We should "desire earnestly the greater gifts" (1 Cor. xii. 31), not shrink from any of them in suspicion and alarm; and employ them, if they are given to us, according to God's will. In the soul of man there are

> Magic casements opening on the foam
> Of perilous seas.

If as we hold communion with God, and open our whole being to His influence, it pleases God to open these casements, we need not fear the peril. We may—"in the body, or out of the body, God knoweth"—find ourselves, like Ezekiel, in scenes far distant, or be "caught up to the third heaven," and learn what we may not reveal to other men. To be so "caught up," if it be "in Christ," is a grace from God, and the revelation made to us a true revelation, however strange may be the form in which it is expressed. The Church has never doubted this.

But, secondly, we should not judge of the value of our experience by its strangeness. Love is the "more excellent way" (1 Cor. xii. 31); and, if we are "zealous of spiritual gifts," it should be chiefly "unto the edifying of the church" (1 Cor. xiv. 12). We are "greater than we know"; and, since life is too short for all our powers to be developed here, we should normally strive for the development of what is most useful. We are here to do the will of God: if we do it as far as we know it, we are pleasing to Him; and if for us the magic casements do not open, there is no cause for disappointment or alarm (cf. 1 Cor. xii. 14–25). Above all, we should not fumble with the casement-latches. It is one thing to be "in Christ caught up," and quite another to cast ourselves down from temple-pinnacles. The "seas" are really perilous, if we launch out into the deep without a guide; we do not know what the relation of the soul to the body may be; and it is always dangerous to meddle with machinery that we do not understand. Above all, we must never attempt to abandon the control of our minds or bodies to influences, whose character we do not know. Spiritualism is very old, and it has always been sternly forbidden to the people of God. Cf. e.g. Deut. xviii. 9–15; Is. viii. 19, 20. The reference in 1 Jn. iv. 1–3 is not to spiritualism, but to "prophetic" utterances, proceeding wholly or in part from the subconscious mind. In our life here we are responsible for the control of our action in accordance with the dictates of reason and con-science. If we in any way deliberately weaken or abandon that control, we do not know what may take its place. It may be—apparently at first it always is—our own subconscious mind, an agent much more susceptible than the conscious to thought-transference and suggestion from other minds, but not at all intellectually or morally its superior. Indeed it may go down to a common or racial mind, whose depths are far from wholesome. We may have, in Mr Studdert Kennedy's words, "Dr Jekyll in the dining-room, Mr Hyde in the kitchen, and God knows who stowed away in the basement." But it may be—and there is much evidence to suggest that it sometimes is—discarnate souls, or "spirits" of some kind, whose character we do not know. How can we be justified in giving *carte blanche* to them to use our brains, and lips, and hands in any way they will? And if these "familiar spirits" are allowed to "possess" us, how can we be sure that they will depart as easily as they came? When Owen Glendower said

> I can call spirits from the vasty deep,

Hotspur replied

> But will they come when you do call for them?

Perhaps, if he had asked

> But will they go when you bid them return?

he would have made an even more pertinent inquiry; the "controls" in the Gospels seem to have had no such desire (Luk. viii. 31). It is no doubt true that spiritualists do not necessarily yield the control of their own personalities to alien influences. Most of what takes place at their public meetings seems to be little more than experimental *clairvoyance*, reminding us of the thought-reading entertainments of our boyhood. Even at their *séances*, it is the medium alone who normally is under control. But to encourage another to do a thing is morally on the same level as to do it oneself; and though it may not bring the same results, it involves the same responsibility.

Thirdly, neither the Bible nor the Church ever encourages us to suppose that we can correct the faith of the Church by occult sources of information; on the contrary, the latter must always be tested by the former (cf. Is. viii. 19, 20; Gal. i. 8; 1 Jn. iv. 1–3), whether the new source of information be prophecy, or dream, or vision, or ecstasy, to say nothing of familiar spirits, or automatic writing. This principle rests, not upon dogmatic prejudice or upon professional jealousy, but upon the conviction that the evidence for the Church's faith is far stronger than that for any occult beliefs which set it aside. No one knows better than thoughtful Christians that at best "we see in a mirror, darkly" (1 Cor. xiii. 12); and that "the human words and ideas in which eternal truths are clad cannot, even through divine skill, convey to us more than a shadow of the realities they stand for[1]." Not even the human mind of the Lord could, as far as we can judge, receive divine truth save in a human translation. But what comparison is there between

---

[1] Tyrrell, *External Religion*, Lecture VI.

5 On behalf of such a one will I glory : but on mine own behalf

the revelation contained in His Person, word, and experience, and any
which we can hope to receive by the methods of spiritualism ? Here we
need go little beyond what is fully admitted by such a scientific investi-
gator as Myers in his *Human Personality*. First, there are the vast
possibilities of conscious fraud on the part of mediums; and, where this is
absent, of inaccurate transmission. Secondly, it is fully admitted that the
"spirits" find communication with us most difficult. *Ex hypothesi*, they
must make use of the brains of others; and every human brain has a
character of its own. They are not, like motor-cars, the result of mass pro-
duction. Each has been gradually formed by the action and experience of
a particular human personality, and bears its impress; and so must colour,
perhaps fatally, every communication which passes through it. Nor is this
all. When the conscious mind is laid to sleep, it is the subconscious mind
which normally assumes control. Even if, as is supposed, an alien "spirit"
may make use of it, how can we distinguish what proceeds from the "spirit"
from that which proceeds from the subconscious mind of the medium and
from the suggestions from other human minds, which it so easily receives ?
Thirdly, what authority in any case as teachers of religious truth, do such
"spirits" possess ? Even if they are truthful, and that is more than we
know, what authority have their beliefs ? Why do we suppose that "there
must be wisdom with great death" ? It is not death, but the Spirit of God,
Who leads us into all truth. Why e.g. should a "spirit" who never here
recognized God Incarnate in Christ, recognize Him any better on the other
side ? We do not find it claimed that the great saints and evangelists of
the past are trying to communicate with us, but "spirits" on the lower
planes of the world unseen. What we find seems to be exactly what we
should expect. The teaching offered to us faithfully reflects the shallow
religious universalism of our own day, just as in the first century it reflected
the current Gnostic asceticism (1 Tim. iv. 1–5). It is just as S. John says.
Spirits which confess not Jesus Christ come in the flesh are not of God.
"They are of the world: therefore speak they as of the world, and the world
heareth them" (1 Jn. iv. 3–5). The teaching that is produced is precisely
what those who welcome it believe already ; its apparent appeal needs no
explanation. The popular religious teacher, like the popular journalist, is
the man who can say impressively what his audience desire to be said.

Those who desire to study the facts for themselves should read Sir
Oliver Lodge's *Raymond*, or (better still) the relevant parts of F. W. H.
Myers' *Human Personality*. Chapter IX is particularly valuable. It
should however be remembered that such books reproduce for the most
part the best and most striking products of the methods employed, and not
the average, or the worst.

5. *On behalf of such a one.* He
was "another man" (1 Sam. x. 6)
then, and for the time not the bearer

of those infirmities in the flesh that
he must bear now.

on mine own behalf. i.e., as Mof-

6 I will not glory, save in *my* weaknesses. For if I should desire to glory, I shall not be foolish; for I shall speak the truth: but I forbear, lest any man should account of me above that which he seeth me *to be*, or heareth from me.

7 And by reason of the exceeding greatness of the revelations—wherefore, that I should not be exalted overmuch, there was given to me a ¹thorn in the flesh, a messenger of Satan to buffet me, that I should not be exalted overmuch.

¹ Or, *stake*

f att translates, "of myself personally," of the man with whom the Corinthians have to do.

6. *I forbear.* S. Paul breaks off, though he had meant to say more about his visions and revelations.

account of me...heareth from me. An important principle. The estimate formed of a man should rest primarily upon personal experience, upon what we see in him, and find to have proceeded from him. Our estimate of S. Paul, e.g., rests upon his writings and the result of his work in the world. In view of all this we find it easily credible that visions and revelations from the Lord were given to him; but claims to them would repel rather than attract us, if his life had been unworthy or unproductive. We might for the moment "account of" him highly, if we were easily impressed by marvels of this kind; but the impression would have no moral influence over us, and would soon disappear.

7. The text here is perhaps corrupt. The R.V. correctly represents the Greek as we have it.

a thorn in the flesh. R.V. margin "stake" seems to be required by the context, and this is according to classical usage. But the use of the word in the LXX on the whole favours the translation "thorn."

The expression "thorn in the flesh" was probably proverbial, and S. Paul adopts it, though it is too weak to describe the real source of his suffering: "stake in the flesh" is too violent a metaphor. The Corinthians doubtless knew to what S. Paul referred, but it is impossible for us to do so. Some light, however, may be thrown by Gal. iv. 13–15, *v.* 15 suggesting eye-trouble. But the most likely suggestion is that S. Paul was frequently prostrated by attacks of malaria, or Malta fever; and that his first visit to the "Galatians" of Pisidian Antioch was due to his having quickly to leave the low-lying Perga (Ac. xiii. 13, 14). That he suffered from epilepsy there is no evidence. That suggestion seems to be due to the erroneous belief that "visions and revelations" imply physical disorder.

a messenger of Satan. "Angel of Satan" is probably right. There was no message from Satan to deliver; and Satan, though never in Scripture called an angel, has angels of his own (Mt. xxv. 41; Rev. xii. 7, 9). Cf. Job i. 12; ii. 6; Luk. xiii. 16; xxii. 31; 1 Cor. v. 5 and the note there. The thought is that, though Satan's action is malicious, it none the less serves a divine purpose.

buffet. The word well suits intermittent attacks of fever.

8 Concerning this thing I besought the Lord thrice, that it
9 might depart from me. And he hath said unto me, My
    grace is sufficient for thee: for *my* power is made perfect
    in weakness. Most gladly therefore will I rather glory in
    my weaknesses, that the power of Christ may [1]rest upon
10 me. Wherefore I take pleasure in weaknesses, in injuries,
    in necessities, in persecutions, in distresses, for Christ's
    sake: for when I am weak, then am I strong.
11   I am become foolish: ye compelled me; for I ought to

[1] Or, *cover me*   Gr. *spread a tabernacle over me.*

8. The thrice-repeated prayer recalls Gethsemane. "The Lord" is the Lord Jesus Christ. In moments of physical suffering it is natural that prayer should be to Him, rather than directly to the Father (cf. Heb. iv. 15), and the Greek word for "besought" is one frequently used of the appeals of the sick in the Gospels. Cf. Jn. xiv. 14.

9. *he hath said unto me.* The Lord's answer has once for all been given. Cf. Deut. iii. 26. In view of the earlier verses of the chapter, it is probable that the voice of the Lord seemed to S. Paul to be heard speaking.

My grace is sufficient for thee. The grace of Christ is His favour, with all the saving and upholding power by which it is manifested. Between "grace" as "favour," and "grace" as "operative power" there is no distinction to be drawn; nor would the Hebrews have drawn any. The grace of the Almighty can never be inoperative.

for my power...weakness. Better literally "the power." The R.V. insertion "my" narrows the meaning. That the power of God in man is made perfect in weakness was the experience of the Lord Himself. "The power" of God "was with him

to heal" (Luk. v. 17), but the perfection of saving power was only reached through death and resurrection. Cf. Luk. xii. 50; Jn. xii. 24. So with S. Paul. "The power" had been with him from the beginning of his ministry, but not as it came to be with him through his deeper sharing of the Cross. Cf. iv. 7 ff., and the notes there. Cornelius à Lapide says that S. Ignatius and S. Francis Xavier prayed daily for the Cross, and were only willing to lose one Cross, if a heavier was bestowed.

rather glory. i.e. glory rather than repine.

rest upon me. Cf. Rev. vii. 15, where the uncompounded verb is used. There is probably in both passages the O.T. thought of the Shekinah. Cf. Ex. xxiv. 15–17; 1 Kgs. viii. 10; Mk. ix. 7; Jn. i. 14; Rev. xxi. 3. The Shekinah was the manifestation of God either in heaven, or on earth.

10. *I take pleasure.* A misleading translation. Better "I am satisfied, or well-pleased."

injuries. Better "outrages." The word suggests the combination of insult with injury.

11. *ye compelled me.* The word "ye" is emphatic.

have been commended of you: for in nothing was I behind
12 ¹the very chiefest apostles, though I am nothing. Truly
the signs of an apostle were wrought among you in all
13 patience, by signs and wonders and ²mighty works. For
what is there wherein ye were made inferior to the rest
of the churches, except *it be* that I myself was not a burden
to you? forgive me this wrong.

¹ Or, *those pre-eminent apostles*   ² Gr. *powers.*

the very...apostles. Better, with
R.V. marg., "those pre-eminent
apostles." Cf. xi. 5. The reference
is to S. Paul's opponents, not to the
Twelve.

though I am nothing. Cf. 1 Cor.
iii. 7 ; xv. 9.

12. *signs of an apostle.* Better
literally "signs of the Apostle." The
Apostle has a particular type of

Christian ministry, which has special
signs to authenticate it, the "patience" being the condition of the
manifestation of the power. Cf.
Ac. xv. 12; Rom. xv. 18, 19; Gal.
iii. 5. The variety of words which
S. Paul employs suggests a similar
variety in the manifestations through
him of the divine power.

There is no definite break. But it may be well to deal at this point with
several difficulties likely to be present to our minds. These chapters,
noticeably the eleventh, moving as they are, do at first a little repel us.
Our difficulties are three: (*a*) We feel that S. Paul speaks, as he says himself, "not after the Lord," and is wanting in Christian humility. (*b*) We
dislike the way in which he speaks of his opponents. Such language indeed
as that of xi. 13–15 is familiar enough in the controversies of the past. The
Fathers use it, and the theologians of the 16th century also. But we avoid
it in our controversies to-day, and are sure that we are right to do so. It
suggests what the world rightly pillories as "*odium theologicum*," and seems
to us inconsistent with the "meekness and gentleness of Christ" (x. 1). "The
Lord's servant"—so says S. Paul himself—"must not strive, but be gentle
towards all, apt to teach, forbearing, in meekness correcting them that
oppose themselves" (2 Tim. ii. 24, 25). (*c*) We do not see the relevance of
S. Paul's argument. The question at issue is whether he is an Apostle, or
not. It is to the purpose to refer to his call on the Damascus road, to
appeal to the "signs and wonders and mighty works" (xii. 12) which
authenticate his mission, and to the result of his apostolic activity in the
Corinthian church itself (iii. 1–3; cf. 1 Cor. ix. 2). But a Christian might
be called to great suffering for his Master's sake, and receive wonderful
revelations, without being any the more an Apostle.

First then, is it the case that S. Paul is wanting in humility? We cannot
feel more strongly that he is open to this charge than he feels it himself
(xi. 1; 16, 17, 21–23; xii. 1). But that only aggravates the difficulty. If
S. Paul knows that he is speaking foolishly, he is the more foolish so to speak.
The true answer to the charge is found in xii. 11. It lies in the fact that

he has to do with people, with whom the native language of Christian humility cannot be employed. Something far more important is at stake than S. Paul's reputation for humility, and to refuse to endanger it would not be humility but vainglory. Those who have been in contact with people like the Corinthians will understand his words without difficulty. Two illustrations may make the matter clear.

Let us first consider the characteristic language of a great scholar. Just because he understands what is meant by knowledge, and the difficulty of the subjects with which he deals, he will be extremely conscious of the gaps in his information, and speak with caution and reserve. An academic audience will understand this, and pay to him all the more attention. But suppose that he is invited by a parish priest to lecture in a great manufacturing town. The parish priest will warn him that there the tone naturally adopted in a University would be quite fatal. If he begins by speaking of the difficulty of the subject and the imperfection of his information, probably a stentorian voice from the body of the hall will inquire why, if he knows nothing about the matter in hand, he has come to speak about it. His audience, who know nothing of his subject, know nothing of its difficulties. Imperfect as his own knowledge may in his own judgment be, it is a thousand times greater than theirs; and he must speak with the authority which, with them, he has the right to claim. It will be contrary to his custom, and go against the grain with him; but he must sacrifice his comfort for his brothers' sake. He must "become foolish"; they have "compelled" him.

Secondly, let us take a different case. Christians who know a little of such men as Dr Pusey or John Keble will not misunderstand the language in which they refer to their own sinfulness, though they may regard it as a little morbid. But what conclusion will the average man of the world be likely to draw, if e.g. he is told that Dr Pusey built a church at his own expense as an act of penitence? Having himself scarcely any sense of sin, he will easily suppose that Dr Pusey must, unknown to others, have been guilty of some appalling wickedness. Before humble Christians speak much of their own sins, they must consider whether their language will be rightly understood. The world is not concerned with the way in which they regard themselves in the light of the holiness of God; if they are seeking moment by moment to do all of God's will that they know, they should (if they find it necessary to speak of themselves at all) say, as S. Paul does (1 Cor. iv. 4), that they know "nothing against themselves."

Now it is such considerations as these which explain S. Paul's language. S. Paul knew his Corinthians. What he writes we can see that he disliked having to write, and felt that he ought not to have been obliged to write (xii. 11). But he wrote only what was strictly true, what under the circumstances it was necessary to say, and what the Corinthians could themselves see to be true (xii. 6). Not to write it would have been not only to let his own cause, and that of those most faithful to him (*v.* 12), go by default, but to let the cause of Christ, the cause of Christian liberty, go by default also.

Secondly, we have to consider the way in which he speaks of his opponents. Here again we must understand the situation. In our own day, very few people take part in serious religious controversy, who are not themselves religious men. But neither in S. Paul's day, nor in the age of the Fathers, nor in the 16th century, was this the case. Apart from a few renegades, all Jews in S. Paul's day claimed to be religious men, and posed as experts in religion (cf. Rom. ii. 17–24; Jam. i. 19–27), though with many of them godliness was simply, in one form or another, a way of gain (1 Tim. vi. 5). S. Paul speaks of his opponents as we do not because he has opponents to deal with altogether different from ours. Controversy in the Church of England sometimes becomes bitter; but we do not describe one another as ministers of Satan, since we do not believe one another to be such. We regard one another as honest, well-living men, to whom godliness is not in the least a way of gain either in money or in reputation. But what were S. Paul's opponents? Probably they were Pharisees, of much the same character as those whom the Lord had Himself addressed in the words recorded in Mt. xxiii. If we condemn S. Paul's words, we must condemn our Lord's also. S. Paul is not the master of language that our Lord was. He has neither our Lord's power of epigram, nor His remarkable wit; and his denunciations do not go home, or carry us with them, as do those of Mt. xxiii. 4–7; 13, 14; 24–27. But S. Paul's charges are much the same; and, if he does not admit the sincerity of his opponents, neither does our Lord. These Pharisees, unlike those with whom the Lord had to do, might call themselves by the Christian name, and in a sense confess the Lord's Messiahship. But what was the confession worth? The spiritual and national pride, which had led the Pharisees to take part in the crucifixion, had not been abandoned. As far as their power went, they were still shutting the kingdom of heaven against men, neither entering in themselves, nor suffering them that were entering in to enter. Moreover, the time had now gone by, when these Pharisaic Christians could offer for themselves any plausible justification. The question at issue between them and S. Paul had been thought out, argued out, and settled by practical experience and the witness of God Himself (Ac. xv. 8–10). The Church had fully considered it, and formulated its decision. With S. Paul stood not only the elder Apostles, but S. James of Jerusalem himself (Ac. xv. 19). Nor was even this all. S. Paul, who knew his men, charges them not merely with the love of power, and personal hostility to himself, but with a corrupt motive, that of desiring to escape persecution (Gal. vi. 12, 13). These "Christian" Pharisees had no intention of breaking with the other Pharisees; their brothers in legalism were far more to them than their brothers in Christ; and, while S. Paul had everything to bear from unbelieving Jews, they had nothing. Indeed they would even escape persecution from the heathen. Judaism was in the eyes of the Romans a "lawful religion," and good relations with the Jews meant good relations with the Romans also. Thus the Pharisaic teachers bore neither the commission of Christ, nor the Cross of Christ. They were just what S. Paul calls them, ministers of Satan, the adversary and accuser of the brethren.

Thirdly, there is the question of the relevance of S. Paul's argument. To this difficulty the answer has been already given. See Introd. pp. xxx f. and the longer notes on ii. 14–16, and iv. 7–12. We have to distinguish between

14   Behold, this is the third time I am ready to come to you;
and I will not be a burden to you: for I seek not yours,
but you: for the children ought not to lay up for the
15 parents, but the parents for the children. And I will most
gladly spend and be ¹spent for your souls. If I love you

¹ Gr. *spent out.*

the call to apostleship and the fulfilment of the call. To be an Apostle of
Christ is to be a representative of Christ; and no one can rightly represent
Christ unless Christ is formed in him by his sharing of the experience of
Christ. S. Paul tells us that he shared both the experience of the Cross,
and the experience of the Resurrection; and thus was made an Apostle
indeed. Each was necessary, if S. Paul was to become all that God meant
him to become; but it is the Cross upon which the chief stress is laid. If
he asks that "henceforth no man trouble" him in his apostolic labours, it
is because he bears "branded on" his "body the marks of Jesus" (Gal. vi.
17). There is a story told of S. Martin which may illustrate his meaning.
The devil appeared to S. Martin gorgeously attired in the *insignia* of
Christ, and demanded the saint's worship. But the saint was not to be
deceived. He did not fix his eyes upon robe or diadem, but upon the hands
and feet of the figure standing before him. "I do not," he said, "see the
marks of the wounds." That is S. Paul's complaint of these ministers of
Satan who fashion themselves as ministers of righteousness; he does not
see the marks of the wounds. If they are Apostles of Christ, it is very
strange that He should never have called them to share His sufferings.

XII. 14–end of the Epistle. This passage contains the final warning and
appeal; but in *vv.* 16–18 S. Paul remembers and deals with yet another
charge which has been made against him.

14. *Behold...come to you.* The
words, like those of xiii. 1, clearly
presuppose that S. Paul has already
twice visited Corinth.

not yours. i.e. not your property.
the children...for the children.
Cf. 1 Cor. iv. 15; Gal. iv. 19. If S. Paul
knew of our Lord's words in Mt. xxiii.
9, he did not interpret them as forbidding the language which he here
employs. As the fatherhood of God
is manifested in the Lord Whom He
has sent, so in its turn this manifested fatherhood is found in the
Apostle through whom the Lord
speaks, and carries out the Father's
mission. S. Paul is a father in God,

not a father taking the place of God.
Cf. the note at the end of this section.

It may be noticed that S. Paul no
more interprets Mt. vi. 19 as forbidding all thrift than he interprets
Mt. xxiii. 9 as forbidding all use of
the title "father," except of God.
Reasonable provision for children
unable to provide adequately for
themselves is a duty, unless some
higher claim upon our time and
labour intervenes. The Apostle, of
course, is simply employing an illustration; but he would not argue from
action which he regarded as unlawful.

15. *And I.* Better "But I." He
will do far more than the parents'

16 more abundantly, am I loved the less? But be it so, I did
    not myself burden you; but, being crafty, I caught you
17 with guile. Did I take advantage of you by any one of
18 them whom I have sent unto you? I exhorted Titus, and
    I sent the brother with him. Did Titus take any advantage
    of you? walked we not by the same Spirit? *walked we* not
    in the same steps?
19 ¹Ye think all this time that we are excusing ourselves
    unto you. In the sight of God speak we in Christ. But all
20 things, beloved, *are* for your edifying. For I fear, lest by
    any means, when I come, I should find you not such as I
    would, and should myself be found of you such as ye would
    not; lest by any means *there should be* strife, jealousy,
    wraths, factions, backbitings, whisperings, swellings, ²tu-

¹ Or, *Think ye...you?*   ² Or, *disorders*

duty; he is ready for the last sacrifice. Cf. Phil. ii. 17, where a sacrificial metaphor is employed.

16. S. Paul was accustomed to deal with his churches by his messengers and representatives. There was a real danger that one of them might misuse his position as Gehazi misused his position in Elisha's house, especially if he were charged with collecting money, as those were whom S. Paul has mentioned in viii. 16–24.

18. *Did Titus...of you?* Titus may have visited Corinth earlier than on the occasion when he carried the severe letter. But cf. note on viii. 6. The present visit is to carry the Epistle, which S. Paul is now writing.

by the same Spirit. The Spirit is not only the bestower of gifts, but the source of the Christian character.

the same steps. Titus placed his feet where S. Paul had trod. The thought of the footsteps of Christ is hardly present here.

19. *Ye think...in Christ.* Cf. 1 Cor. iv. 3, 4. The difficulty of dealing rightly with people like the Cor-

inthians is great. It does not do to act upon the proud maxim of the world "Never explain." If we act upon that, their unworthy suspicions become inveterate. But if we do explain, we seem to put ourselves on trial before them, and their arrogance increases to their own serious injury. There seems to be no other course than the one which the Apostle takes. He deals with the charges and suspicions fully, while telling them that he in no way regards them as his judges, and explains solely in their spiritual interests. Our Lord in the Fourth Gospel speaks just as S. Paul does. Cf. e.g. Jn. v. 30–34. S. Paul, as His representative dwelling in Him, speaks ever in the thought of God's presence, and not to gain the favour of the Corinthians.

20. *For I fear.* S. Paul is anxious to get rid of their suspicions in order that nothing may hinder the effectiveness of the action which he may have to take.

strife...tumults. Moffatt's translation is much better: "quarrels,

21 mults; lest, when I come again, my God should humble
me before you, and I should mourn for many of them that
have sinned heretofore, and repented not of the uncleanness and fornication and lasciviousness which they committed.

XIII. 1. This is the third time I am coming to you. At the
mouth of two witnesses or three shall every word be
2 established. I have said [1]beforehand, and I do say [1]before-
hand, [2]as when I was present the second time, so now,
being absent, to them that have sinned heretofore, and to
3 all the rest, that, if I come again, I will not spare; seeing
that ye seek a proof of Christ that speaketh in me; who

---

[1] Or, *plainly*   [2] Or, *as if I were present the second time, even though I
am now absent*

---

jealousy, temper, rivalry, slanders,
gossiping, arrogance, and disorder."
This and the following verses do not
accord with the view that the last
four chapters belong to the earlier
and severe Epistle. That was concerned with a particular outrage.
What S. Paul has now to deal with
are the sins characteristic of the
Corinthians, as we see them in our
First Epistle.

21. *my God.* S. Paul, like the
prophets of the O.T., stands to God
in a special relation. An ordinary
Christian would not use this language.
Cf. Jn. xx. 17 ; Phil. iv. 19.

humble me. The Corinthians are
his source of pride.

mourn for. The mourning will be
for the spiritually dead.

have sinned...repented not. There
is a change of tense in Greek, as in
our version. But it is not likely that
the second verb points back to
S. Paul's last visit. The point rather
is that sin is an abiding condition,
and repentance a change made at a
particular time.

XIII. 1. The quotation is from

Deut. xix. 15. Those who have sinned
have refused to repent. A formal in-
vestigation will now take place and
punitive action follow.

every word. Better "every matter" or "case."

2. In the arrangement of the
clauses, "I have said beforehand"
and "as when I was present" correspond the one to the other ; and "I
do say beforehand" and "so now,
being absent" similarly correspond.

if I come again. No doubt is implied, S. Paul's plans being now
fixed. But he reproduces the language used some time back.

3. *seeing that...speaketh in me.*
S. Paul claimed not only that he
spoke for Christ, but that Christ
Himself spoke in him. The Corinthians said that this remained to
be proved. S. Paul replies that his
disciplinary action will prove it. The
reference seems plainly to be to such
action as we find described in Ac. v.
1–11; xiii. 10, 11; 1 Cor. v. 3–5.
Cf. xii. 12.

*who to you-ward...powerful in
you.* The Christ Who lives and speaks

4 to you-ward is not weak, but is powerful in you: for he
was crucified through weakness, yet he liveth through the
power of God. For we also are weak ¹in him, but we shall
5 live with him through the power of God toward you. Try
your own selves, whether ye be in the faith; prove your
own selves. Or know ye not as to your own selves, that
Jesus Christ is in you? unless indeed ye be reprobate.
6 But I hope that ye shall know that we are not reprobate.

¹ Many ancient authorities read *with*.

in S. Paul, and so is among the Corinthians, when S. Paul is present, is not
Christ as He was in the days of His
humiliation, but Christ as He is now.

4. *for he was crucified...power of
God.* The Lord's weakness was the
source of His crucifixion, not in the
sense that His enemies were too
strong for Him (cf. Mt. xxvi. 53),
but in the sense that by the Father's
will He had emptied Himself of His
glory, and was fully accepting the
conditions of a human life. S. Paul
regards the flesh of the Lord as a
source of human weakness, but not
(as in ourselves) sinful flesh. Cf. the
careful language of Rom. viii. 3, as
contrasted with that of vii. 14, 25,
and viii. 6–14. Through the power
of God displayed in His Resurrection
and Ascension He is now the living
and triumphant Lord.

For we also. Further explanation
of S. Paul's imminent action. "We"
refers to the Apostles, or to S. Paul
himself.

are weak in him. Cf. iv. 10, 11.
The weakness and suffering of the
Lord are reproduced in S. Paul just
because of his union with Him, but
this leads on to the reproduction of
His divine power. It is in this that
S. Paul will act.

5. *Try...selves.* Put yourselves to
the test, not me.

whether...in the faith. Better "in
faith." It is not the whole body of
Christian truth, which is in question;
S. Paul hardly ever uses "faith" in
this objective sense. It is faith in
the sense of trustful and obedient
adherence to Christ Himself as the
crucified and glorified Lord—the
faith from which the indwelling of
Christ by the Spirit results. Thus
the transition is easy to the question
which follows.

Jesus Christ is in you. The introduction of the human name Jesus
insists strongly that it is the historical
person Who is the indwelling Christ.
It is not S. Paul only who is a Christ-
bearer; all Christians are Christ-
bearers, though He does not work
through all in the same way.

unless indeed ye be reprobate. i.e.
have lost your place in Christ, and
been cast away. Cf. 1 Cor. ix. 27.
The word, originally used of metals
in the LXX (cf. Is. i. 22), is always
applied in the N.T., with the exception of Rom. i. 28, to the rejection
of those who have once known the
truth. It never has the Calvinistic
sense of "not among the elect."

6. *But I hope...not reprobate.*
Better, with Moffatt, "trust that you
will find." S. Paul looks confidently
to the test to be applied to himself.
Cf. *v.* 3. He has entire confidence

7 Now we pray to God that ye do no evil; not that we may
  appear approved, but that ye may do that which is honour-
8 able, ¹though we be as reprobate. For we can do nothing
9 against the truth, but for the truth. For we rejoice, when
  we are weak, and ye are strong: this we also pray for,
10 even your perfecting. For this cause I write these things
  while absent, that I may not when present deal sharply,
  according to the authority which the Lord gave me for
  building up, and not for casting down.

¹ Gr. *and that.*

that they will find the divine power
operative in him. "Hope," as often
in the N.T., is not a word which
suggests uncertainty; it is rather
the confident expectation that God
will fulfil His promises. "Trust"
expresses the meaning better, if this
word retains its proper sense. Un-
fortunately it has acquired, owing to
the weakness of most of our trust,
just that suggestion of uncertainty
which it ought to exclude.

7. The meaning is clear, though
awkwardly expressed. S. Paul, unlike Jonah of old, is far from desiring
the fulfilment of his threats of punishment. Rather he prays that he may
find nothing to punish. His desire
before God is not to have his apostolic powers tested at their expense,
and emerge triumphant, but that
they should do right, even though
he remained open to the charge of
being reprobate. If i.e. he is not
called upon to make good his words,
it will still be possible to maintain
that in no case could he have done

so. But that in his love he is willing
to bear.

8. A very important principle.
Spiritual power, unlike physical and
mental power, cannot be abused.
Cf. *v.* 10.

9. *we rejoice...strong.* Cf. 1 Cor.
iv. 8–10, though the sarcasm of the
earlier words is absent here. It was,
as S. Paul has shewn in iv. 11, 12 and
elsewhere, his very weakness and
suffering that were the conditions of
his influence, and of the blessings
which it brought.

perfecting. i.e. by the correction
of what is wrong.

10. Once again, the expression is
awkward, but the meaning clear.
The Lord's power and authority have
been given to S. Paul, and he will
use them to administer condign
punishment, if it proves necessary.
But the primary purpose of the power
is a purpose of grace. Punishment
is always God's strange work (Is.
xxviii. 21).

The foregoing verses are of great importance for the understanding of
apostolic authority, and indeed of all authority that is "spiritual" in the
proper sense of that word. But this subject has been discussed at length in
the Introduction (cf. especially pp. xx f., xxx f.), and little needs to be added
here. All true authority is derived from God (Jn. xix. 11), but its character
as it is found in the Kingdom of God is different from its character as it is

found in the State. Even in the State "there is no power but of God" (cf. Rom. xiii. 1–7); and the State rightly claims the obedience of its Christian members, as long as it on the whole fulfils its God-given function of maintaining order and justice, and asks nothing that for Christians is unlawful. But the authority is here a delegated authority, which those who have it use as they will; and it may thus be grossly misused. It is not at all true of our secular rulers that "they can do nothing against the truth but for the truth." In the Church, the Kingdom of God, it is otherwise. Here the divine authority and power are not delegated, nor can they be abused. Spiritual authority means the authority of the Spirit, the authority of God in Christ manifested in those in whom Christ personally dwells; and it is only while this union is maintained that spiritual authority continues to exist. Thus it is always possible to challenge spiritual authority, by denying that Christ is really speaking to us in those who claim to represent Him; and this denial is often justified. But to do this is to appeal to Christ against His ministers; and if our appeal is rejected, we must expect Him to vindicate against us the authority of those who bear His commission.

Thus much for S. Paul's teaching. But of course just so far as the Church allows itself either (as in England in the past) to be identified with the State; or, while maintaining its distinctness from the State, to become itself a kingdom of the world; the authority which it possesses sinks to the level of secular authority, and its ministers must ultimately appeal to force, as the State rightly does. The Church may itself employ force, or it may hand over its disobedient members to a convenient "secular arm" to employ force for it; but in neither case is it exercising any "spiritual" authority. The Church may be quite right on the immediate issue of doctrine or morals; if God's methods were trusted and accepted, God's vindication would be given. But spiritual power and secular power cannot possibly be exercised at the same time by the same people; if we employ the latter, we shall certainly be without the former.

One point more. It is only if we understand what spiritual authority means, and fulfil the conditions of its exercise, that the manner of the appointment to the Christian ministry possesses any interest. If there is nothing supernatural about the ministry, and Christ does not "speak in" its members, and exercise His authority through them, what does it matter how they are appointed? If the ministry is only a useful piece of organization, and has no powers but what the laity bestow, obviously the laity should appoint to it. If it has no powers but what the State bestows, obviously the State should appoint to it. Those Nonconformists who appeal to the democratic principle, and the old-fashioned Erastians who subordinate the Church to the State, are quite consistent with themselves in their respective views of the ministry. A ministry which receives nothing from the Apostles, and never attempts to employ an authority like theirs, obviously does not require any Apostolic Succession. But with one that is to speak as S. Paul speaks here, it is otherwise.

11   Finally, brethren, [1]farewell. Be perfected; be comforted; be of the same mind; live in peace: and the God of love
12 and peace shall be with you. Salute one another with a holy kiss.
13   All the saints salute you.
14   The grace of the Lord Jesus Christ, and the love of God, and the communion of the Holy Ghost, be with you all.

[1] Or, *rejoice: be perfected*

11. *farewell.* The margin "rejoice" is probably right.

Be perfected; be comforted. Or (with Moffatt) "Mend your ways, listen to what I have told you."

the God of love and peace. An unique phrase, though the title "the God of peace" is found in Rom. xv. 33; xvi. 20; Phil. iv. 9; 1 Th. v. 23. Love and peace were the chief needs of the Corinthian church.

12. *with a holy kiss.* Cf. Rom. xvi. 16; 1 Cor. xvi. 20 (with the note there); 1 Th. v. 26; and Justin Martyr, *Ap.* I. 25. The use of the kiss probably came from the worship of the synagogue, in which men and women were separated. So the *Apostolical Constitutions* ordain that the men are to salute the men, and the women the women. In view of Jn. iv. 27, and 1 Cor. xi. 3–6 we can hardly doubt that this was the rule from the first.

13. S. Paul probably took the pen from his amanuensis at this point. Cf. 2 Th. iii. 17, 18. This final benediction is fuller than any other that S. Paul gives. As a rule, he simply invokes the grace of Christ; and this may be the reason why Christ's name here comes before the Father's. But the order here found corresponds to the order of revelation. It is the grace of the Lord Jesus Christ (cf. viii. 9) which meets us first; through this we come to recognize the love of God as revealed in it; and finally by faith and baptism we claim and receive our share in the Holy Ghost.

The words, as Bengel says, are "Egregium de S. S. Trinitate testimonium"; but it is not their immediate purpose to bear this testimony; nor is it that of such other Trinitarian passages as Mt. xxviii. 19; Rom. viii. 9–11; 1 Cor. xii. 4–6; Eph. iv. 4–6; 1 Pet. i. 2; 1 Jn. iv. 13–16; Rev. i. 4, 5. All such language is the simple and natural expression of Christian experience. To draw out the doctrinal implications of this experience, and to find suitable language to express them, was not the task of New Testament days.

INDEX

PRINTED BY W. LEWIS, M.A.
At the UNIVERSITY PRESS
CAMBRIDGE

METHUEN'S GENERAL LITERATURE

A SELECTION OF
MESSRS. METHUEN'S PUBLICATIONS

This Catalogue contains only a selection of the more important books published by Messrs. Methuen. A complete catalogue of their publications may be obtained on application.

PART I. GENERAL LITERATURE

Allen (R. Wilberforce)
METHODISM AND MODERN WORLD PROBLEMS. *Crown 8vo* 7s. 6d. *net.*

Bain (F. W.)
A DIGIT OF THE MOON. THE DESCENT OF THE SUN. A HEIFER OF THE DAWN. IN THE GREAT GOD'S HAIR. A DRAUGHT OF THE BLUE. AN ESSENCE OF THE DUSK. AN INCARNATION OF THE SNOW. A MINE OF FAULTS. THE ASHES OF A GOD. BUBBLES OF THE FOAM. A SYRUP OF THE BEES. THE LIVERY OF EVE. THE SUBSTANCE OF A DREAM. *All Fcap. 8vo.* 5s. *net.* AN ECHO OF THE SPHERES. *Wide Demy 8vo.* 10s. 6d. *net.*

Baker (C. H. Collins)
CROME. Illustrated. *Quarto.* £5 5s. *net.*

Balfour (Sir Graham)
THE LIFE OF ROBERT LOUIS STEVENSON. *Twentieth Edition. In one Volume. Cr. 8vo. Buckram,* 7s. 6d. *net.*

Belloc (Hilaire)
PARIS. THE PYRENEES. *Each* 8s. 6d. *net.* ON NOTHING. HILLS AND THE SEA. ON SOMETHING. FIRST AND LAST. THIS AND THAT AND THE OTHER. ON. ON EVERYTHING. ON ANYTHING. *Each* 3s. 6d. *net.* MARIE ANTOINETTE. 18s. *net.* A HISTORY OF ENGLAND. In 4 vols. Vols. I and II. 15s. net each.

Birmingham (George A.)
A WAYFARER IN HUNGARY. Illustrated. *Crown 8vo.* 8s. 6d. *net.* SPILLIKINS: A BOOK OF ESSAYS. *Fcap. 8vo.* 5s. *net.*

Bowen (Frank C.)
THE KING'S NAVY. Illustrated. *Fcap. 4to.* 7s. 6d. *net.*

Bowles (George F. S.)
THE STRENGTH OF ENGLAND. *Demy 8vo.* 8s. 6d. *net.*

Brinton (Selwyn)
THE GOLDEN AGE OF THE MEDICI. Illustrated. *Demy 8vo.* 15s. *net.*

Bulley (M. H.)
ART AND COUNTERFEIT. Illustrated. *Demy 4to.* 15s. *net.* ANCIENT AND MEDIEVAL ART : A SHORT HISTORY. *Second Edition, Revised. Crown 8vo.* 10s. 6d. *net.*

Burns (Robert)
THE POEMS AND SONGS. Edited by ANDREW LANG. *Fourth Edition. Wide Demy 8vo.* 10s. 6d. *net.*

Campbell (Olwen Ward)
SHELLEY AND THE UNROMANTICS. Illustrated. *Second Edition, Revised. Demy 8vo.* 16s. *net.*

Chandler (Arthur), D.D., late Lord Bishop of Bloemfontein
ARA CŒLI. 5s. *net.* FAITH AND EXPERIENCE. 5s. *net.* THE CULT OF THE PASSING MOMENT. 6s. *net.* THE ENGLISH CHURCH AND REUNION. 5s. *net.* SCALA MUNDI. 4s. 6d. *net.*

Chesterton (G. K.)
THE BALLAD OF THE WHITE HORSE. ALL THINGS CONSIDERED. TREMENDOUS TRIFLES. FANCIES VERSUS FADS. CHARLES DICKENS. *All Fcap. 8vo.* 3s. 6d. *net.* ALARMS AND DISCURSIONS. A MISCELLANY OF MEN. THE USES OF DIVERSITY. THE OUTLINE OF SANITY. *All Fcap. 8vo.* 6s. *net.* A GLEAMING COHORT. *Fcap 8vo.* 2s. 6d. *net.* WINE, WATER, AND SONG. *Fcap. 8vo.* 1s. 6d. *net.*

Clutton-Brock (A.)
WHAT IS THE KINGDOM OF HEAVEN ? ESSAYS ON ART. SHAKESPEARE'S HAMLET. *Each* 5s. *net.* ESSAYS ON BOOKS. MORE ESSAYS ON BOOKS. ESSAYS ON LIFE. ESSAYS ON RELIGION. ESSAYS ON LITERATURE AND LIFE. *Each* 6s. *net.* SHELLEY, THE MAN AND THE POET. 7s. 6d. *net.*

Cowling (George H.)
A PREFACE TO SHAKESPEARE. Illustrated. *Crown 8vo.* 5s. *net.*

Dolls' House (The Queen's)
THE BOOK OF THE QUEEN'S DOLLS' HOUSE. Vol. I. THE HOUSE, Edited by A. C. BENSON, C.V.O., and Sir LAWRENCE WEAVER, K.B.E. Vol. II. THE LIBRARY, Edited by E. V. LUCAS. Profusely Illustrated. A Limited Edition. *Crown 4to.* £6 6s. *net.*
EVERYBODY'S BOOK OF THE QUEEN'S DOLLS' HOUSE. An abridged edition of the above. Illustrated. *Crown 4to.* 5s. *net.*

Edwardes (Tickner)
THE LORE OF THE HONEYBEE. *Thirteenth Edition. Crown 8vo.* 7s. 6d. *net.* BEEKEEPING FOR ALL. *Crown 8vo.* 3s. 6d. *net.* THE BEE-MASTER OF WARRILOW. *Third Edition. Crown 8vo.* 7s. 6d. *net.* All Illustrated. BEE-KEEPING DO'S AND DON'TS. *Fcap. 8vo.* 2s. 6d. *net.*

Einstein (Albert)
RELATIVITY : THE SPECIAL AND GENERAL THEORY. 5s. *net.* SIDELIGHTS ON RELATIVITY. 3s. 6d. *net.* THE MEANING OF RELATIVITY. 5s. *net.* THE BROWNIAN MOVEMENT. 5s. *net.*
Other books on the Einstein Theory.
AN INTRODUCTION TO THE THEORY OF RELATIVITY. By LYNDON BOLTON. *Crown 8vo.* 5s. *net.*
THE PRINCIPLE OF RELATIVITY. By A. EINSTEIN, H. A. LORENTZ, H. MINKOWSKI and H. WEYL. With Notes by A. SOMMERFELD. *Demy 8vo.* 12s. 6d. *net.*
Write for Complete List

Forrest (H. Edward)
THE OLD HOUSES OF STRATFORD-UPON-AVON. Illustrated. *Crown 8vo.* 7s. 6d. *net.* Also an edition limited to 250 copies, *Fcap. 4to.* 21s. *net.*

Fyleman (Rose)
FAIRIES AND CHIMNEYS. THE FAIRY GREEN. THE FAIRY FLUTE. THE RAINBOW CAT. EIGHT LITTLE PLAYS FOR CHILDREN. FORTY GOOD-NIGHT TALES. FAIRIES AND FRIENDS. THE ADVENTURE CLUB. FORTY GOOD-MORNING TALES. *Each* 3s. 6d. *net.* A SMALL CRUSE, 4s. 6d. *net.* THE ROSE FYLEMAN FAIRY BOOK. Illustrated. 10s. 6d. *net.* LETTY. Illustrated. 6s. *net.* A CHRISTMAS BOOK. Illustrated. 2s. *net.*

Gibbon (Edward)
THE DECLINE AND FALL OF THE ROMAN EMPIRE. With Notes, Appendixes, and Maps, by J. B. BURY. Illustrated. Seven volumes. *Demy 8vo.* 15s. *net* each volume. Also, unillustrated. *Crown 8vo.* 7s. 6d. *net* each volume.

Glover (T. R.)
THE CONFLICT OF RELIGIONS IN THE EARLY ROMAN EMPIRE. POETS AND PURITANS. VIRGIL. *Each* 10s. 6d. *net.* FROM PERICLES TO PHILIP. 12s. 6d. *net.*

Gotch (J. A.)
OLD ENGLISH HOUSES. Illustrated. *Demy 8vo.* 16s. *net.* Also an edition limited to 50 copies, £2 2s. *net.*

Graham (Harry)
THE WORLD WE LAUGH IN : More
Deportmental Ditties. Illustrated by
" FISH." *Sixth Edition. Fcap. 8vo.
5s. net.* STRAINED RELATIONS. Illus-
trated by H. STUART MENZIES and
HENDY. *Royal 16mo. 6s. net.*

Grahame (Kenneth)
THE WIND IN THE WILLOWS. *Nine-
teenth Edition. Crown 8vo. 7s. 6d.
net.* Also, Illustrated by NANCY
BARNHART. *Small 4to. 10s. 6d. net.*
Also, Illustrated by H. STUART MEN-
ZIES. *Fcap. 8vo. 5s. net.*

Hadfield (J. A.)
PSYCHOLOGY AND MORALS. *Sixth
Edition. Crown 8vo. 6s. net.*

Hall (H. R.)
THE ANCIENT HISTORY OF THE NEAR
EAST. *Sixth Edition, Revised. Demy
8vo. £1 1s. net.* THE CIVILIZATION
OF GREECE IN THE BRONZE AGE. Illus-
trated. *Demy 8vo. 10s. 6d. net.*

Hamer (Sir W. H.), and Hutt (C. W.)
A MANUAL OF HYGIENE. Illustrated.
Demy 8vo. £1 10s. net.

Hewlett (Maurice)
THE LETTERS OF MAURICE HEWLETT.
Edited by LAURENCE BINYON. Illus-
trated. *Demy 8vo. 18s. net.*

Hind (A. M.)
A CATALOGUE OF REMBRANDT'S ETCH-
INGS. Two Vols. Profusely Illus-
trated. *Wide Royal 8vo. £1 15s. net.*

Holdsworth (W. S.)
A HISTORY OF ENGLISH LAW. Nine
Volumes. *Demy 8vo. £1 5s. net each.*

Hudson (W. H.)
A SHEPHERD'S LIFE. Illustrated. *Demy
8vo. 10s. 6d. net.* Also, unillustrated,
Fcap. 8vo. 3s. 6d. net.

Hutton (Edward)
CITIES OF SICILY. Illustrated. *10s.
6d. net.* MILAN AND LOMBARDY.
THE CITIES OF ROMAGNA AND THE
MARCHES. SIENA AND SOUTHERN TUS-
CANY. VENICE AND VENETIA. THE
CITIES OF SPAIN. NAPLES AND
SOUTHERN ITALY. Illustrated. *Each,
8s. 6d. net.* A WAYFARER IN UNKNOWN
TUSCANY. THE CITIES OF UMBRIA.
COUNTRY WALKS ABOUT FLORENCE.
ROME. FLORENCE AND NORTHERN TUS-
CANY. Illustrated. *Each, 7s. 6d. net.*

Imms (A. D.)
A GENERAL TEXTBOOK OF ENTOMOLOGY.
Illustrated. *Royal 8vo. £1 16s. net.*

Inge (W. R.), D.D., Dean of St. Paul's
CHRISTIAN MYSTICISM. (The Bampton
Lectures of 1899.) *Sixth Edition.
Crown 8vo. 7s. 6d. net.*

Jackson (H. C.)
OSMAN DIGNA. *Demy 8vo. 12s. 6d.
net.*

Kipling (Rudyard)
BARRACK-ROOM BALLADS. *241st Thousand.*

THE SEVEN SEAS. *180th Thousand.*

THE FIVE NATIONS. *138th Thousand.*

DEPARTMENTAL DITTIES. *111th Thousand.*

THE YEARS BETWEEN. *95th Thousand.*
Four Editions of these famous volumes
of poems are now published, viz. :—
*Crown 8vo. Buckram, 7s. 6d. net. Fcap.
8vo. Cloth, 6s. net. Leather, 7s. 6d. net.*
Service Edition. Two volumes each
book. *Square Fcap. 8vo. 3s. net each
volume.*

A KIPLING ANTHOLOGY—Verse. *Fcap.
8vo. Cloth, 6s. net. Leather, 7s. 6d.
net.*

TWENTY POEMS FROM RUDYARD KIP-
LING. *423rd Thousand. Fcap. 8vo.
1s. net.*

A CHOICE OF SONGS. *Second Edition.
Fcap. 8vo. 2s. net.*

Lamb (Charles and Mary)
THE COMPLETE WORKS. Edited by
E. V. LUCAS. A New and Revised
Edition in Six Volumes. With Frontis-
pieces. *Fcap. 8vo. 6s. net each.*
The volumes are : I. MISCELLANEOUS
PROSE. II. ELIA AND THE LAST ESSAYS
OF ELIA. III. BOOKS FOR CHILDREN.
IV. PLAYS AND POEMS. V. and VI.
LETTERS.

SELECTED LETTERS. Chosen and Edited
by G. T. CLAPTON. *Fcap. 8vo. 3s. 6d.
net.*

THE CHARLES LAMB DAY BOOK.
Compiled by E. V. LUCAS. *Fcap. 8vo.
6s. net.*

Lankester (Sir Ray)
SCIENCE FROM AN EASY CHAIR. SCIENCE
FROM AN EASY CHAIR : Second Series.
DIVERSIONS OF A NATURALIST. GREAT
AND SMALL THINGS. Illustrated.
Crown 8vo. 7s. 6d. net. SECRETS OF
EARTH AND SEA. Illustrated. *Crown
8vo. 8s. 6d. net.*

Lodge (Sir Oliver)

MAN AND THE UNIVERSE (*Twentieth Edition*). THE SURVIVAL OF MAN (*Seventh Edition*). *Each Crown 8vo.* 7s. 6d. net. RAYMOND (*Thirteenth Edition*). *Demy 8vo.* 10s. 6d. net. RAYMOND REVISED. *Crown 8vo.* 6s. net. RELATIVITY (*Fourth Edition*). *Fcap. 8vo.* 1s. net.

Lucas (E. V.)

THE LIFE OF CHARLES LAMB. 2 Vols. £1 1s. net. EDWIN AUSTIN ABBEY, R.A. 2 Vols. £6 6s. net. VERMEER OF DELFT. 10s. 6d. net. A WANDERER IN ROME. A WANDERER IN HOLLAND. A WANDERER IN LONDON. LONDON REVISITED (Revised). A WANDERER IN PARIS. A WANDERER IN FLORENCE. A WANDERER IN VENICE. *Each* 10s. 6d. net. A WANDERER AMONG PICTURES. 8s. 6d. net. E. V. LUCAS'S LONDON. £1 net. INTRODUCING LONDON. 2s. 6d. net. THE OPEN ROAD. 6s. net. Also, illustrated. 10s. 6d. net. Also, India Paper. *Leather*, 7s. 6d. net. THE FRIENDLY TOWN. FIRESIDE AND SUNSHINE. CHARACTER AND COMEDY. *Each* 6s. net. THE GENTLEST ART. 6s. 6d. net. *And* THE SECOND POST. 6s. net. Also, together in one volume 7s. 6d. net. HER INFINITE VARIETY. GOOD COMPANY. ONE DAY AND ANOTHER. OLD LAMPS FOR NEW. LOITERER'S HARVEST. CLOUD AND SILVER. A BOSWELL OF BAGHDAD. 'TWIXT EAGLE AND DOVE. THE PHANTOM JOURNAL. GIVING AND RECEIVING. LUCK OF THE YEAR. ENCOUNTERS AND DIVERSIONS. ZIGZAGS IN FRANCE. EVENTS AND EMBROIDERIES. 365 DAYS (AND ONE MORE). *Each* 6s. net. SPECIALLY SELECTED. 5s. net. URBANITIES, 7s. 6d. net. *Each* illustrated by G. L. STAMPA. YOU KNOW WHAT PEOPLE ARE. Illustrated by GEORGE MORROW. 5s. net. THE SAME STAR : A Comedy in Three Acts. 3s. 6d. net. THE BRITISH SCHOOL. 6s. net. LITTLE BOOKS ON GREAT MASTERS. *Each* 5s. net. ROVING EAST AND ROVING WEST. 5s. net. PLAYTIME AND COMPANY. 7s. 6d. net. See also **Dolls' House (The Queen's)** and **Lamb (Charles)**

Lynd (Robert)

THE MONEY BOX. THE ORANGE TREE. THE LITTLE ANGEL. *Each Fcap. 8vo.* 6s. net. THE BLUE LION. THE PEAL OF BELLS. *Each Fcap. 8vo.* 3s. 6d. net.

Marie Louise (H.H. Princess)

A CHOICE OF CAROLS. *Fcap. 4to.* 2s. 6d. net. LETTERS FROM THE GOLD COAST. Illustrated. *Demy 8vo.* 16s. net.

McDougall (William)

AN INTRODUCTION TO SOCIAL PSYCHOLOGY (*Twentieth Edition, Revised*). 10s. 6d. net. NATIONAL WELFARE AND NATIONAL DECAY. 6s. net. AN OUTLINE OF PSYCHOLOGY (*Second Edition*). 12s. net. AN OUTLINE OF ABNORMAL PSYCHOLOGY. 15s. net. BODY AND MIND (*Fifth Edition*). 12s. 6d. net. ETHICS AND SOME MODERN WORLD PROBLEMS (*Second Edition*). 7s. 6d. net.

Mackenzie-Rogan (Lt.-Col. J.)

FIFTY YEARS OF ARMY MUSIC. Illustrated. *Demy 8vo.* 15s. net.

Maeterlinck (Maurice)

THE BLUE BIRD. 6s. net. Also, illustrated by F. CAYLEY ROBINSON. 10s. 6d. net. MARY MAGDALENE. 5s. net. DEATH. 3s. 6d. net. OUR ETERNITY. 6s. net. THE UNKNOWN GUEST. 6s. net. POEMS. 5s. net. THE WRACK OF THE STORM. 6s. net. THE MIRACLE OF ST. ANTHONY. 3s. 6d. net. THE BURGOMASTER OF STILEMONDE. 5s. net. THE BETROTHAL. 6s. net. MOUNTAIN PATHS. 6s. net. THE STORY OF TYLTYL. £1 1s. net. THE GREAT SECRET. 7s. 6d. net. THE CLOUD THAT LIFTED and THE POWER OF THE DEAD. 7s. 6d. net.

Masefield (John)

ON THE SPANISH MAIN. 8s. 6d. net. A SAILOR'S GARLAND. 6s. net. SEA LIFE IN NELSON'S TIME. 5s. net.

Methuen (Sir A.)

AN ANTHOLOGY OF MODERN VERSE. 117th Thousand. SHAKESPEARE TO HARDY : An Anthology of English Lyrics. 19th Thousand. *Each Fcap. 8vo. Cloth*, 6s. net. *Leather*, 7s. 6d. net.

Milne (A. A.)

NOT THAT IT MATTERS. IF I MAY. *Each* 3s. 6d. net. WHEN WE WERE VERY YOUNG. Illustrated by E. H. SHEPARD. *Fourteenth Edition.* 129th Thousand. 7s. 6d. net. *Leather*, 10s. 6d. net. WINNIE-THE-POOH. Illustrated by E. H. SHEPARD. 7s. 6d. net. *Leather*, 10s. 6d. net. FOR THE LUNCHEON INTERVAL. 1s. 6d. net.

Milne (A. A.) and Fraser-Simson (H.)
FOURTEEN SONGS FROM "WHEN WE WERE VERY YOUNG." (*Tenth Edition*.) TEDDY BEAR AND OTHER SONGS FROM "WHEN WE WERE VERY YOUNG." Words by A. A. Milne. Music by H. Fraser-Simson. Each *Royal 4to*. 7s. 6d. net. THE KING'S BREAKFAST. *Second Edition*. *Music 4to*. 3s. 6d. net.

Montague (C. E.)
DRAMATIC VALUES. *Cr. 8vo.* 7s. 6d. net.

Morton (H. V.)
THE HEART OF LONDON. 3s. 6d. net. (Also illustrated, 7s. 6d. net.) THE SPELL OF LONDON. THE NIGHTS OF LONDON. Each, 3s. 6d. net. THE LONDON YEAR. Illustrated. 7s. 6d. net.

Newman (Tom)
HOW TO PLAY BILLIARDS. *Second Edition*. Illustrated. *Cr. 8vo.* 8s. 6d. net. BILLIARD DO'S AND DON'TS. 2s. 6d. net.

Oman (Sir Charles)
A HISTORY OF THE ART OF WAR IN THE MIDDLE AGES, A.D. 378–1485. *Second Edition*, Revised and Enlarged. 2 Vols. Illustrated. *Demy 8vo.* £1 16s. net.

Oxenham (John)
BEES IN AMBER. *Small Pott 8vo.* 2s. net. ALL'S WELL. THE KING'S HIGHWAY. THE VISION SPLENDID. THE FIERY CROSS. HIGH ALTARS. HEARTS COURAGEOUS. ALL CLEAR! Each *Small Pott 8vo.* *Paper*, 1s. 3d. net. *Cloth*, 2s. net. WINDS OF THE DAWN. 2s. net.

Perry (W. J.)
THE ORIGIN OF MAGIC AND RELIGION. THE GROWTH OF CIVILIZATION (*Second Edition*). Each 6s. net. THE CHILDREN OF THE SUN. 18s. net.

Petrie (Sir Flinders)
A HISTORY OF EGYPT. In 6 Volumes. Vol. I. FROM THE IST TO THE XVITH DYNASTY. *Eleventh Edition, Revised*. 12s. net.
Vol. II. THE XVIITH AND XVIIITH DYNASTIES. *Seventh Edition, Revised*. 9s. net.
Vol. III. XIXTH TO XXXTH DYNASTIES. *Third Edition*. 12s. net.
Vol. IV. PTOLEMAIC EGYPT. By EDWYN BEVAN. 10s. 6d. net.
Vol. V. EGYPT UNDER ROMAN RULE. J. G. MILNE. *Third Edition, Revised*. 12s. net.
Vol. VI. EGYPT IN THE MIDDLE AGES. STANLEY LANE POOLE. *Fourth Edition*. 10s. net.

Raleigh (Sir Walter)
THE LETTERS OF SIR WALTER RALEIGH. Edited by LADY RALEIGH. Two Vols. Illustrated. *Second Edition*. *Demy 8vo.* £1 10s. net.

Ridge (W. Pett) and Hoppé (E. O.)
LONDON TYPES: TAKEN FROM LIFE. The text by W. PETT RIDGE and the 25 Pictures by E. O. HOPPÉ. *Large Crown 8vo.* 10s. 6d. net.

Smith (Adam)
THE WEALTH OF NATIONS. Edited by EDWIN CANNAN. 2 Vols. *Demy 8vo.* £1 5s. net.

Smith (C. Fox)
SAILOR TOWN DAYS. SEA SONGS AND BALLADS. A BOOK OF FAMOUS SHIPS. SHIP ALLEY. Each, illustrated, 6s. net. FULL SAIL. Illustrated. 5s. net. TALES OF THE CLIPPER SHIPS. 5s. net. THE RETURN OF THE "CUTTY SARK." Illustrated. 3s. 6d. net. A BOOK OF SHANTIES. 7s. 6d. net.

Sommerfeld (Arnold)
ATOMIC STRUCTURE AND SPECTRAL LINES. £1 12s. net. THREE LECTURES ON ATOMIC PHYSICS. 2s. 6d. net.

Stevenson (R. L.)
THE LETTERS. Edited by Sir SIDNEY COLVIN. 4 Vols. *Fcap. 8vo.* Each 6s. net.

Surtees (R. S.)
HANDLEY CROSS. MR. SPONGE'S SPORTING TOUR. ASK MAMMA. MR. FACEY ROMFORD'S HOUNDS. PLAIN OR RINGLETS ? HILLINGDON HALL. Each illustrated, 7s. 6d. net. JORROCKS'S JAUNTS AND JOLLITIES. HAWBUCK GRANGE. Each, illustrated, 6s. net.

Taylor (A. E.)
PLATO : THE MAN AND HIS WORK. *Demy 8vo.* £1 1s. net.

Tilden (W. T.)
THE ART OF LAWN TENNIS. SINGLES AND DOUBLES. Each, illustrated, 6s. net. THE COMMON SENSE OF LAWN TENNIS. Illustrated. 5s. net.

Tileston (Mary W.)
DAILY STRENGTH FOR DAILY NEEDS. *32nd Edition*. 3s. 6d. net. *India Paper, Leather*, 6s. net.

Underhill (Evelyn)
MYSTICISM (*Eleventh Edition*). 15s. net. THE LIFE OF THE SPIRIT AND THE LIFE OF TO-DAY (*Sixth Edition*). 7s. 6d. net. CONCERNING THE INNER LIFE. (*Second Edition*). 2s. net.

Vardon (Harry)
How to Play Golf. Illustrated.
19th Edition. Crown 8vo. 5s. net.

Waterhouse (Elizabeth)
A Little Book of Life and Death.
22nd Edition. Small Pott 8vo. 2s. 6d.
net.

Wilde (Oscar).
The Works. In 16 Vols. Each 6s. 6d.
net.

I. Lord Arthur Savile's Crime and
the Portrait of Mr. W. H. II. The
Duchess of Padua. III. Poems. IV.
Lady Windermere's Fan. V. A
Woman of No Importance. VI. An
Ideal Husband. VII. The Impor-
tance of Being Earnest. VIII. A
House of Pomegranates. IX. In-
tentions. X. De Profundis and
Prison Letters. XI. Essays. XII.
Salome, A Florentine Tragedy, and
La Sainte Courtisane. XIII. A
Critic in Pall Mall. XIV. Selected
Prose of Oscar Wilde. XV. Art and
Decoration. XVI. For Love of the
King. (5s. net.)

William II. (Ex-Emperor of Germany).
My Early Life. Illustrated. Demy
8vo. £1 10s. net.

Williamson (G. C.)
The Book of Famille Rose. Richly
Illustrated. Demy 4to. £8 8s. net.
Also a limited edition, £12 12s. net.

PART II.   A SELECTION OF SERIES

The Antiquary's Books
Each, illustrated, Demy 8vo. 10s. 6d. net.
A series of volumes dealing with various
branches of English Antiquities, com-
prehensive and popular, as well as
accurate and scholarly.

The Arden Shakespeare
Edited by W. J. Craig and R. H. Case.
Each, wide Demy 8vo. 6s. net.
The Ideal Library Edition, in single
plays, each edited with a full Introduction, Textual Notes and a Commentary
at the foot of the page. Now complete
in 39 Vols.

Classics of Art
Edited by J. H. W. Laing. Each, pro-
fusely illustrated, wide Royal 8vo. 15s.
net to £3 3s. net.
A Library of Art dealing with Great
Artists and with branches of Art.

The "Complete" Series
Demy 8vo. Fully illustrated. 5s. net
to 18s. net each.
A series of books on various sports and
pastimes, all written by acknowledged
authorities.

The Connoisseur's Library
With numerous Illustrations. Wide
Royal 8vo. £1 11s. 6d. net each vol.
European Enamels. Fine Books.
Glass. Goldsmiths' and Silver-
smiths' Work. Ivories. Jewellery.
Mezzotints. Porcelain. Seals.

The Do's and Dont's Series
Fcap. 8vo. 2s. 6d. net each.
This series, although only in its in-
fancy, is already famous. In due course
it will comprise clear, crisp, informative
volumes on all the activities of life.
Write for full list

The Faiths
Edited by L. P. Jacks, M.A., D.D.
LL.D. Crown 8vo. 5s. net each volume
The first volumes are :
The Anglo-Catholic Faith (Rev.
Canon T. A. Lacey) ; Modernism in
the English Church (Prof. P. Gard-
ner) ; The Faith and Practice of the
Quakers (Prof. R. M. Jones);
Congregationalism (Rev. Princ. W. B.
Selbie).

The Library of Devotion
Handy editions of the great Devotional
books, well edited. Small Pott 8vo.
3s. net and 3s. 6d. net.

Little Books on Art
Well Illustrated. Demy 16mo. Each
5s. net.

Modern Masterpieces
Fcap. 8vo. 3s. 6d. each volume.
Pocketable Editions of Works by A. A.
Milne, Joseph Conrad, Arnold
Bennett, G. K. Chesterton, E. V.
Lucas, Hilaire Belloc, Kenneth
Grahame, W. H. Hudson, Robert
Lynd, R. L. Stevenson, Jack London
and E. V. Knox.

Sport Series
Mostly Illustrated. Fcap. 8vo. 2s. net
to 5s. net each.
Handy books on all branches of sport by
experts.

Methuen's Half-Crown Library
Crown 8vo and Fcap. 8vo.

Methuen's Two Shilling Library
Fcap. 8vo.

Two series of cheap editions of popular books.

Write for complete lists

The Wayfarer Series of Books for Travellers
Crown 8vo. 7s. 6d. net each. Well illustrated and with maps. The volumes are :—Alsace, Czecho-Slovakia,

The Dolomites, Egypt, Hungary, The Loire, Provence, Spain, Sweden, Switzerland, Unfamiliar Japan, Unknown Tuscany.

The Westminster Commentaries
Demy 8vo. 8s. 6d. net to 16s. net.
Edited by W. LOCK, D.D., and D. C. SIMPSON, D.D.
The object of these commentaries is primarily to interpret the author's meaning to the present generation, taking the English text in the Revised Version as their basis.

THE LITTLE GUIDES

Small Pott 8vo. Illustrated and with Maps

4s. net mostly

THE 62 VOLUMES IN THE SERIES ARE :—

BEDFORDSHIRE AND HUNTINGDONSHIRE
BERKSHIRE
BRITTANY
BUCKINGHAMSHIRE
CAMBRIDGE AND COLLEGES
CAMBRIDGESHIRE
CATHEDRAL CITIES OF ENGLAND AND WALES 6s. net
CHANNEL ISLANDS 5s. net
CHESHIRE 5s. net
CORNWALL
CUMBERLAND AND WESTMORLAND 6s. net
DERBYSHIRE
DEVON
DORSET 5s. 6d. net
DURHAM 6s. net
ENGLISH LAKES 6s. net
ESSEX 5s. net
GLOUCESTERSHIRE
GRAY'S INN AND LINCOLN'S INN 6s. net
HAMPSHIRE
HEREFORDSHIRE 4s. 6d. net
HERTFORDSHIRE
ISLE OF MAN 6s. net
ISLE OF WIGHT
KENT 5s. net
KERRY
LANCASHIRE 6s. net
LEICESTERSHIRE AND RUTLAND 5s. net
LINCOLNSHIRE 6s. net
LONDON 5s. *net*
MALVERN COUNTRY

MIDDLESEX
MONMOUTHSHIRE 6s. net
NORFOLK 5s. net
NORMANDY 5s. net
NORTHAMPTONSHIRE
NORTHUMBERLAND 7s. 6d. net
NORTH WALES 6s. net
NOTTINGHAMSHIRE
OXFORD AND COLLEGES
OXFORDSHIRE
ROME 5s. net
ST. PAUL'S CATHEDRAL
SHAKESPEARE'S COUNTRY
SHROPSHIRE 5s. *net*
SICILY
SNOWDONIA 6s. net
SOMERSET
SOUTH WALES
STAFFORDSHIRE 5s. net
SUFFOLK
SURREY 5s *net*
SUSSEX
TEMPLE
WARWICKSHIRE 5s. net
WESTMINSTER ABBEY 5s. *net*
WILTSHIRE 6s. net
WORCESTERSHIRE 6s. net
YORKSHIRE EAST RIDING 5s. net
YORKSHIRE NORTH RIDING
YORKSHIRE WEST RIDING 7s. 6d. net
YORK 6s. net

METHUEN & CO. LTD., 36 ESSEX STREET, LONDON, W.C.2.
1026